9HEADS

9 Heads — a guide to drawing fashion
by Nancy Riegelman

Published by 9 Heads Media
Mailing address: 9 Heads Media, PO Box 27457, Los Angeles CA 90027–0457, USA
Website: www.9headsmedia.com
Copyright © 2000, 2003, 2006, 2010 Nancy Riegelman

First edition 2000
Second edition 2003
Third edition 2006
   revised 2010
Printed in China

Publisher's Cataloging-in-Publication Data

Riegelman, Nancy

9 Heads — a guide to drawing fashion/ Nancy Riegelman 1st edition
352 p. 33 x 23 cm
LCCN: 00-106285
ISBN: 0-9702463-3-1

1. Fashion Drawing 2. Drawing — technique I Title

Lib. Cong. Class. No. TT509 DDC 741.672

"This book is dedicated to the memory of my dear friend Paul McDonough and my aunt Ruthann Askey." N.R.

Nancy Riegelman was born in San Francisco. She attended the University of California at Berkeley, UCLA and Art Center College of Design in Pasadena, Ca., where she studied drawing and fine arts.

Nancy teaches fashion drawing at the Fashion Institute of Design and Merchandising (FIDM) in Los Angeles and international style at Art Center College of Design. She has been visiting professor at the University Premila Polytechnic in Bombay, India, Seibu University in Tokyo, Japan, the Paris Fashion Institute and the Central Academy of Art & Design in Beijing, China.

Nancy is also a fine artist who has exhibited in museums in the USA and overseas. Nancy lives in Los Angeles.

a guide to
drawing fashion

Nancy Riegelman

9HEADS

contents

Girl with turkey
Demetrios Psillos 2003

preface

This edition of *9 Heads* is the first complete revision of the book since its publication, six years ago. It is published to coincide with the publication of my new book, *Colors for Modern Fashion* and it is necessary to discuss some of the aspects of the new book to understand the changes in this one.

Colors for Modern Fashion is a large book created over a period of several years. This prolonged period of drawing, analyzing and writing about the drawing, collaborating with other artists, illustrators and professionals, and finally revising and editing a large body of work profoundly affected my approach, giving rise to new thinking, and insights into the nature and purpose of fashion drawing. It became clear well before finishing *Colors* that these changes in thinking and approach should also be introduced to its black and white companion. This new edition of *9 Heads*, then, is the re-statement of my approach to the subject, incorporating my most developed thinking and views, both in terms of what the end product should look like, and how best to achieve it. At the outset of this task—naively, and more than a little wishfully—I thought that this might be achieved through the substitution of a few drawings and explanations. Staying true to the approach and philosophy that emerged with *Colors*, though, the process became longer and more involved, resulting in a much larger work with some significant changes from its predecessor.

The process of creating *Colors* strongly reinforced one of my principal convictions about drawing fashion: Drawing is a powerful tool for designing fashion. In a similar way to language, though, in order to be effective drawing has to be used with clarity and precision. In fashion drawing —or indeed any form of technical drawing—where the end result is an *illustration* of another object rather than an end to itself (i.e. a piece of art) ,the first consideration is that the *meaning* of the drawing is clear. For me, there are two aspects to this: First, the shape, dimensions and overall appearance of the garments being drawn must be accurate: silhouette, fit and drape, details and fabric must all be correct. Second, the mood and, if possible, the essence of the garment must be accurately conveyed. The second of these aspects—conveying the mood and essence of garments—is often more difficult to learn (and teach) than the first, but if the first is mastered the second will become easier. All the drawings in this edition of *9 Heads* have been made with these criteria of accuracy, meaning and clarity firmly in mind.

This new edition of *9 Heads* also presents, in many cases, a different style of finished drawing, one where figures are usually more fleshed-out and where garment fabrics are more rendered than in the drawings of the previous editions. These changes are not intended to imply that one type of drawing is preferable to the other, but result from the realization, over a number of years of using *9 Heads* as a course book, that students (who often have no previous formal training in drawing and who have a need to learn the basics of fashion drawing quickly as part of a larger course in fashion design or merchandising) can be easily confused by stylized drawings. My own style tends naturally to a minimal use of line (often employing nuanced line to indicate shading and fabric type) both in the depiction of the garment and the figure. It is my own personal style, though, and one that is highly evolved, resulting from many years of intense drawing and developing my skills and instincts. Copying a style —and particularly one that uses line sparsely—is not necessarily the best way to learn to draw. I have come to the view that when learning to draw it is advisable first to master more fully rendered drawings. Once one is able to make drawings with a full information content (in terms of the use of line in the depiction of the silhouette, and shading of the figure and garments) it is then easier to decide for oneself how this drawing can be abstracted—which elements can be omitted while conveying the same information and having the same overall effect. To try to learn to draw—particularly a form of technical drawing—and do so in an abstract manner at the same time can give rise to uncertainty and mistakes as to what are acceptable and comprehensible techniques for abstraction and what are not.

This edition of *9 Heads* includes, then, as examples of finished drawings, fuller, and, in a way, less-stylized, drawings than its prede

cessor. It is intended that these drawings will make the distinction between style and content in drawing clearer, and encourage the student to make her or his own stylistic decisions once the basics of drawing have been mastered. The decision to introduce pencil for shading and line work (used extensively in Chapter 2) rather than ink was made partly for this reason: it is difficult to add extensive shading to a drawing using only ink line, as one is limited in effect to variations of cross-hatching, and also because printed reproduction of pencil had caused problems and not yielded the required clarity.

Drawings have been included of the main garment categories that focus separately on silhouette, fit and drape and detailing, so the importance of these defining characteristics of garments can be fully appreciated. Other changes that have been made: the chapter on Fabrics has been extended to include detailed descriptions of how to render all the main fabric types and the chapter on drawing flats has been extended, a large number of modern flats included in an Appendix, and a summary description of the various measurements for "specs" also included for the first time. This treatment of flats and specs is not intended to be exhaustive but to provide an introduction to and overview of a technique that is important but varies somewhat between different apparel companies.

An important addition in this new edition is the two new chapters on drawing men and children. Fashion for men and children continues to grow in variety and sophistication, and given the very distinct differences in physical appearance between men, women and children, each deserves it s own special treatment. Drawing children is not easy, and has caused problems for artists for centuries. I made a prolonged study of them when preparing the drawings for *Colors* , the fruits of which carried over to this new edition. In fashion drawing it is important that children and men look realistic and space is devoted at the beginning of each of the respective chapters to examining differences between the sexes and different age groups of children to show how they are drawn accurately.

Finally, this new edition of *9 Heads* has been extended in scope so that together with *Colors for Modern Fashion* the two books constitute a course in all the elements of modern fashion drawing from Beginners through to Advanced. Broadly speaking, *9 Heads* has been expanded so that it covers a Beginners through Intermediate /Advanced level course in fashion drawing, while *Colors* is a complete Advanced course; at the same time *9 Heads* also covers all applications of fashion drawing in black and white and *Colors*, not surprisingly, covers color. Many students will be impatient to move quickly to color, and, recognizing that this is going to happen, *Colors* includes a number of elements designed to help the Beginner to learn the basics. If, however, the student has a serious desire to learn about fashion and fashion drawing in depth, and to acquire drawing—and design—skills that will serve her or him a lifetime, then it is essential to acquire a firm foundation in the techniques, skills and body of knowledge such as that is taught in *9 Heads* in black and white before diving into all the complexities of color.

I am most grateful to all those who have embraced the approach and values that *9 Heads* has sought to promote over the few years since its first publication. I believe the book has achieved some success in pointing the way to improving standards of fashion drawing and, in a way, it is edifying that its omissions and shortcomings are now more readily recognized (and commented on) than before: it is a sure sign that critical awareness and standards are rising. This new edition is a sincere attempt to expand and improve the book wherever it seemed appropriate.

Nancy Riegelman
Los Angeles, 2006

ALL THE VASTNESS OF THE UNIVERSE
WAS IN THE CIRCLE OF HER PUPILS.

OPEN WIDE.

NEVER WAS
IMMENSE LOVE MORE POWERFULLY
SIGNIFIED BY ANY EARTHLY
CREATURE.

BUT SHE SMILED HER SLIGHT, CONCEALING SMILE.

No title (All the Vastness)
Raymond Pettibon, 1990

LEARNING TO DRAW

Speaking from my experience with the thousands of students I have come into contact with over the years, the number of us who are able to draw *instinctively*, without tuition or study, is surprisingly few, perhaps one percent or less. Equally surprising though, particularly for those who have not yet started to draw, is that the number who are *not* able to learn to draw is even fewer.

Every semester a new group of students join my Fashion Sketching 1 class, most of whom have never made a fashion drawing. Within a few short weeks *all* of them (to date there has yet to be an exception) are able to make coherent drawings of the figure and clothing. Within a few months they are able to express a clearly defined figure with contemporary face and hair. Shortly after that they can make drawings of a wide range of modern garments and accessories on the figure that are both clear and pleasing.

For the vast majority of people, drawing is *not* intuitive, any more than speaking a foreign language is intuitive. Language "pills" do not exist and neither do drawing pills. Almost everyone who *can* draw has, in fact, *learnt* to draw at some stage or other in life, either through attending courses or self-tuition. When learning to draw, what is required, whether it is drawing fashion or any other type of drawing, is, just as when learning a foreign language, *commitment*, *motivation* and *constant practice*. If the motivation is sufficient, and the student applies her- or himself enthusiastically to the task, results almost always follow more quickly than expected.

DRAWING FASHION/THE SCOPE OF THIS BOOK

This book is a guide to drawing modern fashion in black and white, for all levels, from Beginners to Advanced. To make drawings of new fashion garments that are coherent and "make sense", that could easily be made in real garments, however, we must become familiar with a basic knowledge of the elements of fashion, those that make up the "language" of fashion. Once we know this language we will be able to frame our ideas for new fashion designs clearly and coherently, just as we would like to be able to frame sentences in a foreign language. The easiest way to learn about fashion, though, and almost certainly the most fun, is to do so visually—first studying photographs and drawings, and then learning how to make those drawings: Learning-about-fashion and learning-to-draw

go hand-in-hand, and improving skills in one of those areas automatically improves skills in the other.

This book covers both of these linked sets of skills: it teaches how to draw fashion, to a level where virtually any type of garment can be drawn on the fashion figure, and it is also designed to serve as a reference work for a large amount of specific information on all types of fashion garments and details that can be drawn on and incorporated into new designs. Every effort is made to make the book as clear as possible—ideas are usually illustrated in several different ways, and text is designed to reinforce the illustrations , and vice-versa, in order that it can serve as a self-tuition guide as well as a textbook for those taking courses.

THE GOALS OF FASHION DRAWING/THE 9 HEADS APPROACH TO FASHION DRAWING

Why do we draw fashion? For two main reasons: One is to illustrate the different ways clothes that already exist can be styled by varying pose, lighting, hairstyle, skin tone, accessories and other variables, perhaps for a movie, musical or theatrical production. The other, and principal, purpose in drawing fashion, though, is to design new garments and accessories.

Fashion design involves presenting well-developed ideas for new garments and accessories that will— or could if so desired— be made up into clothes. Fashion design is the result of *combining* fashion elements in new ways that are appealing, and capture the mood and trends of the time with flair and originality. The overwhelming majority of the fashion elements that are combined in new ways *already exist*, so, if we become familiar with them and learn how to draw them we will be well equipped for making new designs.

Given that design is our main purpose in drawing fashion, what exactly do we wish to accomplish with our design drawings of new garments and accessories? The answer to this question is quite simple: No matter who the audience for our drawings might be—clients, employers, potential clients or employers, college instructors, or friends—*we want our drawings first, to clearly and accurately set out our ideas for new garments, and, then, to impress, to persuade, to convince, to capture the imagination and seduce;* in short we want our drawings first to *explain* our ideas clearly and then to *sell* them. And what qualities do our drawings for new designs for garments have to display to achieve these goals? The answer undoubtedly resembles answers to similar questions in a wide range of enterprises and fields of endeavor: to be effective, fashion drawings have to be clear, accurate, realistic and attractive. This book teaches how to acquire the techniques, skills and knowledge needed to make fashion drawings with these qualities.

DRAWING SKILLS

The main technique required to draw fashion is, of course, independent of the subject matter of the drawing—it is drawing itself. Drawing is the use of line and shading to represent, on the two-dimensional surface of the paper, objects that are three-dimensional, that have depth as well as height and breadth. This book teaches these basic foundation skills of drawing that can be developed so that fashion can be drawn to an advanced level. Drawing skills are acquired through observation and practice, but if systems can be applied that speed up the learning process these are to be welcomed. For example, underlying all good fashion drawing is the ability to draw the human figure—the fashion croquis—in the correct proportions. This book uses a system where the human head itself is used as a unit of measurement for the parts of the figure, not only for its overall length (nine) but for the length and width of all the other parts and how they sit in relation to each other. Using this system can greatly speed up the process of learning to draw the figure; the drawings of the figure produced by those who have learnt using this system tend to be accurate and realistic and particularly well-suited for drawing fashion.

FASHION AS TECHNICAL DRAWING

In fashion drawing, the drawing is, of course, not an end in itself, but the servant of the ideas that are being expressed. Fashion drawing is a type of *technical* drawing, like other types of design drawing, but that is not to say that the techniques employed in fashion drawing should be less than *any* type of drawing, technical or otherwise. As this book shows, it is possible to communicate in a drawing a large amount of information about a garment, including shape, fit and drape and fabric type, as well as mood, market, age range and so on. If this amount of information about a garment that as yet only exists in the designer's mind's eye can be effectively communicated in a drawing, then drawing becomes a very powerful design tool:

quick, effective, versatile and economical. This "enhanced" type of drawing takes drawing beyond the diagrammatic: it communicates with an immediacy and realism that is the next best thing to seeing the finished garment on a model.

When drawing garments on the figure is introduced in the second chapter of the book, again, as with learning to draw the figure itself, wherever possible systems and techniques that facilitate the learning process have been introduced. For a drawing to be effective it has to be accurate and realistic, and experience shows this means accuracy and realism in every aspect of the representation of the garments. All the basic garment types are analyzed, and focus is brought to bear on the defining properties that make each garment unique: silhouette; fit and drape, and fabric. For a drawing to be most effective, and for the garment to appear its most realistic and convincing, each of these properties has to be represented (given the limitations of the medium) as accurately and realistically as possible.

Much modern fashion drawing, for example, is accurate in its depiction of silhouette and fit, but is often curiously negligent when depicting drape and fabric type. How the fabric of a garment fits the body and how, when it is not close to the body, the fabric falls away from the body in folds and drape, whether the body is in motion or in a fashion pose, is crucial information about the appearance and the very essence of the garment. *9 Heads* shows how to represent all these defining properties of a garment in a drawing in chapters on women's, men's and children's clothes. A separate chapter provides a more detailed treatment of how to draw fabric types so they are instantly recognizable.

THE FASHION CROQUIS—THE FOUNDATION FOR ALL GOOD FASHION DRAWING

Fashion drawings, whether new designs or stylings that use existing designs, have as their subject matter, garments and accessories. Accessories are usually solid freestanding objects with forms that are independent of the figure that can mostly be drawn in the same way as things such as buildings or cars. (There are a number of obvious exceptions, such as hair, the most important of accessories, which requires a special approach of its own.) Garments, however, designed with the sole purpose of being worn, take their shape (in differing degrees but overwhelmingly moreso than not) from the body underneath, and the way fashion designers intend their designs to appear can only be fully appreciated when they are shown on the figure. In fashion drawing, then, particularly when presenting original new clothes where cut, drape, fabric and details must be clear, it is usual to show the clothes on a figure. This is why when starting to learn to draw fashion we begin by learning to draw the figure the garments will be displayed on; this figure is the foundation underlying all good fashion drawing: all the elements of a fashion drawing are designed to emphasize and show off the clothing, and the figure in the drawing is also chosen specifically for this task. The type of figure best suited, and that is most commonly used in fashion drawing is an elongated one called the *croquis* (the French word for "sketch"). The croquis figure is equivalent in length to nine heads, as opposed to the natural figure that is closer to eight.

While the croquis is essentially a mannequin to show off the garments, and should never dominate the clothes in the drawing, it is important that it is drawn accurately. The simple reason for this is that, as mentioned, how clothes look on the figure is to a large extent determined by the figure underneath. At the extreme—snug-fitting swim-wear, or body-suits for active sports, for example—the clothes take on almost exactly the same form as the body underneath, like an additional layer of skin; for other less-fitted clothes the shape (or silhouette, as it is known) is determined by where the clothing *touches* the body underneath, and in the parts where it does *not* touch it, how the fabric follows the shape of the figure and then falls away in drape and folds. If the figure can be correctly drawn and the garments to be displayed then correctly aligned on that figure, then the difficult part of the fashion drawing will have been accomplished. Because it provides the essential foundation to all good fashion drawing, the croquis is the first element to be learnt and is the subject of the first chapter of this book.

MODERN CROQUIS AND POSES

It is almost always the case that a poorly drawn croquis will detract from garments and can give an unrealistic representation of the clothing. A well drawn croquis, on the other hand, will bring flair and realism to the clothes and, often, important information on the type of person they are designed for and how they should be marketed. It is not sufficient, though, simply to draw the croquis *accurately*. In order for the portrayal of the garments to be most effective they have to be shown convincingly, in a pose that is modern and fashionable and appropriate for the subject matter. This will often involve the choice of a three-quarter view pose, and also often a modern pose that is a variation of the classic S curve pose. A variety of poses of this type is also included in the chapter and every attempt is made throughout the book to make the poses fresh and modern and to suit the clothes on display.

DRAWING CLOTHES ON THE FIGURE

The chapter on drawing clothes on the figure—the female figure—is at the core of the book. Each of the main garment categories is reviewed, in a sequence that corresponds approximately to their order of difficulty, beginning with skirts and ending with necklines and collars. Examples of silhouette, drape and fit, and details are presented and analyzed, and how to draw the garments is explained in step-by-step detail in the text and images. In most cases drawings of varying degrees of complexity, which might correspond to different amounts of time available, or how advanced the design is, are included, ranging from simple silhouettes to fully rendered concept drawings. Often multiple examples of details or basic style variations of the garment are included. The emphasis is on showing effective methods for showing each garment and indicating what is and what is not good practice and technique in drawing them. Chapter Three on Accessories and Chapter Five, the Encyclopedia of Details are intended as comprehensive—though not exhaustive—sources for detailed information on garments that will complement the information of the other chapters and can be used for inspiration or direct incorporation into new design drawings.

MEN AND CHILDREN

Although the principles of garment design and construction are similar between the sexes and among the ages, there are strong physical differences between men and women, adults and children and between children of different ages. These make for significant differences in design, how the clothes fit and how they are drawn on the figure between these different groups. That consideration, along with the indisputable evidence of the increasing variety of fashion available for children and men has led—after too long a lapse of time since its first publication—to the inclusion in this new edition of separate chapters dedicated to each. Much of the emphasis in these chapters is on drawing the croquis and face , particularly the way the features are differentiated by age and sex, and also showing how to choose poses appropriate to age and activity. A range of modern garments are shown, both on the figure and as flats.

FABRICS

Those who have followed the arguments in this introduction this far will appreciate that the underlying approach and philosophy of this book is one of striving for accuracy and realism in fashion drawings. This extends to the fabric of the garment as well as its other defining elements. Although this book deals only with black and white drawing, and color is unquestionably one of a fabric's major features, much can be achieved in the accurate representation of a fabric using only black and white/greyscale. Indeed, to be able to achieve success in depicting fabrics in color it is important first to learn how to depict fabrics in greyscale, *without* the use of color. In this chapter of the book fabrics are examined according to weight and texture, and a range of garments typical of the type made of those fabrics are presented.

FLATS

Flats—the two-dimensional drawings that serve as the basis for the manufacture of (mainly mass-produced) garments—have evolved into the single most important device for communicating information about modern garments. For anyone working in, or contemplating a career in the fashion industry, it is important to become familiar with flats and to be able to draw them. In this new edition of *9 Heads* the treatment of flats has been considerably extended, and is now divided between Chapter Four: Flats and an Appendix that contains hundreds of examples of women's flats to be used as learning aides or as the basis for new designs. Also, for the first time, explanations of how "specs"—the precise measurements used in the manufacture of garments—are taken and presented are included.

GOOD FASHION DRAWING: DISCIPLINE AND AN ATTENTION TO DETAILS

The opinion I have formed, over the years of both drawing fashion and teaching how to draw fashion to undergraduate and graduate students at colleges of fashion and design, is that the key to successful fashion drawing (as is the case with many other areas of design, art and indeed human enterprise in general) lies in building up a discipline in the approach to the subject. In the case of fashion drawing this discipline consists of developing a

sensitivity to, and continually paying attention to, detail, in all areas, and representing that detail faithfully in drawing. Developing powers of observation and the ability to perceive the details is part of the larger process of learning to understand and appreciate fashion, which is also key in developing drawing and design skills.

The importance of careful observation at all levels cannot be over-emphasized: the imagination is a powerful tool, but it is important, for example before adding a modern hairstyle or makeup to a drawing, or before deciding how loose or tight the fit of a garment should be, to look around oneself to see what hairstyles, makeup or fits are actually being worn. The equally important other side of the same coin is that it is important to avoid generalization in fashion drawing: In drawings where the clothes are elaborate it is often effective to divert attention from the *figure* by making it an abstract or generalized form. This does not work when drawing the garments themselves, though: shoes should be drawn not as "shoe-shapes" but as faithful representations of the actual complexity of shapes and details that make up the shoe. Again, detailed observation is critical to the success of the drawing.

As when learning any new set of skills, learning to draw takes time, and there will be some frustrations along the way. Drawing skills usually develop hand-in-glove (and drawing hands in gloves itself takes some time to perfect) with the increasing knowledge of and a developing eye for fashion itself. Hand/eye coordination improves with constant practice, the trajectory of one's line and one's shading technique become more confident and instinctive and a lighter and more controlled touch evolves. When this starts to happen drawing becomes a pleasurable and rewarding activity; until that point is reached, though (and also in order to reach that point as quickly as possible) a conscious effort should be made to make every mark on the page meaningful, clear and precise. Work slowly and deliberately and progress will come.

As one's skills improve, the rewards are ample: as well as being a powerful tool of communication (and a potential way to earn one's living) drawing in general—and fashion drawing in particular—is a wonderfully relaxing and fulfilling activity. To be able to express one's creative ideas in such a clear and immediate form is highly satisfying and can be a great source of personal pride.

MATERIALS

The materials required for drawing the croquis are few: pencils, paper and an eraser (a few other materials are used when drawing flats and are discussed in that chapter). Fashion drawing is a precise type of drawing, involving the depiction of garments with exact measurements and a clear depiction of often-complex detail; the materials chosen are those that can best reproduce this exactness and detail.

When beginning to draw it is not necessary to use expensive paper—a bond paper is the best choice. Begin by using a fairly hard pencil—an HB lead is ideal—to give a crisp and precise line. Either a regular graphite or a mechanical pencil can be used.

MATERIALS

Graphite pencil HB, 2B, 4B
Mechanical pencil and leads
.005 pen
10% grey marker
Brush
Eraser
Drafting tape
Ruler
11" x 18" or 14" x 17" newsprint
11" x 18" white layout pad
Tracing paper

timeline

| 1877 | 1885 | 1892 | 1907 | 1912 | 1914 |

| 1927 | 1931 | 1931 | 1939 | 1947 | 1950 |

1950   1950   1951   1959   1968   1971

1983   1984   1989   2000   2003   2005

chapter one: proportions of the croquis

preparing to draw

Sit comfortably in a chair with the back straight. Keep the weight on the elbow and rest it on the desk (or other flat surface) so that the forearm and wrist are free to move on the page. If the hand shakes when beginning to draw (this is very common),try the following exercise: Place two dots randomly on a sheet of paper about three inches apart. Place the pencil on one dot and, without removing the pencil from the paper, rapidly draw a line to the other dot. Repeat this excercise until the action of making the line feels smooth and the shaking disappears.

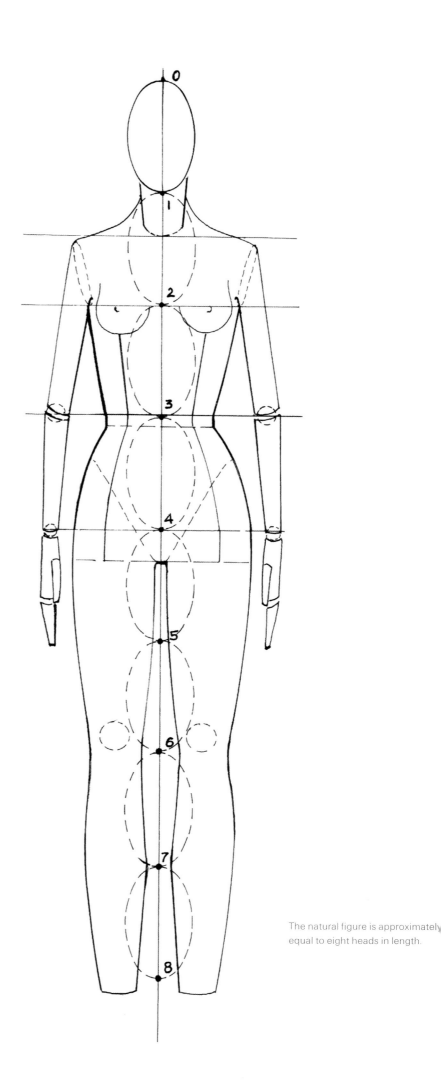

The natural figure is approximately equal to eight heads in length.

planning the figure on the page

PLANNING THE FIGURE ON THE PAGE
To begin drawing the croquis the placement of the figure on the page must first
be planned out. As a rule, the figure will
be centrally placed and fill up the page
so that all the details can be clearly
seen. For the front view croquis, the
position of the figure on the page is indicated by drawing a vertical line that
runs through the figure from the top of
the head to the feet, passing between
the eyes, down the nose, down the center of the neck,between the breasts,
through the tummy and crotch and
between the legs. This line is called the
axis line, and divides the figure into two
symmetrical halves. Place dots on the
page to indicate the top of the head and
the bottom of the legs (where the
ankles will be)and join them. Drawing a
straight line can be difficult, and a ruler
can be used, but it is important to develop the skill of drawing freehand, so
practice joining the dots using hand and
eye: Touch the uppermost dot with the
sharp pencil point and move quickly to
the lower dot. Do not watch the pencil
move but focus on the point at the end
of the line.

Draw the axis line, filling the page from
top to bottom (small figures are like
whispers and do not command attention). Divide the line into nine equally
spaced sections. This will allow us to
indicate the position of the different
parts of the body.

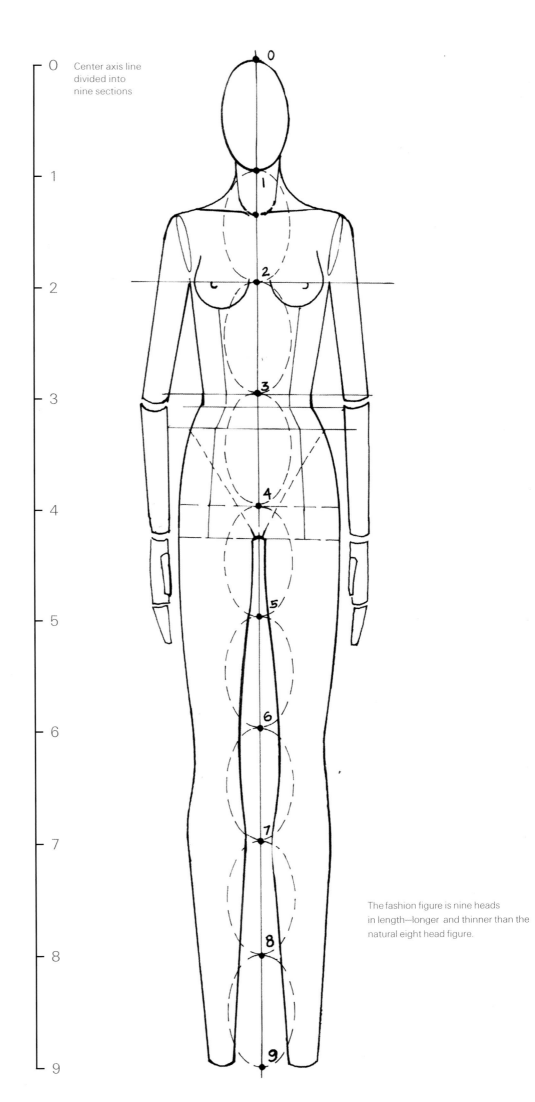

Center axis line
divided into
nine sections

The fashion figure is nine heads
in length—longer and thinner than the
natural eight head figure.

drawing the croquis/ front view

DRAWING THE CROQUIS

We are now ready to draw the croquis. The fashion croquis is based on a scale equal in length to nine heads from the top of the head to the ankles. Begin by drawing a vertical line—the axis line—and marking the nine equally spaced points.

1. Beginning with the head, place an oval the shape of an egg in the first section between 0 and 1. To draw this oval symmetrically (the two sides identical to each other) place two dots on the axis line at 0 and 1, and dots on either side of the axis line midway between 0 and 1, approximately ⅔ of a head apart. Practice making the shape in the air before connecting the dots with the pencil. This oval represents the head, and is slimmer than the natural shape of the head. Think of it as egg-shaped rather than as a hot-dog or watermelon. Move from dot to dot to create a symmetrical oval.

2. Next draw the neck, moving half way down the axis line from 1 to 1½. The neck is slimmer than the head. It is a cylinder, slightly wider at the bottom, that connects the head from the jawline to inside the shoulders at the collarbone. The neck is often elongated to make the figure appear more graceful.

3. Take the length of the head and the neck (1½ heads), and turn it sideways: this is the width of a woman's shoulders. Draw the shoulder line slightly above the base of the neck and slanting down slightly to end at the same level as the base of the neck, also where the collarbone is located. Draw a circle at each end of the shoulder line to represent the shape of the shoulder.

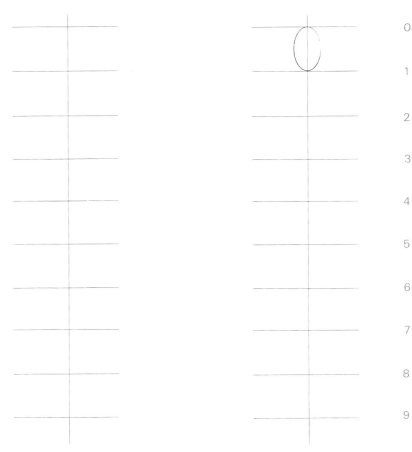

The fashion croquis is based on a scale equal in length to nine heads from the top of the head to the ankles. Begin by drawing a vertical line—the axis line—and marking the nine equally spaced points.

The head is drawn between 0 and 1.

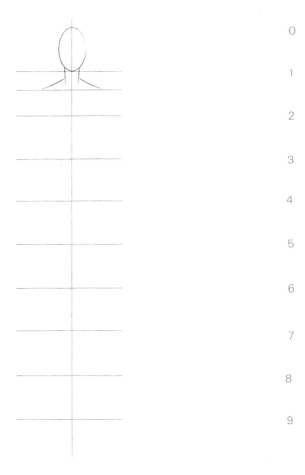

The neck is drawn from 1 to 1½ Shoulders are at 1½ and are 1½ heads wide.

croquis/
front view

4. The armhole is half a head length, extending from 1½ to 2. It slants in slightly from the shoulders, as the body begins to taper towards the waistline, and bends inwards (i.e., it is concave).

5. Place two dots at number 2 at equal distances from the axis (center line), midway between the axis and the sides of the body. These represent the highest parts of the breasts (and will be used as guides for the placement of the princess lines, as

discussed in the next chapter).

6. The waist is at number 3 and can be drawn with a width of three-quarters of a head (the exact width of the waist is a matter of personal taste, but fashion figures are best drawn slim). Make sure the points marking the edge of the waist are equally spaced from the axis line so the waist appears symmetrical.

Armhole is ½ head wide..

0
1
2
3
4
5
6
7
8
9

The position of the shoulders is indicated with circles. Armholes are drawn as ½ head long and slant inwards. The collar bone extends from the base of the neck out to the shoulders.

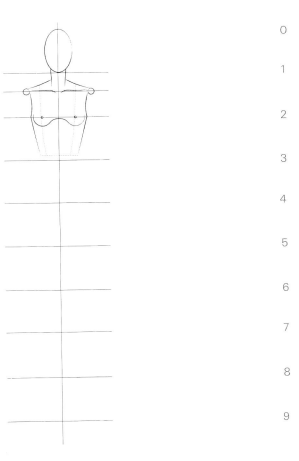

0
1
2
3
4
5
6
7
8
9

The highest point of the bustline is at 2. The torso tapers to the waist, which is ¾ to one head wide.

7. The next dot is just below the waist at 3¼. It is the point at the top of the pelvis and is called the *ilium*, the high point of the pelvis bone. It is important to establish this point precisely on the figure so the drawing is accurate over-all. The ilium is the point at which a woman's hip begins to differ from a man's. At this point a man's hip becomes a vertical line whereas a woman's hip extends out at a diagonal.

8. The next point of reference is the base of the hip, which is at number 4 and is slightly narrower than the width of the shoulders—about 1¼ heads. (The "hips" or "hip area" extends from the ilium at 3¼ to the base of the hip at 4.)

9. Next, mark the crotch between the legs at 4¼.

10. Add the arms connecting the arm-hole to the elbow. The arms are drawn as two lines from the outer edge of the shoulder to a point at 3—the elbow. Tap your own elbow to your waist to feel exactly where the elbow fits—they are both at point 3 on the croquis.

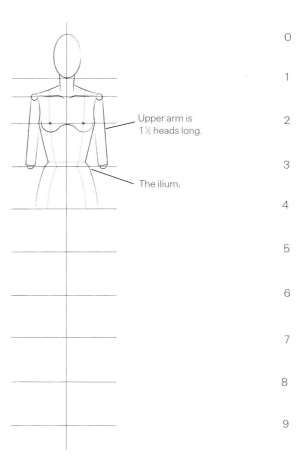

Upper arm is 1½ heads long.

The ilium.

The hips extend from 3 to 4 and are 1¼–1½ heads wide (usually slighter narrower than the shoulders). The upper arms extend from the shoulder to the elbows at 3. The position of the elbows is indicated with a circle.

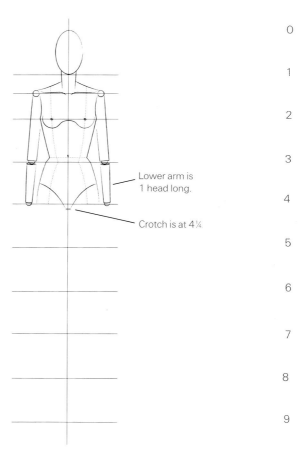

Lower arm is 1 head long.

Crotch is at 4¼

The tops of the legs, where they join the pelvis, curve down to the crotch just below 4. The lower parts of the arms extend from the elbow at 3 to 4.

croquis/
front view

11. Draw a line down from the crotch to number 6, representing the inside edge of the thigh. Number 6 is where the knee is placed. Draw the other side of the thigh from the outside of the hip at 4, tapering down to number 6. Draw these lines elegantly, each with a single movement and without lifting the pencil from the paper. Try not to make chicken scratches (lines made up of lots of smaller lines). The knee is about ¼ of a head wide. At this stage the position of the knees is indicated with little circles. Connect the hip to the knee.

12. The next point is at 7¼–7½ (depending on your own preference). This point marks the widest point of the calf (a large muscle called the *gastrocnemius*). Draw the line from the top of the knee to the calf, making the calf just a bit wider than the knee.

13. Slide from the calf down to a very thin ankle at 9 (or, if preferred, just above 9 for a sporty, younger looking croquis).

14. Finish off the croquis by continuing the arm down to the wrist at 4. Note there is an excellent fit of the wrist with the hip, just as there is of the elbow and the waist (tap the elbow to the waist and the wrist to the hip to see). A helpful proportion to remember is that the upper arm is one and a half heads and the lower arm is one.

Congratulations. You have just drawn your first croquis.

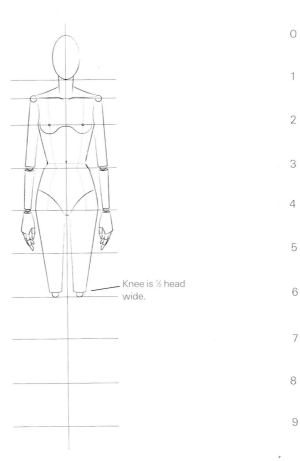

Knee is ½ head wide.

The thighs curve down to the knees at 6. Each knee is approximately one half of a head wide.

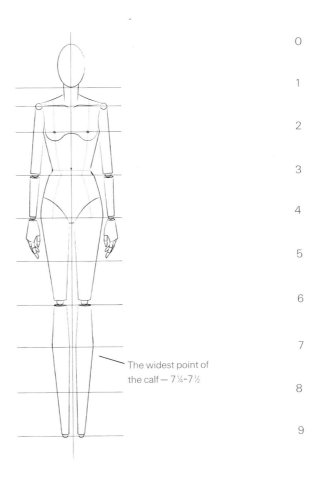

The widest point of the calf — 7¼–7½

The lower legs begin at the knees at 6 and extend to the ankles at 9.

croquis/front view/
exercises

To create a finished realistic look some
muscles should be added to the croquis. Muscles give the rounded,
fleshed-out look to the different parts of
the croquis. How large the muscles are
drawn is a matter of personal preference, but normally, for the fashion croquis , minimal musculature is indicated.
(For drawings of active sportswear larger muscles can be indicated.)

Muscles are longer on their outside
edges than the inside, though they do
not all stand out from the body in the
same direction: for example, the leg
muscles are located at the front of the
thigh and the back of the lower leg, and
are *not* seen when viewed from the
front but *are* seen in side or three-quarter view. The arms, however, rotate
through a wider range of movement
and the biceps and triceps can be seen
in a number of different views.

EXERCISES
The croquis is the foundation for most
fashion drawings and must be drawn
well. Drawing it well requires practice.
Try the following exercises to gain speed
and to learn the croquis measurements:

1. Draw the figure five times with a light
line. Use a mechanical pencil.
2. Draw the figure five times using a
dark line. Use a soft pencil, 2B or 4B.
3 Draw the figure and fill in with a variety of patterns (a pattern is any image
thatis continuously repeated—stripes,
dots, flowers, musical notes, etc.).
Neatness is important.
4. Make a croquis out of cardboard or
paper, make a croquis doily, a croquis
cookie or simply repeat the earlier exercises until completely familiarity with the
proportions of the figure is learnt.

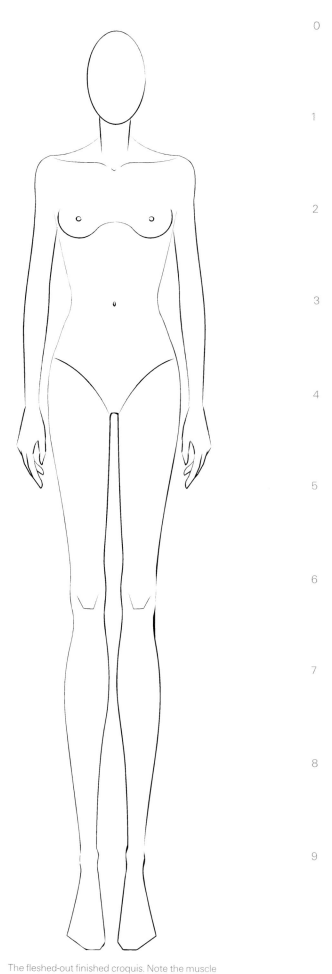

0

1

2

3

4

5

6

7

8

9

The fleshed-out finished croquis. Note the muscle
on the outer side of the thigh is longer than the
muscle on the inner side of the thigh, and the outer
side of the calf muscle is also longer than the inner.

croquis/
back view

THE BACK VIEW CROQUIS

The back view is used in fashion drawing when it is necessary to show the details of the back of a garment, for example, a beautiful train in a wedding dress or a backless evening gown. The overall proportions of the back view are, not surprisingly, the same as the front view, but different parts of the body appear in each view.

1. One small difference between the back view and the front view is that in the back view the neck is turned up and fits inside the skull (touch the back of the skull and feel the soft part where the skull begins). The neck will appear shorter, but is still half a head in length.
2. The shoulder blades are drawn as two lines about three-quarters of a head long and lying about half a head apart on either side of the axis line that runs down the center of the back; they are closest at number 2, bending out above and below that point.
3. The waist is at 3, as in the front view, and is the same width as in the front view. The hips are the same as the front view, ending at 4. The bottom is small and the cheeks rounded. Note that in the drawing the lower hip is located higher than in the actual human figure. Do not draw dark lines under the hip as this is a soft, full, rounded area of the body and black lines tend to make shapes look two-dimensional.
4. The rest of the back view of the figure remains the same as the front view, noting, of course, that from the back we see the elbows and the backs of the feet.

EXERCISE
Draw 10 back views .

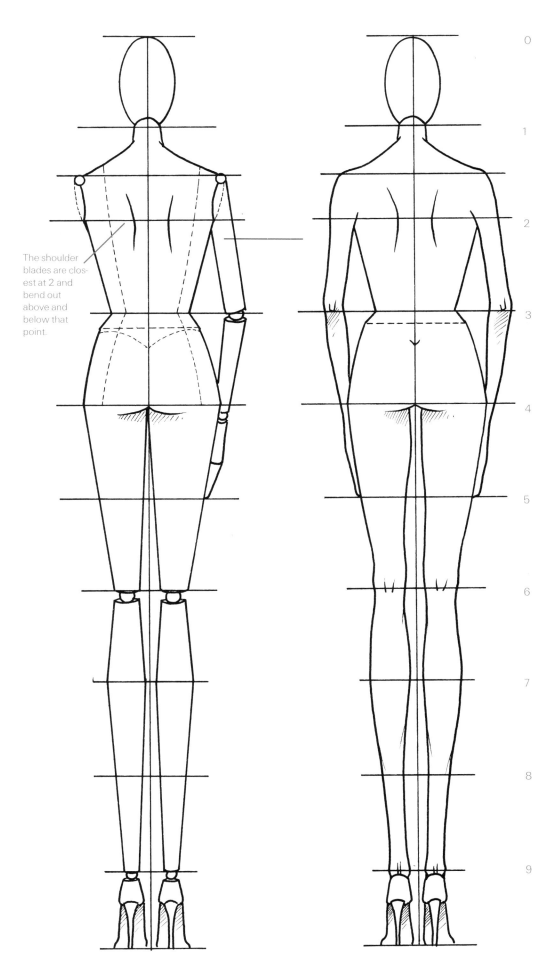

The shoulder blades are closest at 2 and bend out above and below that point.

Back -view croquis. The arms and legs can be thought of as cylinders. The croquis on the right is the final fleshed out version. Note the curves at the knees and elbows and the downward slope and rounded ends of the shoulders.

croquis/side view/ balance line

THE SIDE VIEW CROQUIS

The side view is used in fashion drawings where it is necessary to indicate features seen from the side, such as side seams or how a garment fits the hip and back (for example, jeans, pants and figure-hugging dresses). Contrary to what might be expected, when viewed from the side, the figure is *not* composed of vertical lines; in fact almost every part of the side view figureinvolves lines that are placed at a diagonal to the vertical.

The vertical line passing through the top of the head, though the body and out through the foot just forward of the heel is in the same position the axis line of the front view figure would be if it rotated through 90° to become a side view figure. The side view figure is *not* symmetrical, though, and as axis lines are lines that divide *symmetrical* forms or shapes into identical halves, for the side view it is not possible to draw in an axis line to assist in drawing the figure. The vertical line here is, in fact, the *balance line*, an important concept in fashion drawing, showing how the weight of the body is supported. In upright figures (and most fashion figures are upright), the balance line will be a vertical line stretching down from the topmost part of the head, as though a plumb line had been dropped to the floor. For the upright figure with legs together it will pass between the feet; if the legs are apart it will pass between the legs; if, as will be seen further on, the weight of the body is on one leg, it will run through that leg.

The balance line is a useful aid when drawing side view fashion poses so that they appear balanced, and it is worth taking the time to work out where it is located and to sketch it in before starting to draw.

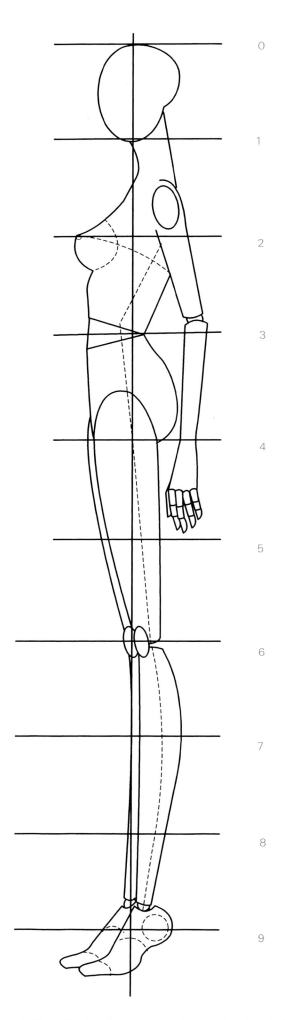

The side view croquis. The profile of the figure is slimmer than the other views. In side view the parts of the body appear in diagonals to the vertical axis. Note the leg extends from the inside of the lower torso and the lower leg from knee to ankle falls on the right side of the balance line. Do not draw the upper part of the figure too far forward or it will look pregnant.

croquis/
side view

1. Begin by drawing the head as an oval, set at a diagonal. (An alternative way to draw the side view head— shown in the diagram at top right— is to draw a rectangle about ⅔ of a head wide, and add a half circle to the top-right corner extending half way down the rectangle. This half circle repre-sents the *cranium*—the back part of the skull—with the neck extending down from it.)

2. The back of the neck starts at the base of the cranium, approximately half way down the head. The front of the neck starts at a point approximately half way back from the front of the head. The neck is half a head long.

3. The upper torso is tipped forward— the balance line runs through(or just in front of) the shoulder, and the waist is positioned in front of it. Use an oval or a rectangle to plot the position of the torso. The line bends around the bust in an arc with the highest point at 2, angles over the rib cage and then extends straight down to the waist. At this point the upper torso meets the lower torso and begins to bend back. Take care not to tip the oval shape of the torso too far from the vertical or the croquis will appear pregnant!

4. The lower torso tilts backwards, fol-lowing the curve of the bottom and creating a curve in the backbone, an area known as the lumbar region.

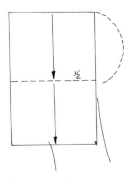

The head can be drawn as an oval or as a rectangle with a semi-circle attached to its top right.

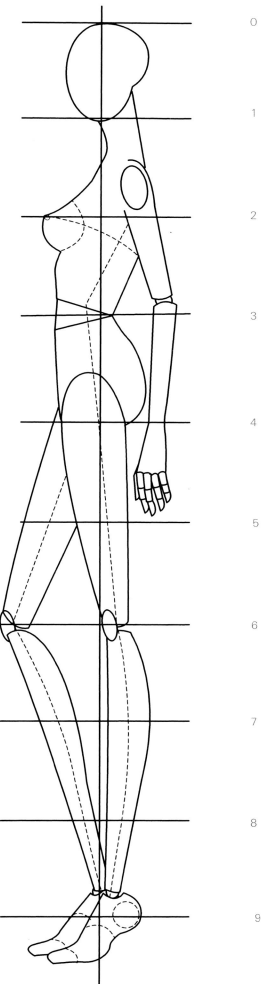

0

1

2   The bust is at 2.

3   The waist is at 3.

4

5

6

7

8

9

Side view croqis with bent inside leg. Note the bent leg still has 9 head proportions–from 4 at the hip to 6 at the knee.

croquis/
side view

5. The legs extend from the ilium to the ankle, with a straight bone in front and the full muscle in the back at 7½.

6. In side view, the shoulder appears aligned with the neck when the arm is at rest. When the arm bends the shoulder pivots, moving forward as the arm moves back and backwards as the arm extends forwards.

7. The knee is on the balance line, and the lower leg curves back behind it.

8. The side view can be varied by thrusting the pelvis forward. This makes the upper body appear to lean backwards. The body must always appear balanced, though, and the vertical balance line must pass through the top of the head and the ankle.

EXERCISE
Draw 10 side view croquis.

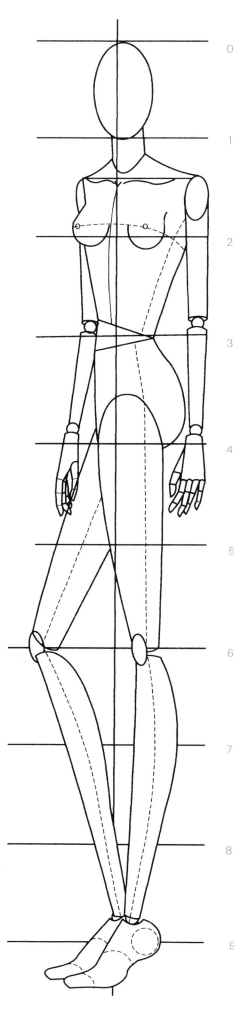

0

1

2

3

4

5

6

7

Note the flow of the curved-line of the side-view figure. The head is forward, neck back, torso at same angle as the head, bottom back..

8

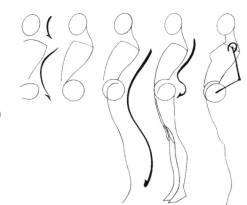

9

Another version of the side view croquis with the torso slightly twisted.

perspective/foreshortening

The next view of the figure to be discussed is the three-quarter view—an example of what is known as a "perspective" drawing. Before moving on to this view a simple introduction to the theory of perspective is required.

The word "perspective" comes from the Latin *perspicere*, meaning *to see through*. In English, to see something in perspective—a problem or proposal, for example—means to see it in a detached way, from different points of view. In drawing—and art in general—perspective has a different, but closely related meaning: Perspective is the way objects are presented on a flat, two-dimensional plane—paper or canvas, for example—so that they appear in the same way as the actual three-dimensional objects appear to a viewer in real life.

Perspective is introduced into a drawing with a number of different devices that imitate the way real objects (or different parts of the same object) appear in relation to each other. For example, to show that an object is in front of another object, one is drawn so that it *overlaps* and partly *obscures* the other. If an object is *closer* to the viewer than another object, it is drawn *larger*, and the object further away *smaller*. This last type of perspective device is known as *linear perspective* and was first used extensively by artists at the time of the Italian Renaissance to make art—particularly the human figure—appear more three-dimensional and life-like.

To make a realistic drawing of an object—for example a fashion model—is quite straightforward when she is standing directly in front of us, with arms by the side and legs together (that is, when all the limbs are in one plane, a plane that is parallel to the surface of the paper). Drawing our fashion model correctly when she is turning away from us, or when an arm is extended or one leg is in front of the other, however, is more difficult: to appear correct the drawing has to be drawn "in perspective".

In modern fashion drawing, issues of perspective do not arise as frequently, and are not as complex as in fine art. Much of the time, in fact, they do not arise at all: the pose

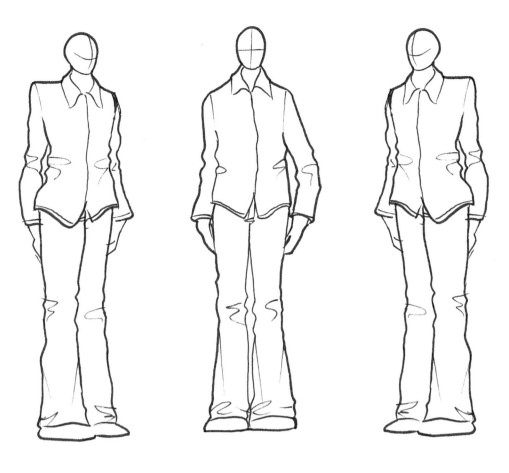

Jo's view of Carl—
a three-quarter view

Bill's view of Carl—
a front view

Sam's view of Carl—
a three-quarter view

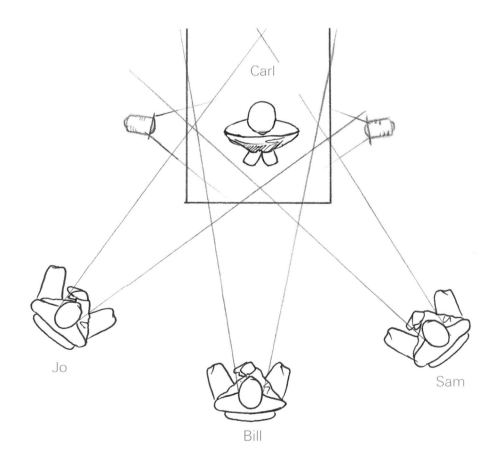

Point of view/angle of view. The model on the catwalk, Carl, is viewed by three members of the audience, Jo, Bill and Sam, each viewing Carl from a different angle. Jo and Sam's views of Carl, shown in the top part of the diagram, are angled— both three-quarter views. The part of the figure turned away from them appears compressed, or "foreshortened". Bill sees Carl straight on and sees both sides of the figure as symmetrical, without foreshortening.

perspective/
foreshortening

is chosen to show off the garments, and a front view with all limbs parallel to the surface of the paper is frequently all that is needed for this purpose. If more than one figure is included in the drawing then the figures can be placed at equal distances from the point of view so that they are drawn the same size.

On certain occasions, though, perspective also has to be employed in fashion drawing: front-view drawing is not always the best choice, and a *three-quarter view* (sometimes called the *oblique view* and discussed in detail in the next section) can give a clearer picture of a garment that has important features on the sides or back as well as the front. There are, too, times when a drawing of a *group* of figures is best composed with the figures arranged at different distances from the viewer's point of view, so that if the drawing is to have the correct appearance of *depth* the figures have to be drawn in different sizes.

Another example where perspective should be employed is that (already referred to above) where a figure has limbs in different planes—for example, one leg in front of the other or one arm coming forward and the other going back. Situations such as these are particularly common when drawing active sportswear, where many of the poses show the body caught in mid-action with limbs spread in all directions, but also arise from time to time with all types of garments. For these, and a number of other types of situations that arise from time to time, if we wish for our drawings of garments on the figure to appear three-dimensional, and as realistic and convincing as possible, we have to know the basics of perspective. These are reviewed over the next few pages before moving on to discuss the three-quarter figure—the view that employs *foreshortening*—one of the basic techniques of perspective.

FORESHORTENING
When an object is viewed at an angle, either to one side or from above or below, so that all of the object is *seen* but it appears to be *compressed*, or *shorter* than when seen straight-on front view at eye level, it is said to be *foreshortened*.

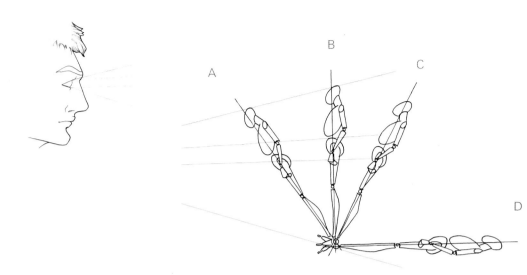

Fixed point of view/changing position of object. The figure is viewed successively inclining towards the viewer (A), upright (B), reclining away from the viewer (C) and flat on the ground (D).

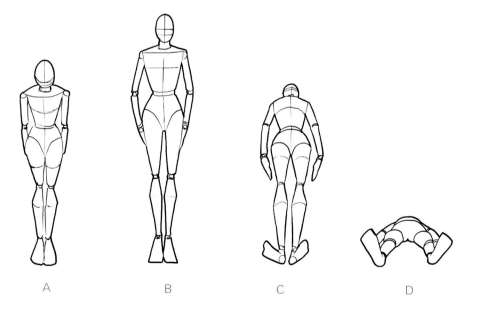

How the different positions of the figure in the top diagram are seen by the viewer. The upright figure, B, is straight on, perpendicular to the point of view and is not foreshortened. In the other positions, A, C and D, the figure is not vertical with respect to the point of view and they appear compressed or "foreshortened".

perspective/
foreshortening

The effect of foreshortening depends on the
point of view, and this can change either
because the viewer changes her or his point of
view (for example, looking at an object from in
front and then from behind, or above and then
below) or because the object itself changes
position—for example, a fashion model turns
around or someone passes us on an escalator.
Foreshortening occurs in the following views:

THREE-QUARTER /OTHER ANGLED VIEWS.
If an object is viewed at an angle, the side that
is turned away from the viewer's point of view
appears foreshortened.

EYE LEVEL
When seen at eye level from the front an object
does not appear foreshortened in any way. If
the eye level changes—if the object or the viewer's eye level moves up or down—the object
appears foreshortened.

RELATIVE DISTANCES OF OBJECTS (OR DIF-
FERENT PARTS OF THE SAME OBJECT)
Though more often described in terms of *linear
perspective*, illustrated at right with vanishing
lines, different objects that are at different distances from the viewer's point of view stand in
a relationship of foreshortening to each other—
the object further away appears compressed or
shortened in relation to the nearer object, even
though we may know they are of the same size.
In fashion drawing this effect is more commonly seen when different parts of the body are in
different planes, as, for example, when a hand
extends out from the page towards the viewer:
the hand will appear relatively large and the
rest of the body foreshortened in comparison.
In fashion drawing it is not common to make
drawings from a point of view other than eye
level, nor is it common to introduce "depth" into
a drawing—objects at different distances from
the viewer's point of view. What is very common, though, and is important to master, is the
three-quarter view, discussed in the next section.

LINEAR PERSPECTIVE
An in-depth knowledge of linear perspective is
not required for most fashion drawing, but as it
is one of the most common devices of repre-
sentational art it is useful to know the basic
principles. Linear perspective is, as mentioned,
the way three-dimensional objects are realistically represented on a two-dimensional surface—for us, paper. When linear perspective is

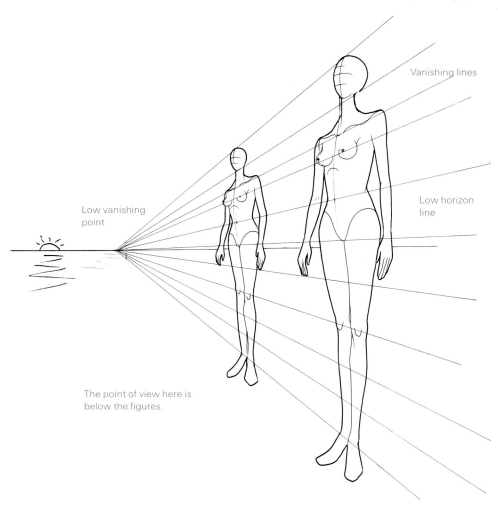

Low vanishing point

Vanishing lines

Low horizon line

The point of view here is below the figures.

Linear perspective, low eye level/low horizon line. Vanishing lines converge at low vanishing point on the horizon.

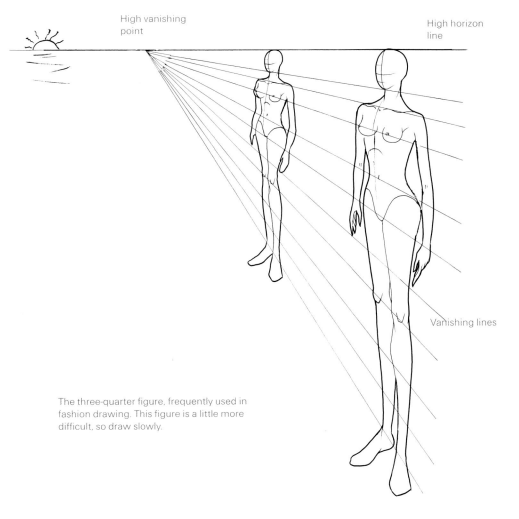

High vanishing point

High horizon line

Vanishing lines

The three-quarter figure, frequently used in fashion drawing. This figure is a little more difficult, so draw slowly.

Linear perspective, high eye level/high horizon line. Vanishing lines converge at high vanishing point on the horizon.

31

perspective/
foreshortening/exercise

written about in books (and many books have been written on the subject) rail tracks or telephone lines are often shown converging to the horizon—the *vanishing point*. When a drawing contains objects receding in space in more than one plane (planes are flat surfaces)—buildings, for example, a favorite of Renaissance writers on perspective, where the different sides of the buildings seen in the drawing represent different planes—then there can be more than one vanishing point. If a drawing contains only one vanishing point then it is called *one-point perspective*, if two, *two-point perspective* and so on. The relations of objects in multi-point perspective drawings can, if so desired, be plotted out geometrically and become highly complex. In fashion drawing, and even then only rarely, no more than two- or three-point perspectives are normally shown.

DRAWING IN PERSPECTIVE

Drawing in correct perspective is more easily learned from studying and copying photographs with foreshortened elements (active , youthful or sports poses, for example) than from trying to apply the theory. It is useful to bear in mind that, when viewed in perspective— in three-quarter view, for example— three -dimensional objects such as cylinders, cubes, spheres and others can all be considered as being made up of combinations of two-dimensional shapes—square, rectangles, ovals. This is also true for the human figure, whose parts often resemble three-dimensional cylinders and spheres, (though the corresponding two-dimensional shapes that appear in the perspective drawing are not quite as regular of course as with geometric forms). When drawing the foreshortened figure, look carefully at where different parts appear in relation to each other. When drawing foreshortened limbs, check to see where joints line up on the vertical balance line or which other parts they are aligned with.

Drawing in perspective is one of the most difficult parts of drawing and requires practice and constant observation to master. When beginning to draw fashion it is best to choose poses that are simple, with relatively few elements of perspective, and gradually to explore more complex poses as skills and experience build.

EXERCISE

Select photos of figures with foreshortened limbs from the sports or arts pages of newspapers or magazines and trace them.

Perspective/Foreshortening.
Views involving complex perspective are not common in fashion drawing, but it *is* common for parts of the body to be in a different plane to the torso. Here, the hand with the mike extends forward from the body. The hand appears proportionately larger than the other parts of the body, and the arm—in three-quarter view—is greatly foreshortened.

How the foreshortened left arm is drawn. When drawing foreshortened parts of the body it is often helpful to think of Bibendum (the Michelin Man) whose limbs are made up of concentric circles (or ovals, depending on the angle). Draw in the circles (or ovals if in three-quarter or other angled view) at the extremities of the limbs, gauging their correct sizes and then fill in the circles/ovals in-between.

croquis/three-quarter view/center-front line

Armed with our knowledge of the basic principles of perspective, let us move on to discuss the figure in three-quarter view. The three-quarter view is the view of the figure partially turned away from the viewer, at an angle to the plane of the paper. It is used frequently in fashion drawing because it conveys more information than the side, front or back views separately, allowing for side seams, armholes, openings, bows and a variety of details to be shown that cannot be seen from the other viewpoints. In three-quarter view the figure also appears more three-dimensional than in other views; it must, however, be drawn correctly, with the foreshortening—the compressed effect of the turned figure—depicted accurately, or the figure will appear distorted.

A line that is helpful when drawing three-quarter figures is the *center-front* line. The center-front line is a vertical line indicating the center front surface of the figure (in the front view figure it would also be the axis line), running from the neck through the center of the torso to the center of the feet. As the figure turns and appears to compress (or foreshorten), the center-front line tracks where the center of the figure appears. This provides valuable guidance for correct placement of the parts of the body on the turned, foreshortened figure. Many of the poses of the figure with garments used throughout this book are in three-quarter view, and in all these cases the center-front line is an invaluable guide for ensuring that the garments appear correctly positioned on the angled figure.

The foreshortening of the three-quarter view figure appears on the side where the figure is turned away. If the center-front line is included in the drawing then approximately three-quarters of the figure appears on the side of the center-front line where the figure is turned towards the viewer— of this, about one quarter is the partial side view, two quarters is the near-front view— and one quarter is on the side turned away.

The three-quarter figure, frequently used in fashion drawing. This figure is a little more difficult, so draw slowly. Begin drawing three-quarter figures straight on—viewed at eye level—before moving to more difficult views from above and below.

1. Draw the head as a simple oval. Draw in the center-front line dividing the head and neck in the proportions 3 to 1. The shoulders are drawn in the same proportions.

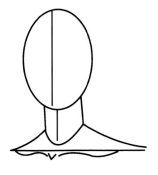

2. Add the bust at 2. Make sure the bust overlaps the arm on the side turning away. On the near side the point of the bust is at about ⅓ the distance between the center-front line and the edge of the figure.

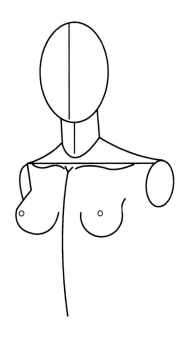

The plane of the torso shows more foreshortening than the legs or arms, which are almost cylindrical and do not foreshorten as much as flatter forms.

3. Draw in the upper torso, tapering to the waist at 3, and the upper arms. The breasts are located midway between the center-front line and the edge of the torso. In the three-quarter figurethe edge of the breast on the side turned away is seen in profile, curving from the shoulder, and partly covers the arm on that side. Make sure the breasts are at the same height (2) and at right angles to the c-f line. The top of the arm on the side turned away is a convex curve.

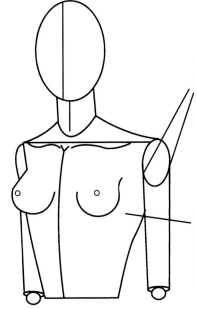

The upper arm on the nearer side extends down from each side of the ellipse of the armhole. Upper arms extend to the waist.

In the three-quarter figure more of the side of the figure is seen. Make sure to show space between the breast and the edge of the torso.

croquis/
three-quarter view

Foreshortening is difficult to represent accurately. It takes place whenever objects in the drawing are at an angle that is not parallel to the surface of the paper, i.e., whenever objects are drawn at an angle, and not in front view..
In fashion drawing it is easiest to show the figure in a vertical upright pose. When the figure *turns,* from a *front* view to a *three-quarter* view it is still vertical. This means that although the features of the figure compress on one side, because it is still vertical the angle of lines such as the shoulders, waist and hips, do not change, remaining at the horizontal. (If, as seen in the last section, besides changing the vertical plane, the horizontal plane is also changed and the figure viewed from either above or below, then foreshortening is introduced into that plane also and the part of the figure furthest away from the point of view—whether it is higher or lower—will appear foreshortened.) Before moving to more difficult views drawn from above and below, though, begin drawing three-quarter figures straight on—viewed at eye level. Note that the torso, which is a flat plane, shows more foreshortening than the legs, which are almost cylindrical and do not appear to foreshorten as much as flatter forms.

In fashion drawing the figure is secondary to the garments and should not distract from the garments, but in matters of foreshortening and perspective the mind/eye seems to be usually much more tolerant than seems to be the case for shape and relative proportions. Every effort should be made to draw perspective and foreshortening correctly, and obvious distortions corrected, but, generally speaking, less-than-perfect accuracy in this area is easier to overlook. Some of the greatest *artists*, let alone fashion designers, in fact never master perspective drawing. In fashion drawing it is more important that features are of the correct relative proportions and in their proper locations than to get perspective absolutely correct.

4. Draw in the hips and the line of the pelvis on both sides, extending to the crotch. Proportions for the hip/pelvis area are also in the ration ¾/¼ Draw in the lower arms to the wrist at the same level as the crotch.

5. Draw in the legs. The leg turned away is slightly smaller than the nearer leg. The knees are indicated as ovals, pointing in the same direction as the figure.

Note that although the three-quarter figure shows foreshortening on one side because of rotation in the vertical plane it is still drawn upright and vertical—there is no rotation in the horizontal plane. The angles of the lines of the shoulders, waist and hips are all parallel to each other and horizontal.

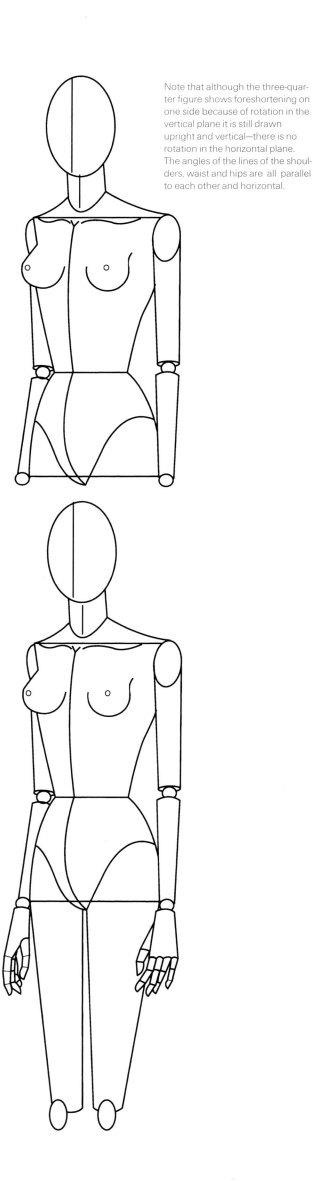

croquis/three-quarter view/exercise

EXERCISE

Draw ten three-quarter figures. Look for these views in a magazine. Trace the edge of each figure.

6. Finish by drawing in the lower part of the legs. Because the leg is cylindrical in three-quarter view it appears less fore-shortened than the torso and the flatter parts of the body.

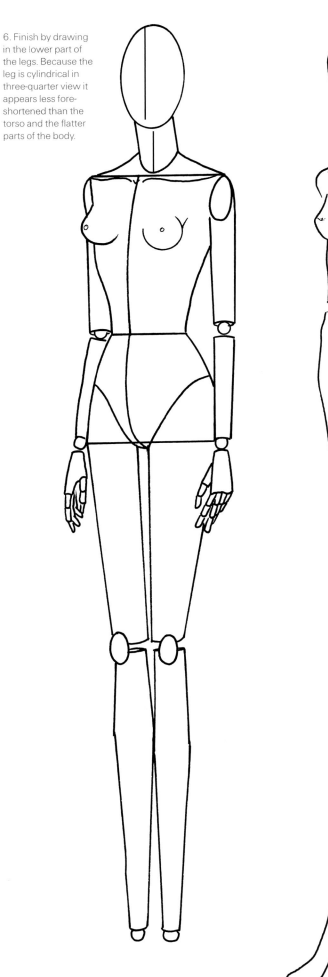

The completed fleshed-out three-quarter figure with natural curve in the center axis.

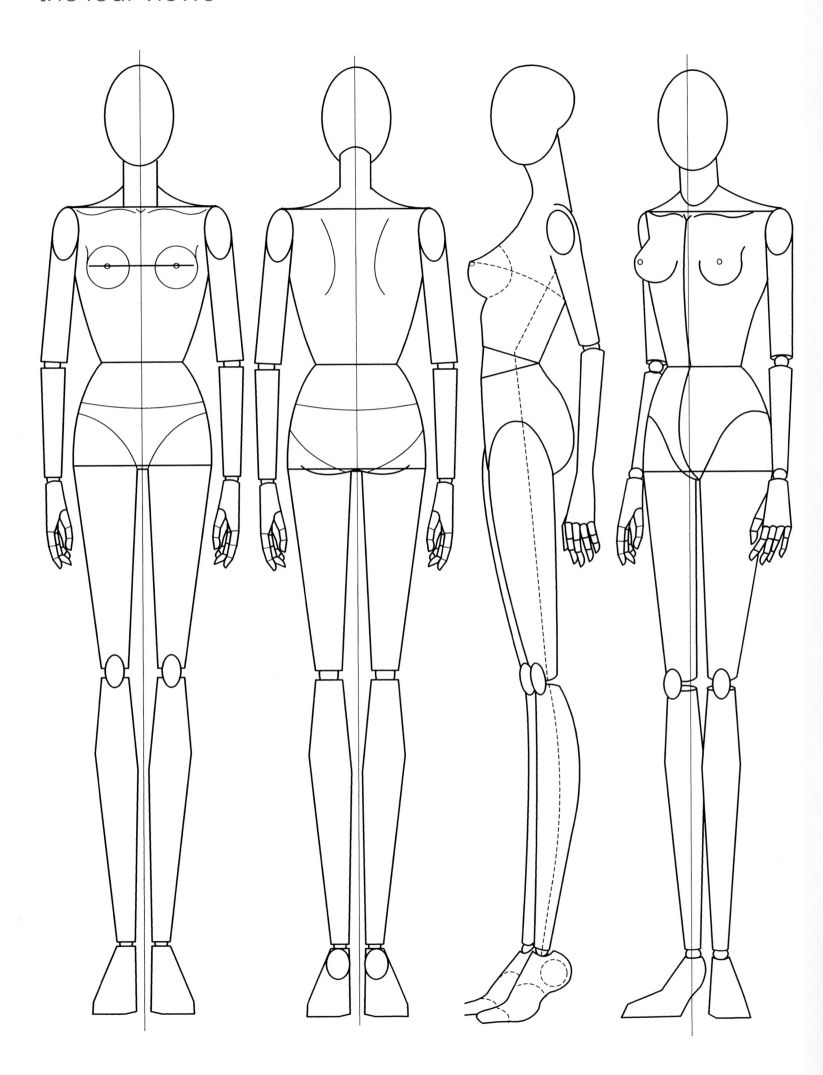

shading and value/ light and shadow

SHADING AND VALUE/LIGHT AND SHADOW

Real objects are three-dimensional; they have height, width and depth. As discussed in the preceding section on perspective, when objects are viewed at an angle, in three-quarter or another partial view, we can *see* they are three-dimensional, and not cardboard cut-outs: we see part of the side of the object as well as the front. To draw these angled views so they appear realistic we use, as we have seen, the technique of *foreshortening*, imitating on the paper— a two-dimensional surface—how we actually see three-dimensional objects. In order for our drawings of objects to appear *fully* realistic, though, we have to reproduce not only the way that the two-dimensional sizes and shapes that represent a three-dimensional form have changed when they are seen at an angle, but also the way in which some parts of an object appear *light*, some parts appear *in shadow* and other parts appear in-between.

Seeing is the process in which the brain interprets *reflected light* that enters through the eyes. The objects we see appear in *color,* and this is because objects of "different colors" (as we rather inaccurately refer to them—color is a property of light, not objects) in fact absorb all the component parts of white light—the colors of the spectrum—with the exception of the color we see. For example, a blue object absorbs all the colors of the spectrum *except* blue, which is reflected. The colored light that is reflected and perceived by our eyes (in coordination with our brains) appears to be of different degrees of light and darkness. Where the surface of an object is *flat*, a lot of light is reflected from it, and that part of the object appears *light;* where the surface of the object is not flat, but bends away from the light, less light is reflected from it and it appears *partly in shadow,* darker; where the surface of an object is completely hidden from the light it appears *completely in shadow.* We see the extremes of darkness and light as *black* and *white.* This is true for objects with color as well as objects without color. For example, take a shiny, red silk dress:

Shading gives these fashion accessories a three-dimensional appearance.

shading and value
color/greyscale

the lightest parts, where most light is
reflected, appear white, as highlights; the
darkest parts, in the depths of the folds,
appear *black*. The rest of the dress
appears as red, of differing degrees of
light and dark. If we were to make an
accurate drawing of this same red dress in
black and white, we would see the same
white and black at the extremes; the
lighter and darker shades of red would be
seen as different shades of grey.

VALUE/TONES, SHADES & TINTS
The lightness or darkness of a particular
color is referred to as its *value*. LIghter colors are said to have *higher values,* the
highest value being white; darker tones
are said to have *lower values*, the lowest
value being black. The range of greys—
each different grey is called a *tone*—
between black and white is known as a
greyscale. Colors themselves have value,
both *intrinsic value*, the value of a particular color (colors such as yellow are high
value, and others such as blue, are low
value, and the rest are in-between) and
value that refers to whether they are a
darker or lighter tones of the color—for
example, a low value *navy blue* or a high
value *sky blue*. Darker tones of colors are
known as *shades* and lighter versions are
known as *tints*. Every tone of a color has a
corresponding value of grey in the
greyscale, so a black and white drawing
(or photograph) can reproduce the same
range of values as the color drawing (or
photograph).

This book is concerned with the principles
involved in drawing fashion in so-called
black and white, which means, in effect,
that we are interested in how to represent
the range of values in a drawing in
greyscale. It is important to master drawing in grey-scale/ black and white before
advancing to drawing fashion in color,
where value differences must also be
shown, but in a range of colors.

In drawing, the way light and shadows
form in and around objects is represented
by using *shading*. Shading means making
an area darker by making a denser application of the drawing medium being used.

Color v. black and white/greyscale.
Every color has a corresponding
greyscale tone of the same value.
Some colors, such as yellow are
light—high value—colors and .others
such as blue are low value.

shading/gradation of tone/ shading geometric forms

SHADING

Shading, also often known as *rendering*, is the key to making objects in a drawing appear three-dimensional. In order for the shading to give a realistic effect, though, it must show the full range of variations of light and dark displayed on the surface of an object, from the lightest highlights, which appear white, or almost white, to the darkest shadows, which appear black, or almost black. Not only must the full range of values be shown, but the order and way in which they appear must be realistic. The way different tones of light change across a surface is known as *tonal gradation,* or *gradation of tone.* If, for example, a surface moves gradually into shadow, gradually bending away from the light, a continuous gradation of tone can be observed. If, on the other hand (particularly in shiny objects) a raised part of the surface, seen as a white highlight, sits immediately adjacent to a hidden part, which appears black, then there will be no gradual gradation of tone, but the dark and light will stand in strong contrast to each other. This juxtaposition of the light and dark—known as *value contrast*—will heighten the light of the highlight and the dark of the shadow.

SHADING OF GEOMETRIC FORMS

Many of the three-dimensional forms of both the human figure and the clothes it wears (which mostly take the shape of the different parts of the figure) are similar to simple geometric forms, such as spheres, cubes or cylinders. To understand the principles of shading, then, it is helpful to examine how these forms are shaded when drawn on paper to appear three-dimensional. (It is also helpful to note that when drawing these three-dimensional forms theycan be broken down into combinations of two-dimensional shapes: a cube is formed of a square and two parallelograms, a cylinder a rectangle with ellipses at each end and so on.) The methods for drawing three common three-dimensional forms that show up frequently in fashion drawing are

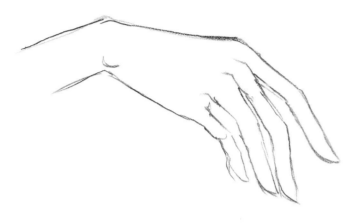

Top, hand without shading; bottom, shaded hand.
Shading is the key to making objects in a drawing appear three-dimensional. In order for the shading to give a realistic effect it must show the full range of variations of light and dark displayed on the surface of an object, from the lightest highlights, which appear white, or almost white, to the darkest shadows, which appear black, or almost black.

shading of geometric forms

described below. It is important first to decide on the location of the light source and where light will fall on the object, just as it would for the lighting of a real object. The further a part of the surface of the object is from the light, the more in shadow it will be; the closer it is to the light source the lighter it will be. In drawing, because light areas are made by leaving the page unmarked, and dark by applying shading, it is usual to work from light to dark, showing the transition from the areas which receive most light, and are brightest, to the areas which receive little or no light and are in the deepest shadows.

1. Sphere. Start with a highlight at the top—a small area of light. This is the area that is facing the light source and receiving most light. Outside this small area the sphere bends away from the light and moves into shadow. At the bottom of the sphere its surface receives no light at all and is completely in shadow. The sphere is shaded by making it progressively darker as it bends away from the light. If the sphere rests on a table top it casts a round shadow known as a cast shadow. The point at which the sphere touches the table is very black and is known as the *tangency*. This area is drawn with a thick black line.

2. Cube. A cube has six square faces set at right angles to each other. Start by drawing the face that is in front view and parallel to the plane of the paper with four equal sides. For the other two faces, create two parallelograms, drawing parallel lines that slant (in this case) to the right for the top of the cube and a third parallel line to indicate the side face. If the cube is lit from the front the front view face will appear light. The base of the cube is dark as as t is at a tangent to the table top. Cast shadows appear to have the same shape as the cube and reflective light extends out in any direction.

3. Cylinder. The cylinder is shaped as a rectangle in one of its cross-sections and a circle in the other. When drawn at an angle to appear three-dimensional it is shown as a rectangle with ovals, or ellipses, at either end. It appears frequently in fashion draw-

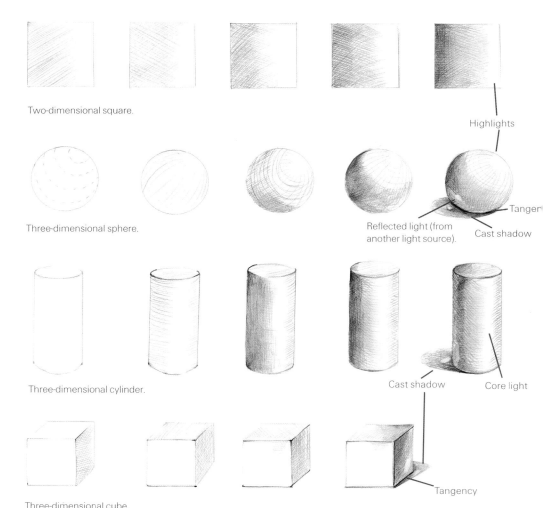

Two-dimensional square.

Highlights

Three-dimensional sphere.

Tanger

Reflected light (from another light source).

Cast shadow

Three-dimensional cylinder.

Cast shadow

Core light

Three-dimensional cube.

Tangency

Building up shading on three-dimensional forms.
Each form can be viewed as made up of two-dimensional shapes which take on a three-dimensional appearance when shading is added. Shading is made with successive layered applications, with the parts in shadow receiving the densest applications and the highlights or corelights being shown by the unmarked white of the paper. Many parts of the body and the garments that cover them resemble these basic forms. When considering how to shade a part of a garment it is useful to decide which geometric form it resembles.

shading the body/
light source/

-ly in fashion drawing as a form used to express arms, legs, fingers, the neck, the nose, toes and lips, the drapes and folds of fabric.

SHADING THE BODY/LIGHT SOURCE
Just as with geometric forms, to draw the *body* so it appears realistic it also must be shaded so that the patterns of light and dark in the drawing appear similar to the patterns of light and shadow that appear on it in real life, with the lightest and darkest parts as well as all the tones bet-ween clearly represented. Once the basic croquis is drawn the direction of the light source must be decided (in a drawing, unless we are making a drawing of an object that is in front of us, it is the artist who decides on the direction of the light source). If the light is from the *front* then the front of the figure will be lit and both sides will have shadows as they recede from the light; if lit from the *right* side the right side will be lit and the left in shadows; if lit from the *left*, the left will be lit and the right in shadows. It is also possible to have two or three separate light sources in a drawing and different parts in light and shad-ow—for example, the body might be lit and the head in shadow, or *vice-versa*— resulting in complex interplays of light and dark

Deciding on the position of the light source does not mean that all the parts of the body that are in light will be uniformly light and those in shadow will be uniformly dark: In the areas of the body that are turned towards the light, those parts that are most raised will be lightest and those that are hidden or receding from the light will be darker; there will be a gradation of tones from light to darker. In the areas that are in shadow there will be a similar range of values, but both the lightest and darkest values will be darker than those of the parts in light. *In general, when shading the human figure, shadows will tend to appear around the bust, the head, including eye sockets, base of nose, base of mouth, cheekbones, under the chin and jaw line, under the hair line, around the neck, behind the ears, around the tummy, under the arms and armholes, between the fingers, around the legs and crotch and, if the level of detail extends to it, between the toes.*

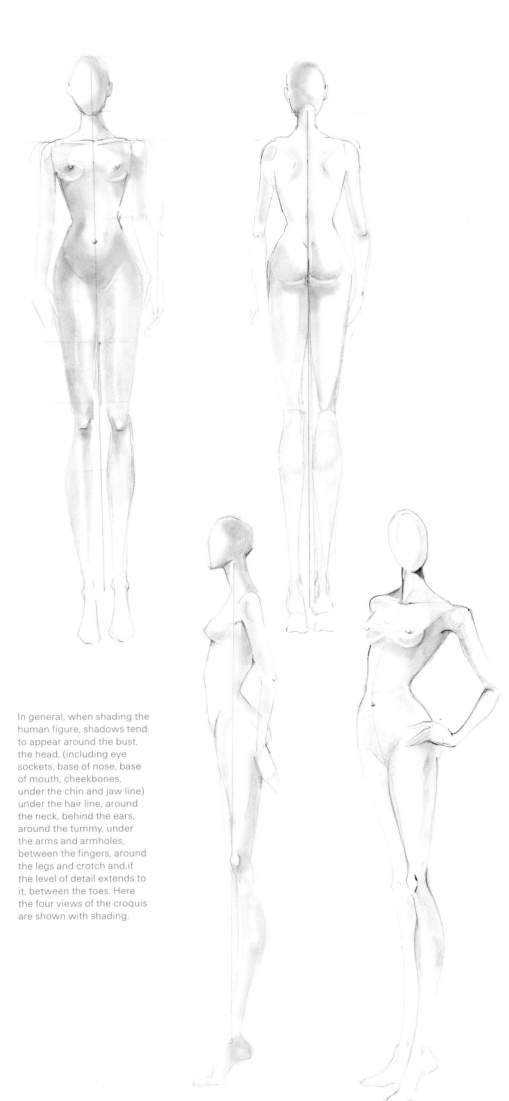

In general, when shading the human figure, shadows tend to appear around the bust, the head, (including eye sockets, base of nose, base of mouth, cheekbones, under the chin and jaw line) under the hair line, around the neck, behind the ears, around the tummy, under the arms and armholes, between the fingers, around the legs and crotch and,if the level of detail extends to it, between the toes. Here the four views of the croquis are shown with shading.

shading/ink v. pencil
line weight and quality

INK v. PENCIL

Up to this point drawings have been made with pen and ink. Ink drawings have a clear, graphic line that is ideal for illustrating structure and shape. For shading, however, pen and ink is limited: very little variation of line thickness and weight is possible, and variations of darkness—light shadow through to heavy shadow—have to be indicated by varying densities of applications of lines, known as *cross-hatching*. *Pencil* is a much more versatile medium for shading, as it is easily possible to use leads of different degrees of hardness that apply more or less graphite to the paper that give different degrees of light and dark and also to vary the line thickness and weight with slight movements of the hand and wrist. For the remainder of this chapter, and in the next two chapters, where the emphasis will be on creating realistic, three-dimensional drawings with detailed shading, pencil will be used

LINE WEIGHT AND QUALITY

When learning to draw it is important to be aware of the type of lines one is drawing right from the beginning so that good habits form early (bad habits are easy to acquire and difficult to change!). All drawings are made with lines, and the types of lines that are chosen and the way they are employed greatly affect the end result of the drawing. Lines have a variety of characteristics, including, besides location and direction, *weight* (the amount of pressure used to make the line and how light or heavy it appears in consequence), *thickness* and *texture*. The overall way that line is used in a drawing—the total of the individual choices made on use of line—is referred to as *line quality*.

A detailed description of the use of line in drawing *garments* is included in Chapter Six: Fabrics. At this stage, while still learning to master drawing the croquis, the following guidelines should be applied:

A THICK BOLD line will give the figure a strong, graphic presence and make it appear to have physical weight on the page.

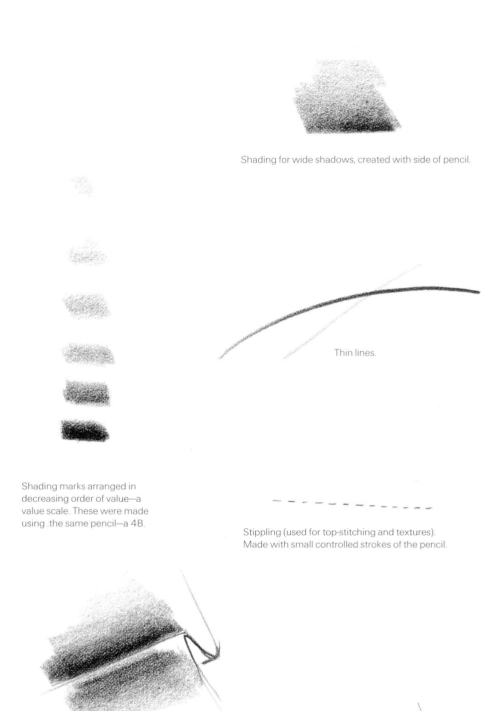

Shading for wide shadows, created with side of pencil.

Thin lines.

Shading marks arranged in decreasing order of value—a value scale. These were made using .the same pencil—a 4B.

Stippling (used for top-stitching and textures). Made with small controlled strokes of the pencil.

Shading for objects with highly contrasting values (for example, shiny fabrics). A dark value is used immediately next to a light value.

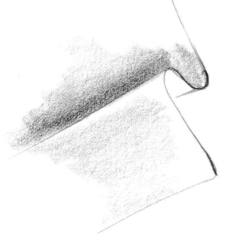

Shading for objects with values closer together (for example matt fabrics like linen or cotton). A medium-dark value is used and gradations appear between it and the lightest value.

shading/lineweight and quality/nuanced lines/ exercises

A THIN line will do the opposite, making the figure appear light and ethereal. A line that is important in fashion drawing is called a NUANCED LINE. A nuance is a slight or subtle change of meaning, and a nuan- ced line is one that changes subtly from thick to thin or from dark to light.

NUANCED LINES

Nuanced lines are used to express the quality of light. Light, as already mentioned, reflects off flat surfaces but does not bend, so when a surface bends away from the light it moves into shadow. A nuanced line, as described below, is able both to express areas of the body that are flat, and therefore well lit, and also areas that bend away from, and therefore do not receive, light. Areas in light are indicated by making the line outlining the edge of the area *thin*, and areas away from the light by making the line *thick*, indicating shadow. A nuanced line becomes thicker round the chin, armhole, waistline, crotch, elbow, knee and ankle, areas where the body bends into shadow, and thinner along the flat planes—the length of the arm and leg, the outside curve of the hip, the side of the neck.

A nuanced line is made by pressing down on and lifting up on the pencil with one fluid movement. The line should be made in one continuous movement to appear smooth and elegant. (When making lines, a common mistake is to move the pencil slowly down the page with little strokes, called chicken scratches. This is a definite "do not do" as it gives the illusion of texture as opposed to the outline of the figure.)

EXERCISES

1. Practice drawing and shading spheres, cubes and cylinders. Use the full range of values of dark and light and show highlights, cast shadows and corelights.
2. Fill a page with lines of different weight and thicknesses.

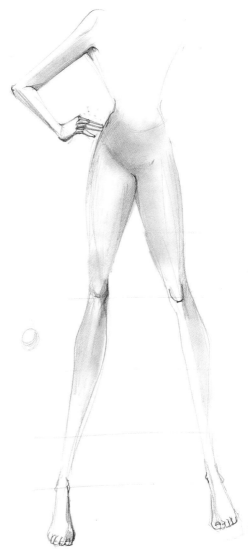

Shading techniques: Using the same pencil, varying the pressure of application. The range of darks and lights can be achieved using a single pencil—here a 2B— and varying the pressure with which it is applied. The continuous, even gradation of tone in the shading is achieved by smudging the pencil immediately after application using a stump or cotton swab.

Nuanced line.

Thicker and darker nuanced line.

A bow drawn with a thick bold line has a strong graphic presence.

A bow drawn with a thin light line has a delicate, ethereal presence.

lineweight and quality/
shading with pencil/exercises

Skilled line use will develop with experience. When starting to draw, the beginner should try to be aware of the appearance of the mark being made on the paper as well as on creating accurate shapes and proportions .

TECHNIQUES FOR SHADING WITH PENCIL

Shading with pencil is made easier if different pencils of different degrees of hardness are used, but in principle all effects can be achieved using only one pencil with differing amounts of pressure and more or fewer applications. It is best to use a 4B or 6B pencil for the darkest areas and an HB for the lightest areas.

In shading, the aim is to achieve an even and continuous application of tone that gives the appearance of mist or smoke, either of the same even value or shifting value from light to dark. The individual pencil marks are not usually seen (unless we want a particular special effect). To do this, apply pencil in a motion similar to the shape of the object being shaded— a circular motion for a sphere, long strokes for cylinders such as arms and legs and so on— and then *smudge the pencil almost immediately*. Smudging can be done with a stump (a pencil without lead) or a cotton swab. Smudging with the finger is not advised as there are oils in the skin that mark the paper.

EXERCISES

1. Draw the four views of the figure and shade. Show shadows in the arms, legs, tummy, bust and face.
2. Practice drawing nuanced lines. Draw the four views of the croquis using nuanced lines.

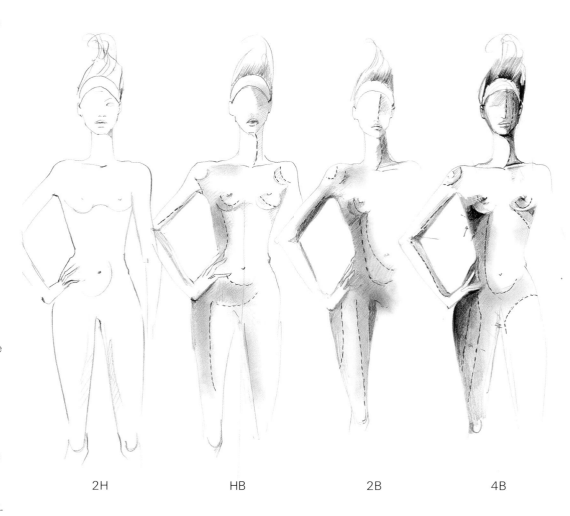

2H   HB   2B   4B

Shading techniques: Using pencils of differing degrees of hardness. These drawings were made using successively darker pencils—2H, HB, 2B and 4B, as shown above from left to right. The areas where the different pencils are used are indicated by dotted lines. The lighter pencils are used in the parts where the body is lightest and reflects light. and progressively darker pencil is used for the parts that bend away from the light. The underside of the arm and the inside of the leg are darkest and are shaded with the 4B pencil.

face/
front view

The face is an oval: as mentioned, it is an egg shape rather than a hot-dog or watermelon. In fashion drawing the face is not as important as in real life, where it conveys much information. In fashion drawing the face is mainly a complement to the clothing (and indeed is often treated like an accesory). If the face is to convey additional information in drawing, such as mood, attitude or a particular expression then that information should be simple and direct.

The fashion face is beautiful, but smaller than in real life. Like the real face, however, it is perfectly symmetrical (moreso in fact than most real faces) and it is important to measure carefully, for the smallest shift in the eye or mouth can make the face appear to look insane or like a cartoon. Much practice is required in order to become proficient.

The features of the face are all approximately the same size. The nose is the least important feature and should be drawn minimally: often the base is all that is needed. The eyes are very expressive and provide information on mood, often providing useful indications as to the style of the clothes in the drawing. Eyes are slimmer than is often thought and the eyeball is only about one-third of the total space of the eye. The fullest part of the face is the mouth: the bottom lip a full upward curve and the upper lip a full curve with a small indentation.

When drawing the face either work down from the eyes or start from the nose or mouth. Draw the face after drawing the other parts of the body and garments; as the face is so seductive it is easy to spend too much time on it. It is, after all, really only an accent to the clothes! Always keep the pencil sharp so the line can be made as precisely as possible.

The starting point for the face. Begin by drawing an oval and divide in half vertically and horizontally. The face is curved, not flat, and the lines bend round the surface.

½

The fashion face with all features added before final fleshing out and shading.

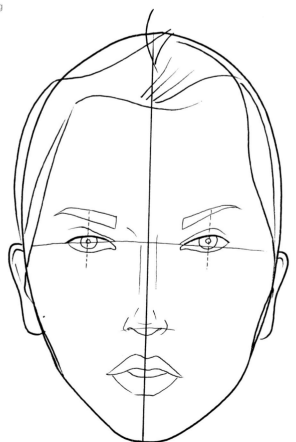

face/front view/ exercises

FACE—FRONT VIEW

Let's begin by drawing the front view of the face.

1. Draw the oval shape of the face and draw in the vertical axis line, dividing the face into two equal parts. Add another line cutting the face exactly in half horizontally, so the face is divided into four parts. The horizontal line marks the the eye level. The eyes should never be placed above this line as the face will then appear extremely old. (As babies, our eye level is only one third up from the bottom of the head; it gradually moves up as we mature, ending up almost exactly in the middle of the head. This is true for men and women.)

2. Having divided the head in half for the eye level, divide the distance between the eyes and the bottom of the head in half again. This point is the bottom of the nose.

3. Divide the distance between the bottom of the nose and the bottom of the head in half again. This point is the bottom of the mouth. It is important to place the mouth close to the nose. The jaw begins below the ears, level with the center of the mouth and the chin is directly under the mouth, no wider or smaller than the mouth. It is important the chin and mouth are the same size. The jaw tapers in on both sides of the face until it meets the chin (above the jaw—between the ears and the beginning of the jaw—the outline of the head also tapers, but less so).

4. The top of the ear is aligned with the top of the eye, and the bottom with the bottom of the nose.

5. The hair line is approximately ⅛ to ¼ of a head length from the top of the head and extends across the eyes—like an umbrella for the eyes—and then moves down from the eyes to the ears. The outside edge (or silhouette) of the hair cascades from the top of the head (the crown), moves close to the skull to the eye level and then falls softly to the shoulders. Slim down the hair and head so that the eyes float down to the clothes.

EXERCISES

1. Select 10 front view faces from a magazine and copy, bringing out shading and line quality. Avoid smiles.

2. Practice drawing the features separately. Refer to the sections below if needed.

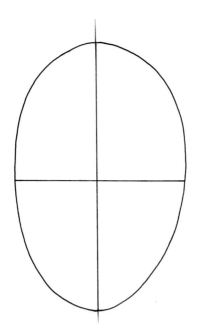

Eye level

1. Draw an oval and divide it vertically and horizontally into four equal segments. The horizontal lne is the level of the eyes.

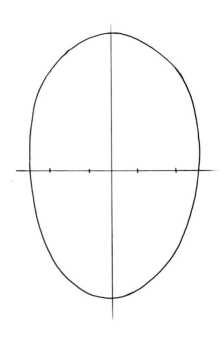

2. Mark out the position of the eyes. All features on the face are the same size. The eyes are placed one eye-width apart and one eye width in from the side of the head.

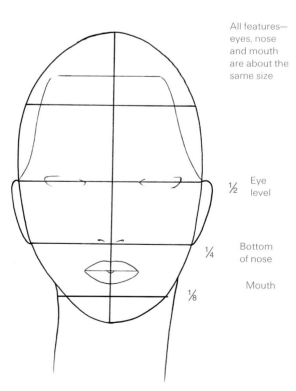

All features—eyes, nose and mouth are about the same size

½ Eye level

¼ Bottom of nose

Mouth

3. The bottom of the nose is indicted at ¼. Divide the space between the bottom of the nose and the chin in half and this indicated the position of the center of the mouth. Ears fit between eye level and the top of the nose.

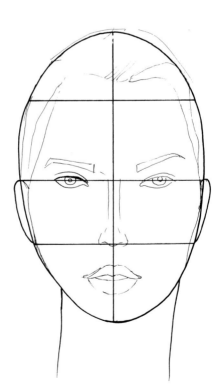

4. The hairline is approximately ⅛ to ¼ of a head length from the top of the head and extends across the eyes, like an umbrella for the eyes. Fill in the details. Keep the head slim.

face/
front view

The finished face is eye-catching
and a little provocative.

Front view face. Artifice and high style combine in this rendering of a wedding veil inspired by a design of Comme des Garcons. Note the flower petal motif of the veil continuing to the false eyelashes.

face/
side view

SIDE VIEW FACE

The side view face has the same proportions as the front view, the difference being that the features of the face
that extend out—the nose, lips, chin
and eyelashes—are, in side view, seen
in profile: they appear as quite different
shapes from their appearances on the
front view face. As with the front view
face, these shapes that represent the
features have to be drawn in teh correct proportions and locations.

The basic shape of the side view head
is an oval, most of which is contained in
a rectangle. When beginning to draw
the side view face it is easiest first to
draw such a rectangle, extending it by
adding an arc where the upper back
part of the head will be, and then plot-
ting the rest of the shape of the head
Divide the rectangle in half horizontally
and the bottom half in half again, and
also divide the original retangle in half
vertically.

1. Begin by drawing the nose. The
slope of the nose starts halfway down
the head. It is about two-thirds of a
head in length and one third at the
base. The angle of the nose can be varied as preferred. The tip of the nose is
rounded and the base curves round
into the upper lip.

2. In profile the mouth is shaped like a
heart sitting on its side, with the lower
lip slightly further back on the head
than the upper. In reality, on the head
the mouth is close to the nose and so
must be kept close in a drawing. It lies
on the same vertical axis as the nose,
directly beneath. The corner of the
mouth aligns with the outer edge of the
eye.

In profile, the jawline is seen in outline.
It is curved, and starts in alignment
with the center of the mouth.

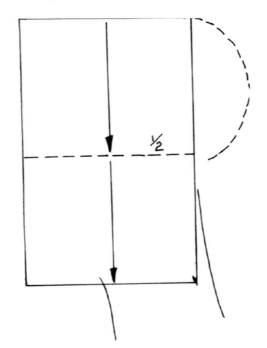

1. The basic shape of
the head in side view
can be seen as a rec-
tangle plus an arc. Eye
level is at ½

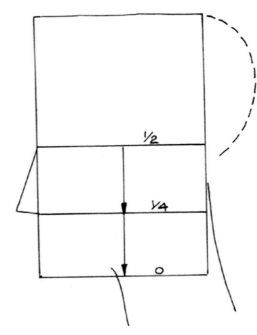

2. Nose is between
½ and ¾

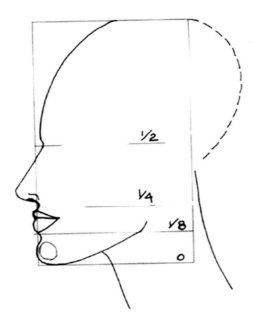

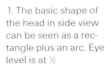

3. The mouth sits directly
under the nose. Chin is
directly under mouth.
Jawline slopes up to mouth
level.

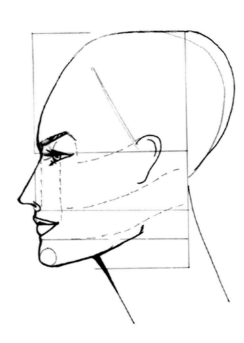

4. The eye is at ½. The ear is
at the level of the eye and
top of nose. Hairline slopes
from forehead to ear.

The proportions of the side view face.

face/side view/ exercise

3. The eye is a wedge shape that sits halfway down the head; the top of the wedge shape represents the bottom of the eyelid. The eyeball is in the front of the eye, just behind the front of the eyelid, and the lash extends out from the eyelid. The eyelash starts at the front of the head just above the eye and extends up around the eye. (If drawn downwards it gives the eye and face a sad look.) The ear is behind the center of the rectangle and its mid point aligns with the center of the eye. It is about one quarter of a head in length and can be drawn with one or two lines. The hairline begins near the top of the head, falls in a close to straight line to the middle of the front of the ear and continues from the lower back of the ear to the back of the head above the jawline.

EXERCISE

Select 10 side view faces from a magazine and copy, bringing out shading and line quality. Avoid smiles. Pay attention to the location of the hairline. Keep the face and neck slim.

Note that the side view head slants diagonally forward. The back of the head—the cranium—is rounded.

The forehead extends to ½—the eye level—where the nose begins. The nose extends down to just above ¼ and then turns back to the base, directly under the mouth. There is a small semi-circular indentation between the base of the nose and the mouth. The mouth is directly beneath the nose.

The ear is the same height as the eye and the top of the nose.

The chin is the same size as the mouth, is directly beneath the mouth and curves back to form the jawline. The jawline extends to the level of the top of the mouth, directly below the ear.

The eye is the shape of an inverted triangle. The eyeball sits in the front of the eye and is drawn as a slim ellipse. The eyelash curves out beyond the eye; the eyebrow begins above and in front of the eye and extends back behind the eye. Add a darker, more detailed line to the eyelashes. Fill in the silhouette of the hair noting that the hairline extends ¼ way down from the top of the head, extends out to the same level as the eye and then slants down to the ear.

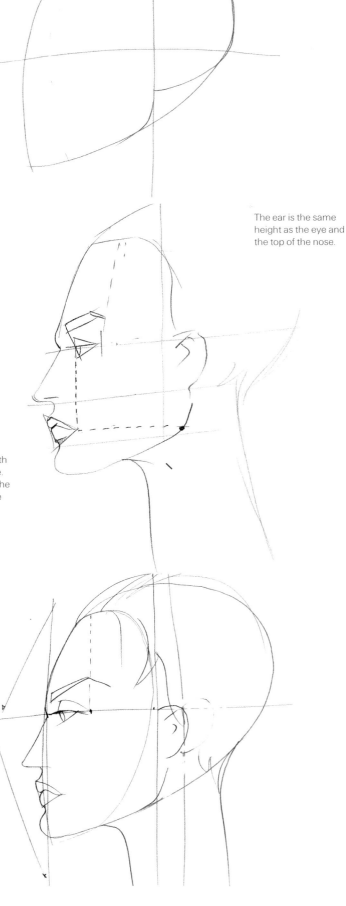

Drawing the side view face.

face/
side view

The completed face. Shading is applied around the cheek and under the jaw-line. Note that the features are full but when seen in profile in the side view are only half the width they appear in front view. Note also that the plane of the forehead ends in a line from the corner of the eye and the hairline slopes to the front of the ear.

face/
three-quarter view

THREE-QUARTER VIEW FACE

The three-quarter face is the face drawn at an angle, so that one side is foreshortened, and the features on this side appear smaller than on the non-foreshortened side (though the features on each side of the face are the same size as the others on the *same* side). Begin drawing three-quarter faces seen from an eye level point of view, i.e., not seen from above or below. This makes it easier to draw them in correct perspective, as foreshortening only takes place in one plane, and also means that the vertical positioning of the features on the head is the same as on the side or front view face.

1. First draw an oval, with curvature on one side more rounded, representing the side closest to the point of view, and flatter on the other, representing the side further away that is foreshortened. Draw in the center-front line, curving around the front of the face. In the three-quarter face this is located so the foreshortened part of the face on one side of it is about one third the total area of the oval and the other section is about two thirds the area of the oval. Draw in a line to divide the head in two sections horizontally, also bending round the surface of the face. As when drawing the side view of the face, draw in another line between that line and the bottom of the head, and divide that area in two again with another line. These lines will make correct placement of the features easier.

2. It is possible to start drawing the face from any point, but it is usually easiest to start at the nose and mouth. First, draw in a line to represent the base of the nose, in the same position as in the other views, just over one quarter up from the bottom of the head. This line cuts through the center-front line, about one third of its length on one side and two-thirds on the other, curving around the surface of the face; for the three-quarter face — the face at 45° to the plane of the paper—all features on the horizontal plane of the face are in these proportions. Draw in the profile of the nose, starting on the center-front line at eye level half way down the head and connecting to the end of the baseline marking its bottom edge.

The three-quarter face is often drawn tilted slightly down: it is an expressive pose and is no more difficult to draw than when level. Begin by drawing the head as an egg shape with greater curvature on the nearer side. Draw in the center-front line dividing the head approximately in the ratio ¾ to ¼, and divide it in two horizontally to indicate the level of the eyes.

The most difficult features to draw in the three-quarter face are those on the side that is turned away. The eye on that side appears foreshortened and is partly obscured by the nose; it must be drawn directly from the line of the nose. The eyebrow is foreshortened and extends from the corner of the eye to the side of the head

Add shading and definition to the features. Shadow can appear under the jawline, under the lower lip and in the eye socket.

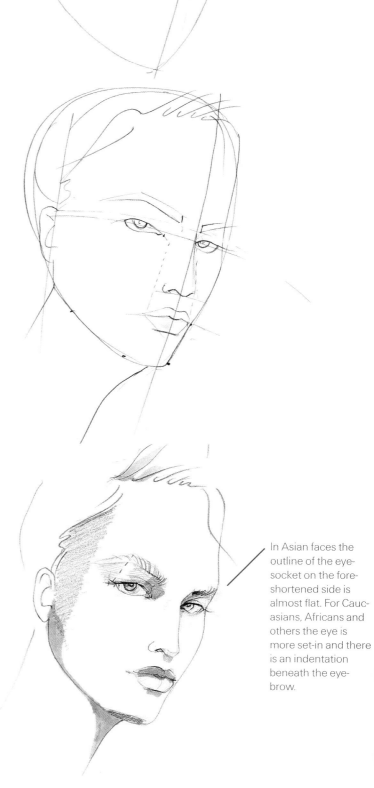

In Asian faces the outline of the eye-socket on the fore-shortened side is almost flat. For Caucasians, Africans and others the eye is more set-in and there is an indentation beneath the eye-brow.

face/
three-quarter view

3. To draw the mouth, first indicate the middle of the mouth where the lips meet by drawing a line parallel to that marking the base of the nose, also split ⅓/⅔ on either side of the center-front line. Add half-circles above and beneath to represent the lips, giving the top line an indentation, lining up with the center of the base of the nose.

4. The chin is a sphere the same width as the mouth, and in the three-quarter face is shown as an oval with less curvature on the foreshortened side. The chin sits directly under the mouth and extends to the jawline.

5. The eye nearer to the point of view sits approximately one eye's width in from the ear and slightly lesser distance from the center-front line running through the nose. The inner edge of the eye aligns with the corner of the mouth. On the foreshortened side of the face, the eye is drawn immediately next to the bridge of the nose.

6. On the foreshortened side of the face, the line of the forehead extends to the eyebrow. The amount of indentation of the eye socket varies among different races—in the African race the eye socket is well set-in whereas the contour is almost flat for most Asians, for example. The profile extends out at the cheekbone and then slopes back to the center-front line in the middle of the jaw.

The complete shaded three-quarter face.

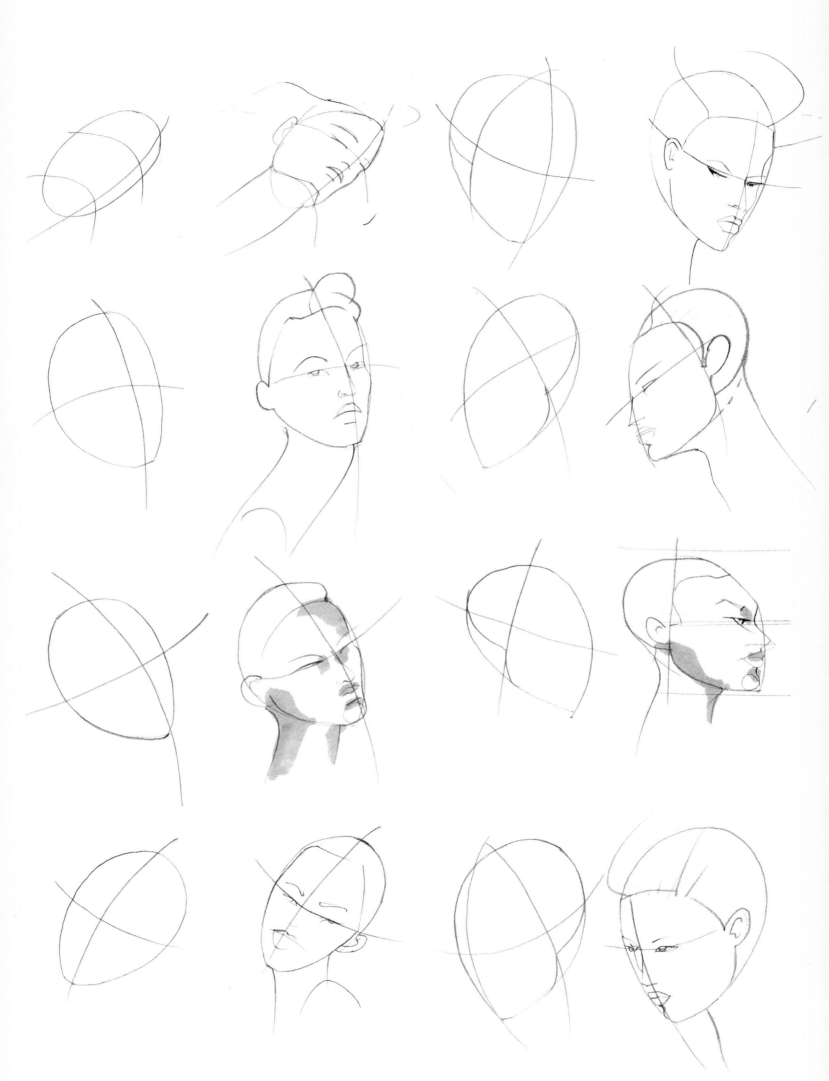

face/ front/side/three-quarter view/different eye levels

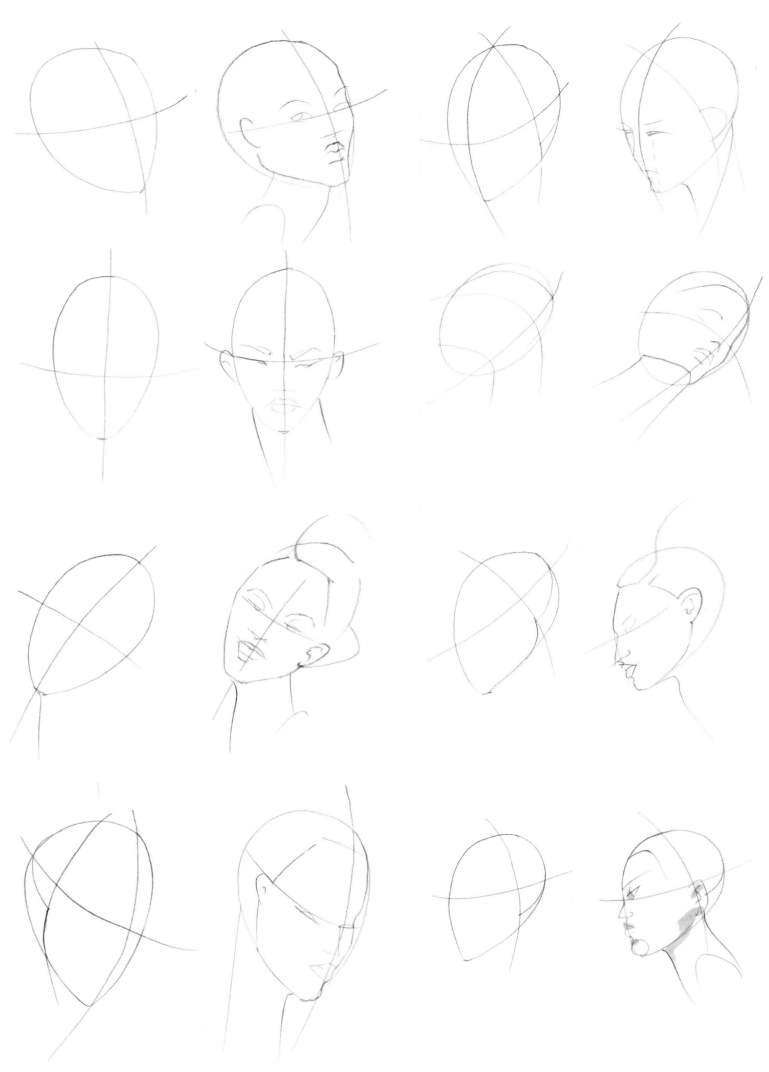

face/ front/side/three-quarter view/different eye levels

face/ front/side/three-quarter view/different eye levels

eyes

The eye must be drawn with care and precision because it expresses so much of the emotion of the face. Slanting the eye down makes the face appear sad, drawing a straight eye makes a person appear bored, drawing the eye up at the outer edge makes the person appear happy. The eye is shaped like an almond, or goldfish.

The eye is drawn slanting upwards, beginning at eye-level (half-way down the head). At eye level the face is five eye widths across. The eyes are positioned one eye length from each edge of the face and there is one eye length between them—the "third eye". See page 46 for accurate sizing and positioning of the eye on the face.

1 The eye is slim. The upper line can be drawn with three movements: Starting with the inner edge of the eye, closest to the nose, draw the line of the eye up for a third of the distance, flatten it out as it stretches over the eyeball for one third and down for the final third. The lower line of the eye arcs up to the outer point of the eye.

2. The eyeball itself is one third of the width of the eye and sits slightly under the eyelid. The upper part of the eyeball is slightly darker because a shadow is cast from the eyelid onto the eyeball. The pupil is the darkest point of the eye with often a pinpoint of light on it. The outer edge of the eyeball is also dark.

3. Remember that the whites of the eyes are slim. There is a second line that can be drawn at the lower edge of the eye to indicate that the eye is recessed in the eye socket. The upper edge of the eye is often drawn with a darker line to give it drama and sophistication. Longer eyes give a sense of sophistication to the face, rounder eyes make a person appear younger.

1. The upper line of the eye can be drawn with three movements starting from the inner edge. The lower line of the eye arcs up to the outer point of the eye. Note the eye turns up at the outer corner.

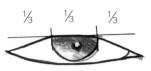

2. The eyeball itself is one third of the width of the eye and sits slightly under the eyelid. The upper part of the eyeball is slightly darker. The pupil is the darkest point of the eye with often a pinpoint of light on it.

3. The whites of the eyes are slim. There is a second line that can be drawn at the lower edge of the eye to indicate that the eye is recessed in the eye socket.

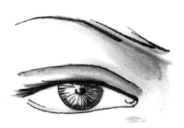

4. The complete eye

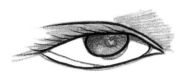

The eye is shaped like a goldfish

The eye turns up at the outer corner

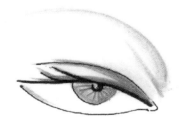

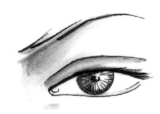

More eyes

eyes/eyebrows/
three-quarter eyes/
do not do's

4. Lashes can be drawn with curved lines that sweep outwards from the upper and lower edges of the eye. Eyelids are parallel to the upper line of the eye. Eyebrows are wider than the eye, and arch up at the edge of the eye. Do not make the eyebrow into an Alpine mountain or Indian tepee by drawing a point in the middle.

5. The eyelid is the same shape as the eye and can be made higher to show a more deep set eye.

6. Draw in eyelashes subtly, using a simple, dark tone. Eyelashes grow from the edge of the eye upwards and outwards with the last eyelashes dipping down for a flirtatious look.

7. Do not make the eyelashes straight or they will appear to injure the eyelid. Do not make the eyeball a full circle as it will the eye look as though it is in shock.

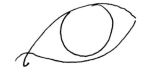

DO NOT DO:
Eyeballs in shock!

DO NOT DO:
Steel eyelashes

DO NOT DO:
Alpine eyebrows

Three-quarter eyes

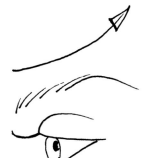

Positioning of three-quarter eyes

Lovely eyebrows

Eyes as seen when head tilts
back—an advanced position.

60

mouth

The mouth is sensuous and expressive. In fashion drawings we use it as an accessory to the garments, indicating mood and attitude. The corners of the mouth tell all!

1. Begin by drawing an oval as wide as the eye socket.
2. Draw a line through the center of the oval.
3. Make an indent in the top of the lip to match the V at the bottom of the nose (see the next section for how to draw the nose).
4. Because the mouth is lush and round and full, make the center and the two bottom parts of the mouth darkest.
5. Leave a spot of light at the center of the bottom lip to express light and shine—a little dew drop.
6. Curve the edges of the mouth up to express happiness and down to express sadness.

1. Begin by drawing an oval the same width as the eye socket.

2. Draw a line through the center of the oval.

3. Make an indent in the top of the lip to match the V at the bottom of the nose

4. Make the center and the two bottom parts of the mouth darkest.

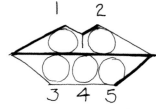

5. Leave a spot of light at the center of the bottom lip to express light and shine

6. Curve the edges of the mouth up to express happiness and down to express sadness

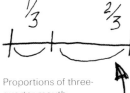

A mouth can be broken into five circles

Shaded

Soften lines

Shaded three-quarter

Proportions of three-quarter mouth

Shaded three-quarter

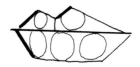

Setting three-quarter mouth with circles

Shaded open

mouth/side view/three-quarter view/do not do

Take a triangle

Cut in half

Round the tips like ice cream cones

Lips are like a heart

DO NOT outline the nose—
it looks like an elephant foot

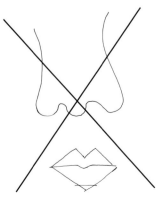

DO NOT make the mouth pointed

62

nose

The nose is a delicate arrow. On a woman the nostrils angle at a slight V.

1. When beginning to draw it is best to ignore the bridge of the nose—the tendency is to draw too hard a line, which makes the nose the focal point of the face, as opposed to the eyes or mouth. Do not outline the nose—it makes it look like an elephant's foot!

2. The nose is as long as the eye is wide. Be careful not to exaggerate the length. (We expect the nose to be longer than it is because it pokes out at us.)

3. The nose begins halfway down the head and ends three-quarters way down (or one quarter up) the head.

4. Add shadow at the base to give the nose an upward tilt.

The base of the nose turns up.

The tip of the nose—the part that sticks out the most— is shaped like an arrow. Shading can be applied under the tip of the nose to make the tip appear to protrude.

Nose in three-quarter view. The silhouette of the bridge of the nose is at an angle between that of the side view and the vertical of the front view. The nearer nostril becomes a slightly fuller curve and the further nostril is almost completely hidden.

ear

The ear is positioned at between ½ and ¼— between the level of the eye and the bottom of the nose. The ear is shaped like a hook or question mark. To indicate more detail in the ear, add a second line in the shape of an S inside the top edge. (Note that detail of the ear is not necessary in most fashion drawings.) It is essential that the position of the ears is drawn correctly, corresponding to different positions of the head: when the head bends back the ears appear lower on the head, and when the head bends forward the ears appear higher.

Shading can be applied to the interior of the ear if the rest of the face also has detailed shading.

S defines a simple ear

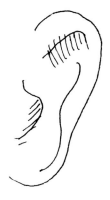

Simple ear with shading

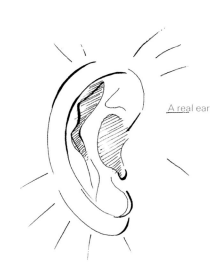

A real ear

hair/straight/curls/ do not do's

HAIR

Hair is drawn by first sketching the outline with simple shapes, adding the texture and shading, and finally the details of the different parts of the hair (a process that is quite similar to drawing a fashion garment, as will be seen in the next chapter). The outline of the shape of the hair follows the inside hairline (where the hair meets the forehead and sides of the head) and then traces the basic shape of the hair on top. The hairline is one quarter of the distance down from the top of the head, extends across the distance of the eyes (an umbrella for the eyes) and falls to the ear.

1. Draw the shape of the hair starting from the inside line of the hair or from the top of the head, called the crown. Draw the shape close to the face until the eye level is reached.

2. Straight hair can be drawn easily by breaking up the edge of the hair shape using straight lines. A technique for making straight hair is the following: choose a small piece of paper with a straight edge and place on top of the piece you are drawing on. Line up the straight edge of the small piece of paper with the edge of the hair and draw parallel lines from the small piece to the drawing paper, so creating a nice even edge for the hair.

3. When drawing curls, fill in the basic shape of the hair. Do not draw lots of lines inside the basic silhouette of the hair, especially lines which overlap, as this makes the hair look like a bird's nest. Break up the outer edge of the shape with half circles of different sizes.

6. Do not let hair get too wide above the eye level: it does not normally grow out horizontally!

7. Do not make parts (partings) larger than the head itself.

8. Draw braids as intersecting chains which are dark where the chains overlap.

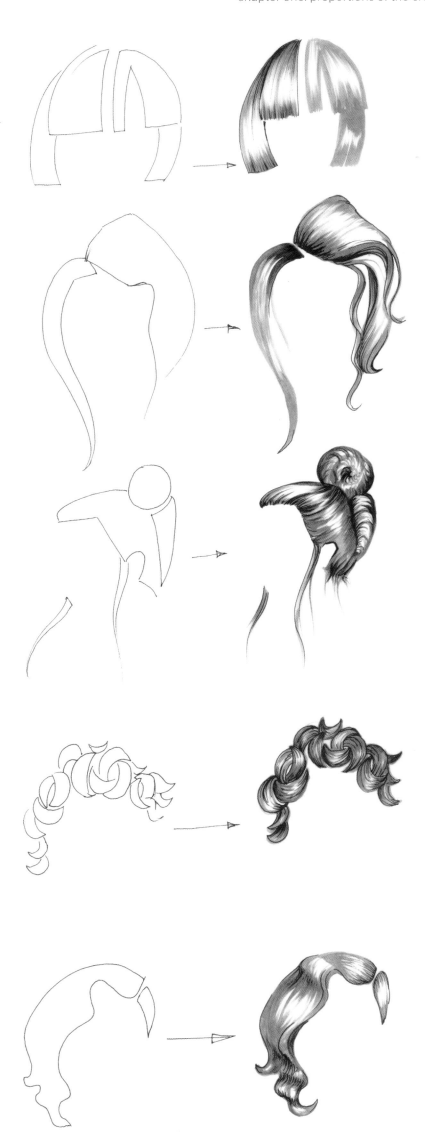

hair

9. Draw long hair by shading the skin and adding tone behind the silhouette of the hair. All hair, including blonde, has very dark and very light areas. The dark areas tend to be closer to the face. Looking at photographs of hair styles is extremely helpful when drawing hair.

10. Using the sharp edge of an eraser, make quick strokes to add highlights where you decide.

EXERCISE

1. Look at fashion magazines to find hairstyles that you like and trace them. Fill in the silhouette with pencil as if it were flat.

2. Copy hairstyles, beginning with simple shapes, remembering that hair has to grow from the skull. Draw a part (a parting) in the hair, remembering that the part is on the head and cannot be drawn beyond the head. Now draw a few lines for the hair from the part to indicate the direction of the hairstyle.

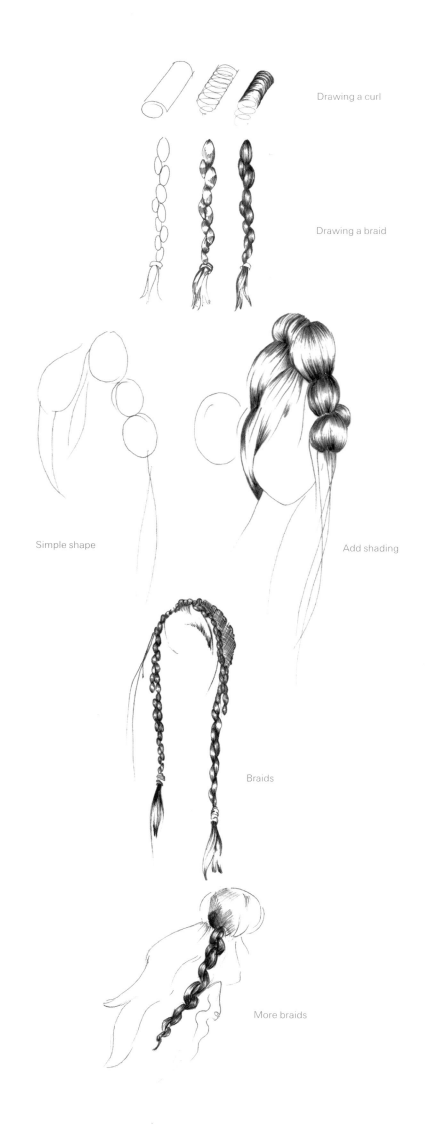

Drawing a curl

Drawing a braid

Simple shape

Add shading

Braids

More braids

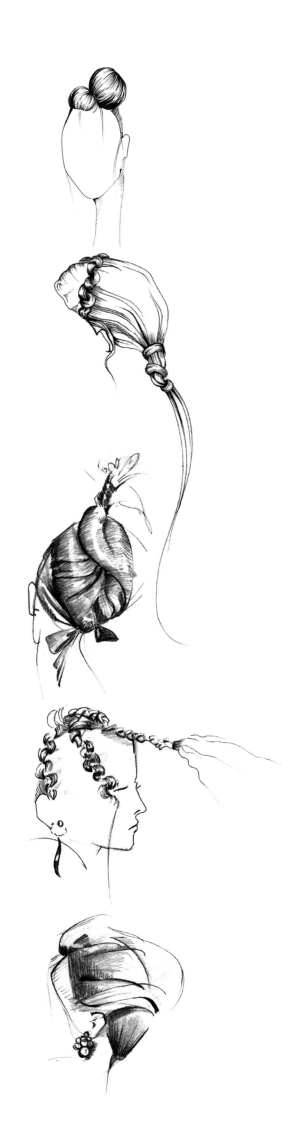

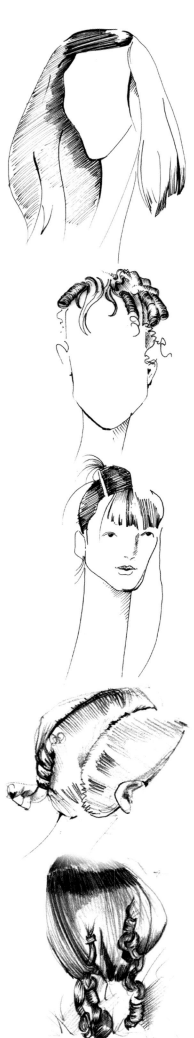

Twists and turns of the hair.
Look for simple shapes and highlights

hands

HANDS

The hand is much larger than we expect: it is equal in size to one head (Do you remember being frightened as a child and covering your face with your hands?) The hand is a wonderful tool in fashion drawing, so should not be hidden. It is very effective for drawing attention to an important feature—for example the collar, waist, or an important pocket—simply by pointing it. The hand should not point away from the figure, however, as it will lead the eye out of the drawing—to a neighbor's work or to a blank space! And do not point the hand to the ground as there is nothing there!

The hand can be used also to express different attitudes in a drawing. If the fingers are spread the figure will appear to have energy; if the hands are dropped to the sides of the body the figure will appear to be at rest. The hand and fingers are long, tapered and elegant.

A good way to begin learning to draw the hand is to place your own hand on the page and trace around it. Do so three times—it is nice having a perfect model for this part of the body so conveniently to hand (so to speak!). Note that the wrist is much slimmer than the hand; by tapering the arms down to slim wrists in our drawings elegant forms can be created regardless of whether a full-bodied or a slimmer croquis is being drawn.

1. Start by drawing a palm as a rectangle measuring half a head. The finger area is also a rectangle, and also half a head.
2. Divide the edge of the palm into four equal areas. It's easy to begin by dividing the line in half and then each half in half again. Each finger is very thin, and they are all the same width. Finger number one is almost half a head. Finger number two is the longest finger—half a head long. Finger number three, the ring finger, is the same as number one, comparatively long. Finger number four—the pinkie—is the baby, approximately two-thirds the length of finger number three.

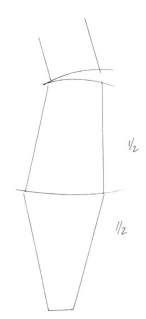

Both the palm and the fingers are half a head.

Divide the palm into four sections.

Shape the fingers.

Slim down the fingers.

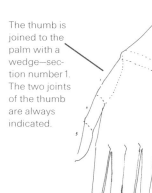

The thumb is joined to the palm with a wedge—section number 1. The two joints of the thumb are always indicated.

Add the thumb.

Define the joints in the fingers.

The completed hand.

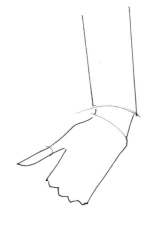

Appearance of the hand on the hip, or when made into a fist.

hands/exercises

3. First draw in each finger as a single line then stop to check the measurements. Flesh out the finger by adding a second line, making sure that the finger remains the same width from top to bottom. If we wish to add a fingernail, be careful to place it directly on the finger, not crooked and not protruding from the tip. It is best not to draw nine-inch nails.

4. There are three separate joints in each finger.

5. The thumb is made of two equal-sized bones. It can be tricky to draw as it is so different from the rest of the hand. The thumb fits into the hand halfway up the palm. It is important to include a wedge between the wrist and the thumb so that all these areas fit together.

6. The side view of the hand is made from a triangular shape about half a head high, and with one side thinner than the other. The first finger is drawn out from the thin point of the triangle, almost one half a head in length. Finger number two extends out from the same point, a little longer. Finger number three extends from the same point and is a little shorter. Think of the open blades of a Swiss Army knife when drawing the fingers of the side view hand. To finish the drawing, add the thumb by placing a wedge from the wrist to halfway up the palm and fit the thumb onto the wedge. DO NOT attach the thumb to the wrist—a common mistake.

EXERCISES
Draw your own hand. Draw your friends' hands. Fill three pages with as many hands as you can draw.

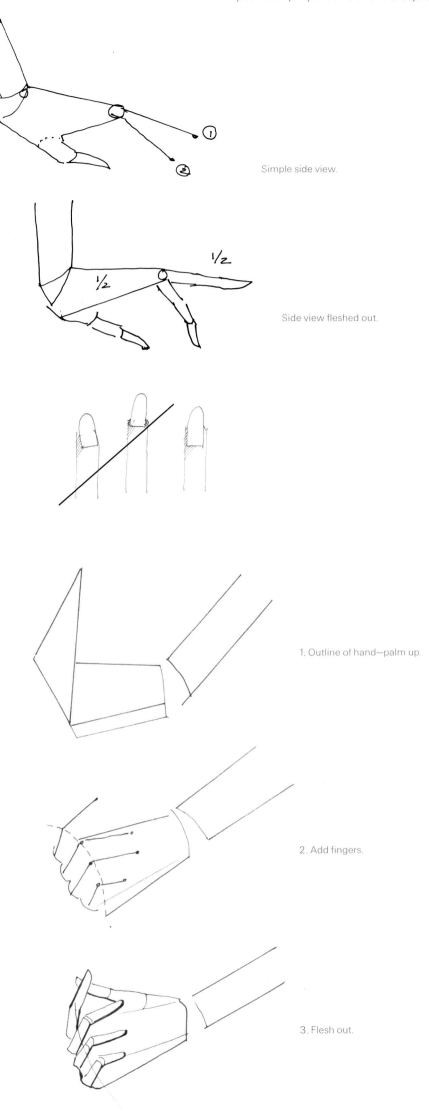

Simple side view.

Side view fleshed out.

1. Outline of hand—palm up.

2. Add fingers.

3. Flesh out.

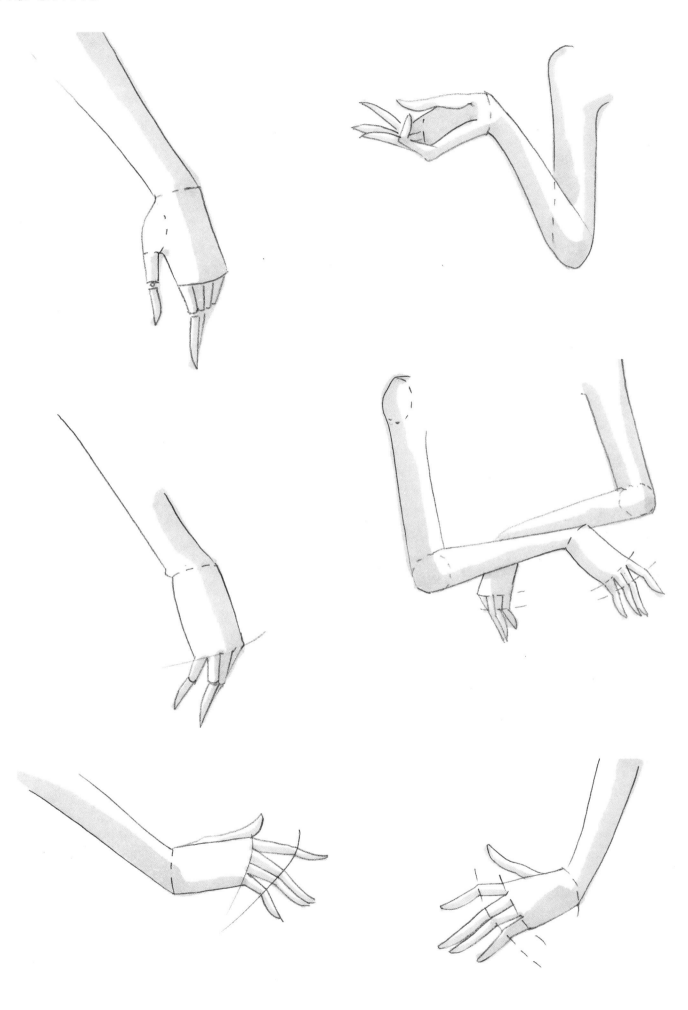

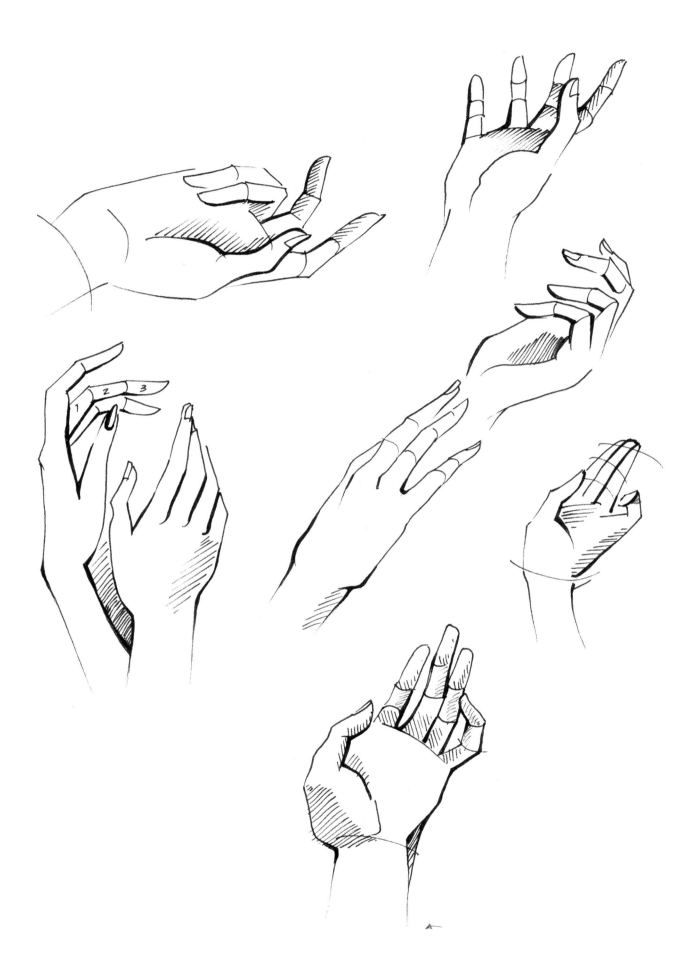

hands

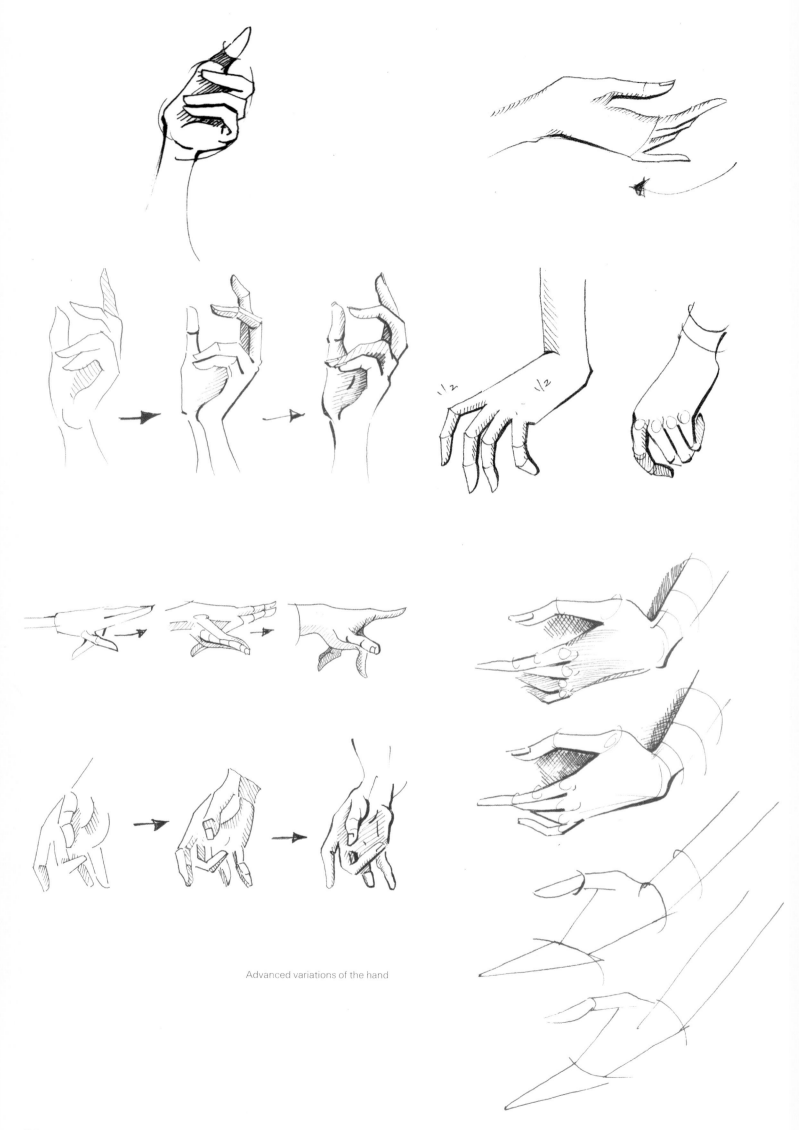

Advanced variations of the hand

hands

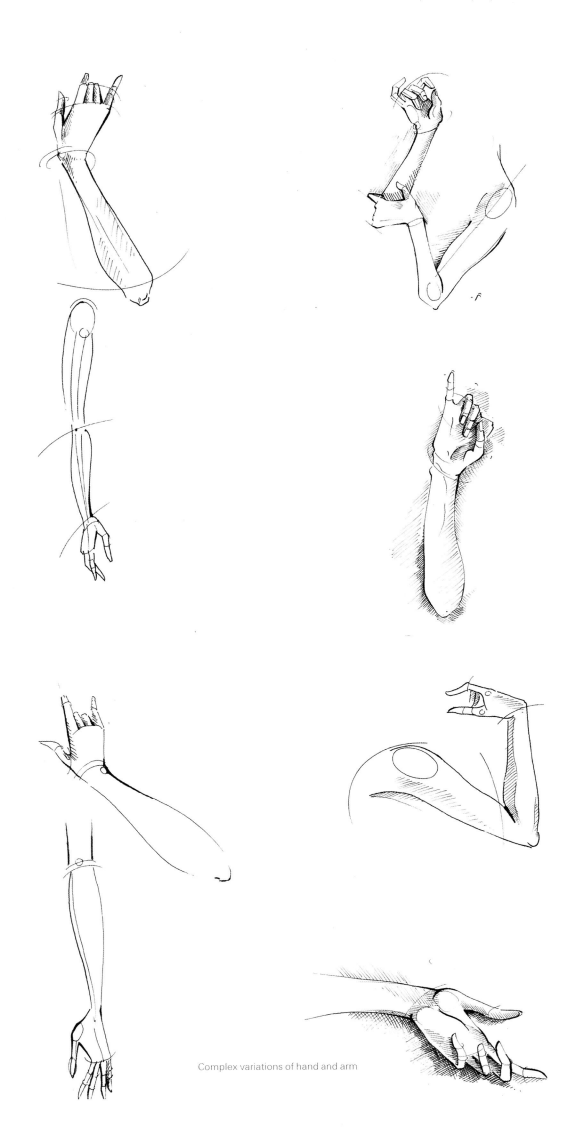

Complex variations of hand and arm

feet/exercise

FEET

The foot is equal to one head in length and is long and slim, just like the hand. It is made up of the ankle bone, which is higher on the inside and lower on the outside, engineered to support the weight of our body: (think of the construction of the arch of a bridge).

1. The foot is often drawn at an angle, to express grace. It is slim, as mentioned, and is made of a rectangle for two thirds of its length and a triangle for the remaining third. The ball of the foot is the widest point and tapers into the large toe. The toenail appears to rest on the top of the toe like a crescent moon. The remaining four toes are shorter and are drawn at an angle up from the inside of the foot.

2. The arch of the foot can be expressed by drawing a curve from the ankle to the ball of the foot.

3. When drawing a shoe on the foot, remember that all lines bend around the form.

4. The foot from the side is also one head and can be drawn as a triangle. Divide the foot into three equal parts placing a circle at the heel, a square at the arch and a triangle at the toe.

5. To draw the foot with a high heel, slant the middle—the arch— at an angle and draw the toe as a triangle which rests flat on the ground.

6. A three-quarter foot is also usually drawn as viewed from above so it appears as a triangle slanting at a 45° slope. The foot can also be regarded as composed of different shapes—the heel a circle, the arch a square and the toes a triangle.

7. The back of the foot can be drawn by tapering down from below the back of the knee to the ankle. At the ankle the leg becomes very thin and resembles a cord (this is the *tendon*). From the tendon the heel can be drawn as a circle measuring one third of the foot. The arch is a square, one third of the foot. The toes are not seen.

EXERCISE

Draw three pages of feet, with or without shoes.

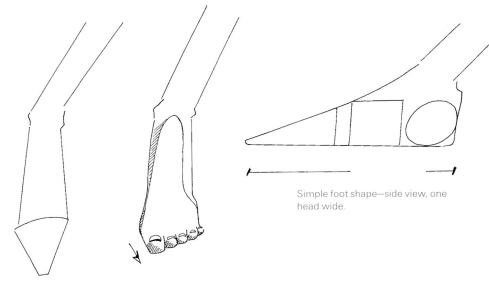

Simple foot shape—side view, one head wide.

. Simple foot shape—front.   Add the toes.

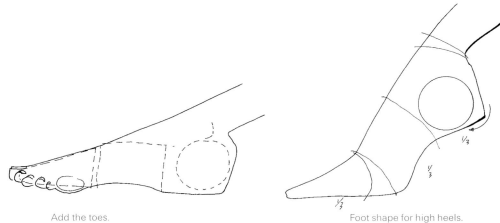

Add the toes.

Foot shape for high heels.

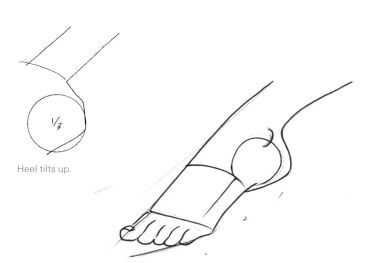

Heel tilts up.

Three-quarter foot

feet

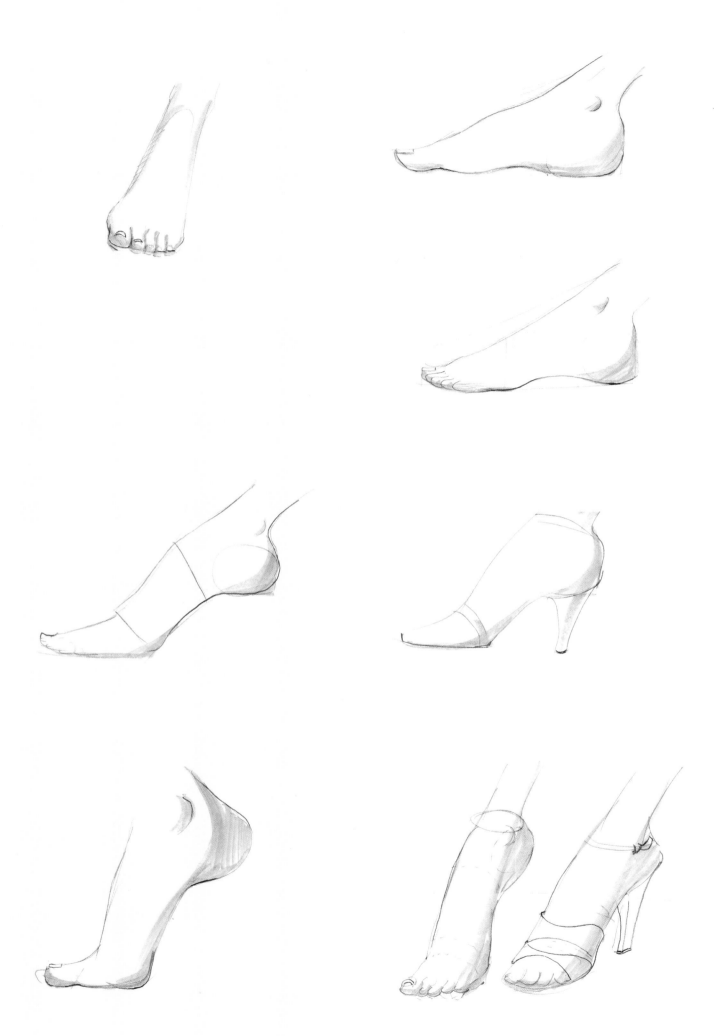

fashion poses/ S curve

FASHION POSES/THE S CURVE

Fashion garments usually look their best when seen in poses that show off the drape and flow of the fabric as well as the design features, and also emphasize the silhouette. The poses best suited to achieve these ends, both on the runway and in drawing, are those that introduce angles into the figure. The vertical and horizontal lines and axes of simple, "feet-together and arms-by-the-side" poses seem to suggest stability and an absence of movement, whereas angles—which create diagonals in the figure—suggest the opposite—energy, dynamism and movement. Angles can be introduced into a pose simply by bending an arm or even just tilting a hand, leaving the rest of the body static. In the S curve—a classic fashion pose—the figure itself forms a long, elegant diagonal.

In the S curve pose the weight of the figure is shifted onto one leg, moving the hip up and shoulder down on one side of the figure, causing a compression, or "crunching" of shoulder and hip on that side and a stretching, or elongation, on the other side, particularly useful for showing the flowing lines of, for example, a long elegant evening gown.

To understand the S curve pose in order to draw it, it is best first to experience what it feels like: Stand up and place all the weight on one leg—let's say the right leg—making sure the right leg is behind the left leg. Notice that the right hip is pushed up. The hip is one large bone and the center and the sides of the hip all shift to the right. The leg that is not bearing the weight is free to move to any angle. Look in a mirror: the body is forming the shape of an 'S'. Note that when the weight shifts onto one leg, in order to balance and not topple over, that leg shifts to the vertical; all the weight of the body is supported on that leg. The line of the vertical weight-bearing leg corresponds to the balance line when it is drawn.

Let us begin by drawing an S curve figure where the top part of the figure remains upright, and the shoulders horizontal.

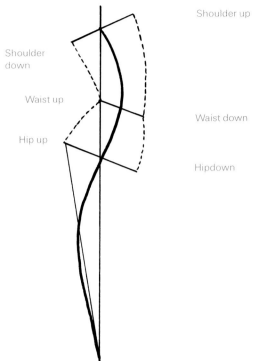

Shoulder up

Shoulder down

Waist up

Waist down

Hip up

Hipdown

When the weight of the body is shifted onto one leg it forms the shape of an S. Shoulders go down, hips go up. Here the weight is on the leg on the left and the body is compressed on the left, stretched on the right.

The tumbling cups show the planes of the shoulders and the hips when the weight is on the left.

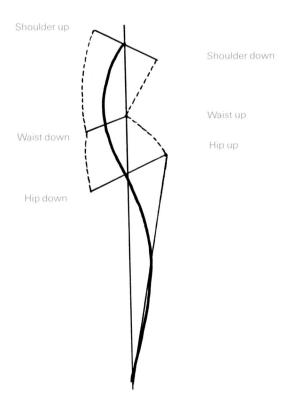

Shoulder up

Shoulder down

Waist down

Waist up

Hip up

Hip down

Here the weight is on the right leg. The body is compressed on the right, stretched on the left.

The tumbling cups show the planes of the shoulders and the hips when the weight is on the right.

fashion poses/
S curve

Let the left leg be the weight-bearing leg. First draw in the position of the head, and then the ankle on the weight-bearing leg; connecting them with a vertical line. This will be the *balance line*. In the S curve figure the line of the hips, which in the normal front view pose is a horizontal through point number 4, tilts at an angle to show the hip moving up on one side and lowering on the other, so that the higher end on the left now sits at around 4¼ and the other end at around 3¾. Draw in the left leg to the left of the balance line and then the right leg angled away. Remember that although the position of the hips and legs have changed, all proportions remain the same and can be measured out along the legs: The knee is two head lengths down from the hip, which, in the weight-bearing leg is at 6, the same as in the regular front view figure. Draw in the upper part of the figure as in a front view croquis.

Draw the figure again and drop the shoulder on the left side (hip up, shoulder down), so that the shoulders move to about 1¼ and 1¾. Dropping the shoulder towards the raised hip accentuates the S curve of the figure. When the shoulder drops, the head often moves away from the vertical, so the balance line should be located by extending a line vertically through the ankle of the weight-bearing leg. The bust- and waist-lines also shift so they are parallel to the shoulder line.

In the S curve pose the non weight-bearing leg is free to be positioned anywhere that gravity permits. Angling the leg out from the figure gives a long line that can used to show off long garments, but any number of positions are possible. The head can also be placed at any angle, so altogether a large number of different poses are possible simply by changing the position of the leg and head. Try a side view head with a straight body; try a three-quarter head, move the shoulders down and the hip up. Examine the page of stick men poses for ideas on different S curve configurations.

The S curve figure is more advanced. Work slowly and carefully.

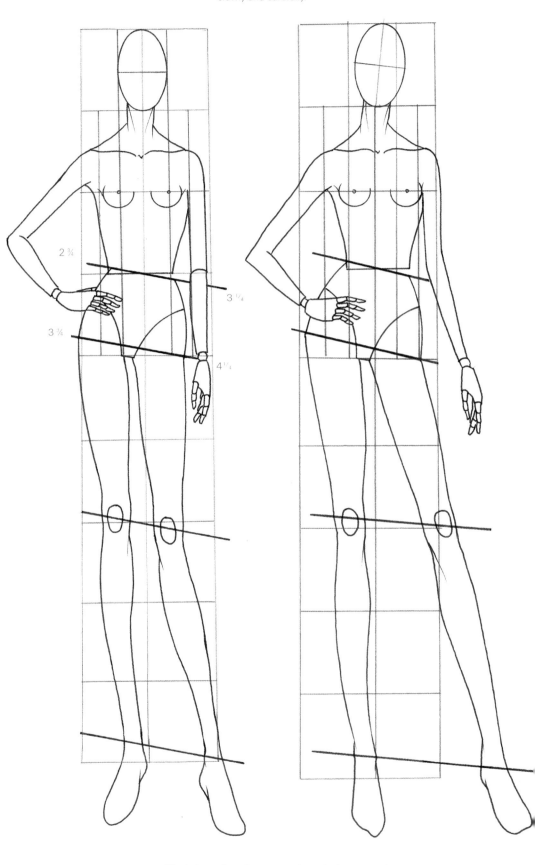

2¾

3 ¼

3 ¾

4¼

The balance line always runs through the support leg. The non-support leg is free to extend away from the body at any angle. When learning the S curve pose it is often helpful to draw the figure on a grid. Note the hip moves up on the weight-bearing side, down on the other. In this drawing the shoulders remain horizontal.

fashion poses/
S curve/3/4 view

Note also that when the arm moves, the structure of the body remains static as long as the arm is parallel to or below the shoulder. When the arm moves above the shoulder, the armhole moves with the arm, close to the head (check in the mirror to observe that the armhole is next to the neck).

THREE-QUARTER VIEW S CURVE

When drawing S curve poses in three-quarter view, just as for straight poses in three-quarter view, draw in the center-front line and make sure the two sides of the body are in the ¾ / ¼ proportion, with the side turned away being foreshortened. It is important to keep these proportions all the way down the figure: a common mistake is to draw the hips on the three-quarter figure symmetrically, without foreshortening on one side, giving the figure a distorted look. Remember also that in three-quarter view we see the side of the body as well as the front: leave space to show this side plane all the way down. Also, pay attention to the positioning of the knees and feet in the three-quarter figure: they must correspond with the alignment of the figure.

Three-quarter S curves are not the easiest pose to draw but are a common and important pose in fashion drawing. It is helpful to study three-quarter S curve poses in fashion magazines to become familiar with how the proportions of the figure appear when it forms this pose.

EXERCISE

Pick favorite pictures and poses from your scrap file. Draw a line through the center of the bust, waist and hip. If the line moves to the right the weight is on the right hip, if it moves to the left the weight is on the left hip. Create a croquis using the above rules that expresses this shift in weight. After drawing this croquis, add eyes, nose, mouth, hair, hands and feet.

Congratulations, you are now at the intermediate stage of drawing.

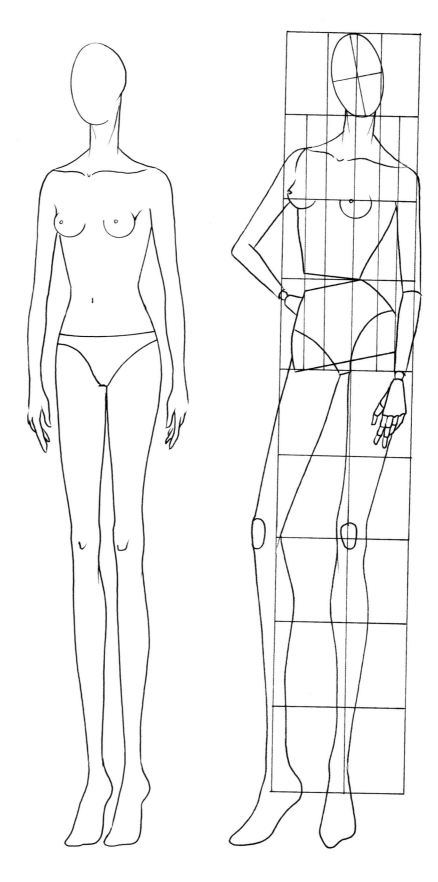

The three-quarter figure and the three-quarter S curve figure. The same principles apply when drawing S curve figures in three-quarter view as for non–S curve figures in three-quarter view.

83

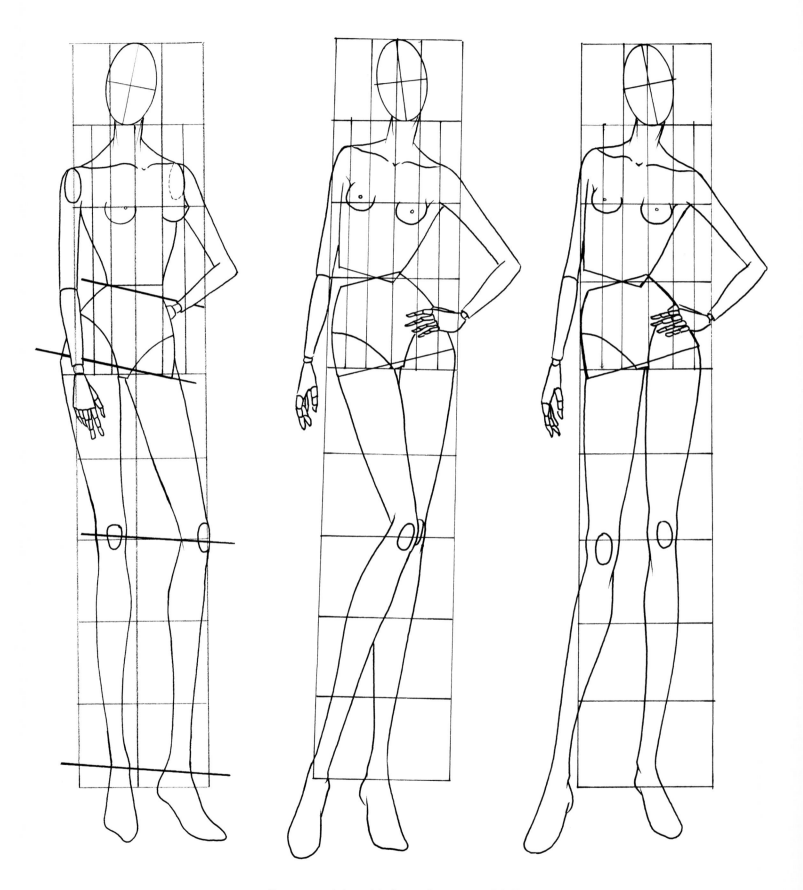

Numerous variations of the S curve figure are possible. Here the figure on the left has the hip up but the shoulders are still horizontal. The shoulders of the middle and right figure have dropped, so the mid-section of the torso is compressed.

fashion poses/
S curve/variations

S curve poses, shaded figures. Left, weight on left leg; middle, weight on the front leg; right, weight on the right leg.

fashion poses/
S curve

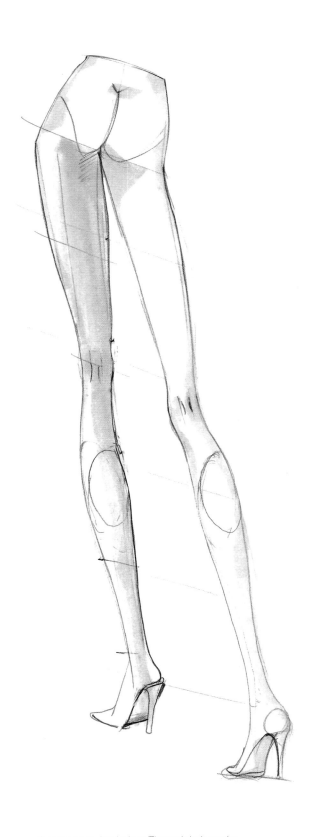

Walking S curve pose. When walking, the body also forms an S curve at the moment when one leg is forward and the other back: the hip on the forward leg side is up and on the back leg side is down. This can be seen when models walk on the catwalk swinging the hips: first one hip is up and then the other, giving movement and drape to the garment.

S curve pose, back view. The weight is on the left leg, pivoting the hip up on the left side.

S curve pose, weight on right leg.

S curve pose, weight on left leg, pushing the left hip up.

fashion poses/
S curve

S curve pose, front view, weight on left leg,
pushing the left hip up, right leg partly extended.

S curve pose, side view, weight on right (nearer)
leg, pushing the right hip up, left knee cocked.

fashion poses/
S curve

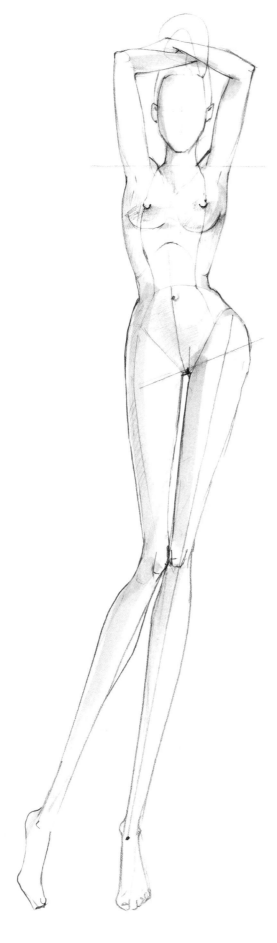

S curve pose, front view with arms over head, weight on
the leg on the right

S curve pose, body in three-quarter view, weight on the
leg on the right.

fashion poses/
S curve

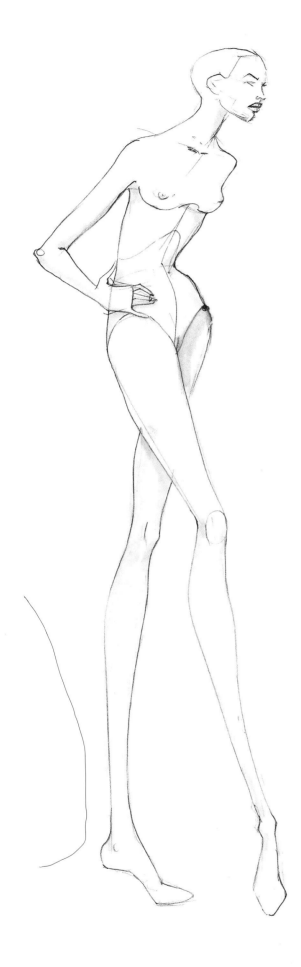

S curve pose, three-quarter view, weight on the back leg.

Back view S curve walking pose. This pose is caught in mid stride with the weight on the left leg. Note the exaggerated drop in the left shoulder. The diagram of the cone to the right shows the shape of the foreshortened lower right leg, as it appears in the drawing.

fashion poses/
S curve

Fashion poses. Left, lower part of the body shown in three-quarter
view; second from left, S curve pose, back view, weight on right leg;
third from left, S curve pose, three-quarter view, weight on left leg;
right, side view, left leg back, right forward, weight evenly distributed.

fashion poses/
S curve

S curve pose, three-quarter view, weight on the front leg. The back leg is slightly foreshortened.

S curve pose three-quarter view, weight on the front leg. The left side of the body is foreshortened, as is the upper arm on the right.

fashion poses/
S curve

S curve pose, three-quarter view, weight on the front leg. The back leg is slightly foreshortened: the cylinder at right shows how its shape is drawn.

S curve pose, three-quarter view, weight on the front leg. The lower back leg is foreshortened: the cylinders show the shapes of the front leg and the lower back leg. The right forearm is also foreshortened as it extends behind the head.

fashion poses/
S curve/seated pose

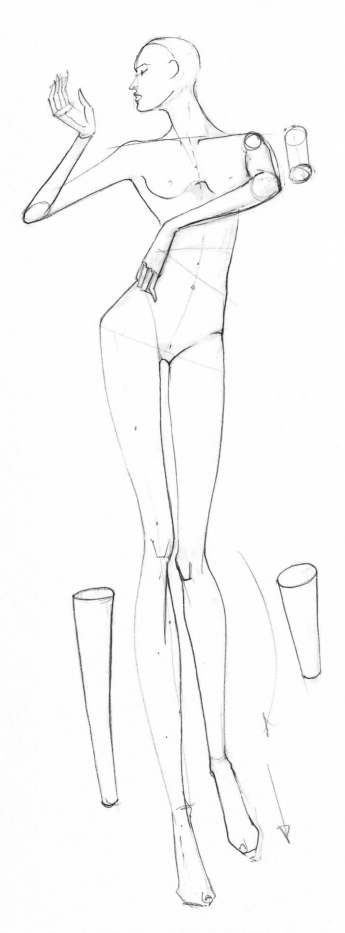

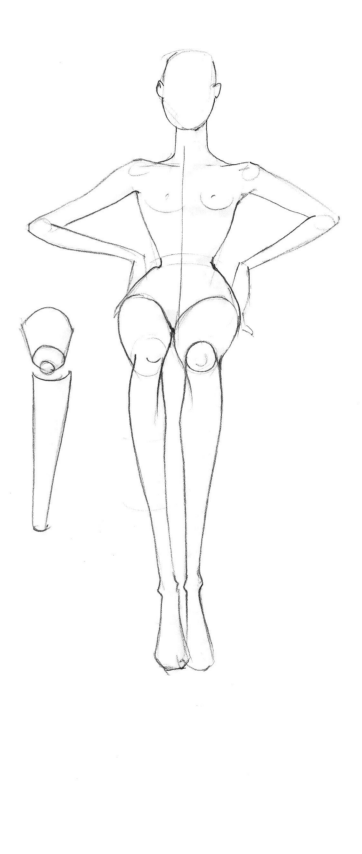

S curve pose, front view, weight on the front(left) leg. The arms extend out from the body; the right upper arm is foreshortened and, to a lesser extent, the left lower arm. The back leg is also slightly foreshortened.

Seating pose. The plane of the lower part of the legs is in front of that of the torso, closest to the point of view, so these parts of the body appear proportionately larger. Because of the angle they are viewed at, the upper legs appear much foreshortened. The shapes of the lower and upper legs are seen in the diagrams at left.

The finished woman— flesh her out!

the complete figure/ with clothing

The croquis with clothing

different racial/
ethnic characteristics

Every fashion figure tries to create expressions of beauty, health, energy, seduction, humor and the ideas of what is fashionable at the moment. Fortunately there are enormous variations from one race to another and each may be a wonderful variation on the theme of beauty. The Asian face is drawn with a higher eyebrow, slimmer eyes and less eyelid. Hair is dark and straight and the mouth is round and full. The Japanese face has pale skin and slim, delicate bones. The Korean face has fuller eyebrows, stronger bones and a stronger chin. The Chinese face is round with round dark eyes with limited shading at the eyelids, noses with straight bridges but full bases and a soft, round mouth. Hair is very black and very straight.

The black, or African, woman has dramatic deep-set eyes and stronger eyelids which require more shading. Eyebrows are stronger and can be drawn with a full arch. The nose is drawn with a broader base, the mouth is round and wide and the lips are full; the cheek bones are high, the hairline is high and the forehead is rounded. There are many variations on skin tone depending on specific nationality and genes. Skin tone can range from aubergine to cinnamon.

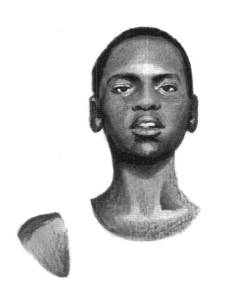

different racial/ ethnic characteristics

Northern Europeans have strong bones, thin, strong noses and wide mouths and eyes. The eyes are set wide apart but do not require a great deal of shadow at the lid. The mouth is wide but can be drawn with a thinner lip or full. Skin tone is usually light. Hair is usually fair but there are many exceptions.

Southern Europeans are principally the Latin races. They have round deep set eyes and wide arched brows, full wide mouths, high cheek bones and strong chins. Hair is often blue-black, full and lush. The Latin eye tends to have a flirtatious down-curve at the end of the lash.

different racial/
ethnic characteristics

chapter two:
drawing clothes on
the figure

beginning to draw/
learning about fashion

BEGINNING TO DRAW

This book teaches how to draw fashion realistically and accurately so that it can be used as a powerful tool of design. When learning to draw with a view to *designing* fashion though, it is important to focus first on developing the skills that will allow new designs to be presented effectively. In fashion, as in other areas of design, presentation is an important part of the overall design and production process (after all, fashion itself is an important part of how we humans present ourselves visually). Until a certain level of proficiency in being able to communicate ideas effectively in drawing is achieved it is best to concentrate on learning to draw: when one begins to make *design* drawings the designs will always look better if they are drawn well.

LEARNING ABOUT FASHION

Fashion drawing is a type of technical drawing; its primary purpose is to convey information about garments, and this information included in the drawings has to be clear and meaningful. This means that (unless one has spent many years following fashion and has made a recent decision to learn how to draw it) when learning to draw it is important at the same time to learn as much as possible about fashion in all its aspects—the appearance of different types of garments, their construction, contemporary designers' work, fashion poses, hair and makeup styling, the differences among fashion in different markets, and the many other components of contemporary fashion. This book contains a large quantity of technical information about modern fashion garments, in both visual and textual form, that the reader should become familiar with and use as constant reference when drawing and designing. This information should be supplemented as much as possible, though, by taking every opportunity to look at and read about fashion with a view to acquiring knowledge of the subject and developing an "eye" for fashion trends.

Fashion design ideas are more effective if the drawings that present them are attractive, clear and show a knowledge of the technical aspects of fashion. This is a design for a dress for the "designer" market.

beginning to draw/
learning about fashion

The fashion design process itself is one of developing, refining, adapting, and combining, in new ways, elements of fashion that have often existed for hundreds of years. Just as with a written and spoken language, though, new design creations have to "make sense": they have to be composed of real elements put together, from a construction and style point of view, in viable combinations. The larger the "vocabulary" of fashion elements that one has acquired, then the larger the number of design possibilities—new combinations of existing elements—that can be devised.

When beginning to study fashion it is important to make an effort to see and touch *real* garments, not just to look at pictures. This can be done by visiting stores (across a range of markets, so the very best designer clothes can be experienced as well as cheaper versions of similar garments, and more popular everyday wear), attending fashion shows and costume exhibits and viewing videos and fashion shows on TV. A variety of the best fashion magazines should be read or subscribed to. These will often show some of the best designers, the best models, the best photography and the most modern poses and styling. It is important *not* to restrict oneself to one's own existing preferences and tastes in fashion, and to look at a wide range of garments: not only do tastes changes, but in the modern world trends are picked up from a very broad base of influences and cut across markets and different areas of design.

Collect images from magazines and other sources, study them and then catalogue them according to interests and priorities, in a scrapbook or separate files as source material for different types of clothing (skirts, desses, jackets, tops, active sportswear, lingerie/swim-wear, coats, and so on), different poses and body types, different styles of hair and makeup, accessories and other categories. The more information that is collected, the better: it is quite common to refer to dozens of images of existing garments when making a fashion drawing.

Striving continually to learn more about fashion and improve drawing skills will improve design skills. This outfit is designed for the junior market. Note the youthful pose, chosen to show the mood of the garments and the type of person they are designed for.

planning the drawing

PLANNING THE DRAWING

When beginning to draw, the emphasis is on developing basic drawing skills as quickly as possible more than thinking about design. Rather than making drawings of new garments, it is best to practice copying existing garments. Copying professional photographs of existing garments is excellent practice for learning to draw the fashion croquis and clothes on the figure, and much can be learnt from the way the clothes and model have been styled and posed for the shot. When beginning, trace the silhouette, drape and folds and details of the garment using tracing paper and then transfer to drawing paper. This is a great help in understanding how to form the basic shapes of garments and how they are constructed. Once basic drawing skills have been acquired, it is then possible to move on to making drawings of new garments.

When drawing new garments, time invested in planning out the various elements of the drawing beforehand will be amply rewarded, resulting in a superior end product and making for a quicker and smoother execution of the design drawing. Most good design is a result of painstaking crafting of ideas, and professional designers spend many months preparing a new collection. Do not spend *too* much time planning, though, or the spontaneity will begin to disappear. Have a clear idea of the principal elements of the drawing and refine them as the garment begins to take shape on the page.

It is common to have fabric swatches to hand when making a drawing, so that the design is made with a particular fabric in mind. This can inject a good dose of realism into the drawing: the visual and textural qualities of the fabric, how it folds and falls, its character and mood are all experienced directly and conveyed in the drawing. The cost of the fabric is also known, which is an important consideration when designing for a particular market. The fashion industry categorizes clothing into various classes corresponding to a view of the type of person who will wear them—the different "markets" for the clothes. These classes of clothing include junior, missy, designer, young

Time invested in planning the drawing makes for a better product and smoother execution of the design drawing. Before beginning to draw it is best to have a clear idea of the garment that is to be drawn: what type of garment it is, who is going to wear it and what occasion it is intended for. This outfit is designed for the "missy" market; the pose is youthful but serious and self-assured.

planning the drawing

designer, career, active sportswear, budget, contemporary and other specialized markets. If designing a garment for a particular market then research will have shown that the garment must meet a number of specific design criteria appropriate for that market, and the economics of making a garment for that particular market segment will define within narrow limits the fabric and method of fabrication to be used. For those learning to draw fashion who are planning to work in the fashion industry, a rapid familiarization of the markets the company manufactures for will take place once in the workplace, but it is useful to develop awareness of the different categories of clothing so that designs and drawings have a relation to the realities of the marketplace from an early stage. For those *not* contemplating a career in fashion, these categories will be of interest but it is more important to direct efforts to learning to draw a wide range of different garments.

Before beginning to draw it is best to have a clear idea of the garment that is to be drawn: what type of garment it is, who is going to wear it, what occasion it is intended for. Visualize the garment as clearly as possible, not just the appearance, but also how it will fit, how the fabric will feel and how it will drape on the body. If only one, or a small number of features of the garment is going to be dominant—such as the silhouette, for instance— this has to be thought out first, and the other elements of the garments elaborated in subsequent steps. Rough sketches can be made of the different features of the garment to help work towards the final versions. Ideas for details and accessories can be jotted down, but these (unless, of course, it is an accessory that is the subject of the drawing) can be worked out and included as the drawing progresses.

It is helpful to have to hand the clippings made from magazines on different garments, poses and styles. These will provide inspiration and help clarify ideas.

The power of drawing in fashion design: This dress, for the "designer" market, contains so much fabric it would be very difficult to design by draping the fabric. Drawing allows a clear realistic version of the final design to be seen quickly and easily.

choosing the pose

CHOOSING THE POSE
The first decision when planning a fashion drawing is the pose. In choosing the pose of the croquis, the first consideration is always "what pose will show off the garments the best?" If important design details are located in the side or back of the garment it will be necessary to choose a pose that will show them off effectively: a three-quarter view pose will be most appropriate. If a garment has plentiful and elaborate drape an S curve pose will raise the hip on one side of the figure causing the fabric to drape at an angle, showing it to best effect.

Besides the practical considerations of presenting the garment, the pose should also suit the type of garment and occasion. For example, a dramatic designer evening gown should be set off with an equally dramatic pose, as well as dramatic hair and makeup styling; an active sportswear outfit is usually best shown on a pose that relates to the sport in question. More everyday garments can be paired with more naturalistic poses. Observe women's body language (which is quite different from men's) and note the type of gestures made with the hands and arms and face; except for the cases mentioned of showing off dramatic designer wear and active sportswear, and also for energetic teenagers, the limbs are mostly kept close to the body and gestures are not as expansive as those used by men, though poses are often struck that show off the curves of the body. Bear in mind also the effect of the pose on the overall composition of the drawing: for example, use the hand as a pointer to draw attention to the important parts of the garment; do not point it outside the drawing or it will suggest there is something more interesting out there.

It has become popular in the styling of contemporary fashion photography—responding to trends in fashion merchandising— to present the model in a more complex setting, and to show glimpses of her inner life; the fashion becomes part of a bigger story and is identified with a lifestyle or particular activity. If taking a similar approach in fashion *drawing*, poses should also be suited to the story being created.

The poses on this and the following two pages are young, energetic, sexy, fun and sassy. They show a different attitude to how we see ourselves in our clothes: now, clothes are chosen to express our personalities rather than our bodies showing off the clothes.

modern fashion
poses

Center-bottom—Bad Pose. This is a poorly conceived pose: the silhouette of the pant legs is unclear because the legs are too close together, the arms hide the details of the belt and the hair covers the face. When deciding on a pose it is important that all the essential information on the garments can be clearly seen.

defining the garment/
the fashion silhouette

DEFINING THE GARMENT
Moving on to the garments themselves, what are the features that define a garment, those that make it unique and different from other garments? The principal defining features are SILHOUETTE, DRAPE AND FIT, DETAILS, FABRIC. These elements are introduced below, and discussed and illustrated in detail in each of the sections on different types of garments. Each feature usually provides some information about other features besides itself and, in fashion drawing, it is important that each piece of information presented is consistent with every other piece of information. For example, a lightweight fabric will drape in small folds and form small bumps at the hem, whereas a heavier weight fabric will drape in wider folds and form smoother, larger waves at the hem; the drawing must show this consistency between fabric, drape and silhouette. These interrelations among the features are also commented on below.

THE FASHION SILHOUETTE
The silhouette is the contour, or outside edge, of a garment—its basic shape. The silhouette is the single most defining feature of a garment, providing detailed information on the type of garment and indicating drape and fit, often also indicating fabric type and details. The silhouette is the key to understanding the garment and must be drawn accurately or the garment will be misunderstood. Garments are three-dimensional, and the silhouette of the garment is also three-dimensional, although in a drawing it has to be represented on a two-dimensional surface. If a garment has interesting silhouette features at the side and back as well as the front a pose has to be chosen that will allow these to be seen: typically a three-quarter view pose.

When drawing the silhouette of garments it is important, no matter what level of proficiency one has attained, always to bear in mind that garments *bend around the body*. Special attention must always be paid to make sure the collar bends around the neck; sleeves end in cuffs or hems that bend around the arm (unless there is a crease or pleat); in a skirt or the skirt of a dress the body of the skirt and the hem bend around the body.

Silhouette. The silhouette is the single most defining feature of a garment. As well as the basic shape of the garment the silhouette provides information on fit and drape and also often fabric type and details. For a complex garment like this dress, besides the silhouette— here indicated by the thick black line—it is helpful to sketch in the outlines of the constructional details inside the silhouette, here drawn with a lighter line.

defining the garment/ details/fabric

DRAPE AND FIT.

Drape and Fit are the opposite sides of the same coin.

DRAPE is the way and the degree to which a fabric forms folds when it hangs or is moved in different ways (drape in *garments* is caused by the movements of the body underneath). The actual appearance of drape in a garment depends on a number of factors: (i) the type of fabric—the basic fabric type, its thickness and weave, (ii) the quantity of fabric used, and (iii) the way the fabric is incorporated into the construction of the garment. The appearance of different fabrics and how they are drawn is discussed below and at length in Chapter Six: How to draw fabrics, and examples of the drape of different fabrics in a variety of garments of different constructions are included throughout the book.

FIT is the relation between a garment and the body underneath. A *fitted* garment is one that sits uniformly close to the body. For most garments some parts are fitted and others are not (or are said to be loose-fitting). In the parts where the fabric is not fitted there will be a larger quantity of fabric present than is needed solely to cover that part of the figure, and the excess fabric will drape into folds. Drape and Fit are often important design features of a garment and must be clearly and faithfully represented in drawings.

DETAILS

Details are the smaller parts of a garment that either form part of the garment's construction, and are then known as "constructional details" or are included for decoration; sometimes they are a combination of the two. Examples of details are seams, pleats, buttonholes, gathers, darts, ease, shirring and top-stitching. Decorative details include trim, pockets, zippers.

Details are often important features of a garment, particularly in those that are tailored and of better quality. If a drawing is going to serve as the basis for technical construction drawings (flats) then it is important that constructional and other details are clearly and accurately shown.

The finished, detailed fashion drawing. This drawing contains a large amount of information about the garments: the complex silhouette is clearly perceived; the different types of fabric used in the construction are indicated by the variations in drape—both crisp and softly draping folds and a stiff underskirt. The detailing is very important in this garment, and this is skillfully rendered at the shoulder, down the left side of the figure and at the wrist and feet/ankles. Note that all the elements of the drawing—the hair, the shoes—accentuate the flow and drape of the dress.

defining the
garment/fabric

FABRIC

Fabric is at the core of fashion design, and the greatest fashion is almost invariably an inspired combination of beautiful fabric and exquisite design. Even when clothing is not high-fashion, the fabric of the garment is often its most important aspect, either for reasons of appearance or function, or both (for example, a leather miniskirt or an active sportswear garment featuring a new high-tech fabric to wick perspiration from the body).

Pointers to the type of fabric used in the construction of a garment are found in the accurate depiction of the silhouette and drape and fit, as discussed above, but for the most effective presentation of new garments though, it it best to draw them so they appear realistic and accurate in as many ways as possible. If fabric of the garment can be immediately recognized, with a high degree of certainty, then this makes a significant contribution to achieving a realistic and accurate depiction of how a finished garment will look.

Because of the importance of fabrics in fashion and fashion drawing and because the techniques for rendering different fabrics accurately are relatively advanced, a separate chapter of the book is devoted to them. It is best to focus first on mastering how to draw the different fashion garments—the subject of this chapter— before perfecting techniques for drawing fabrics. In this chapter, which covers how the principal fashion garments are drawn, the fabrics of the garments are identified by no more than simple classifications into heavy or light-weight, shiny or matt, or soft or crisp. The different fabric types that are used in this chapter are drawn in the following ways:

SOFT FABRIC is depicted with a soft pencil—a 2B or 4B.

LIGHT AREAS of a fabric tend to be thin and shadowy areas wide.

SHINY FABRIC requires a contrast of very dark shading in the interiors of the folds—the valleys— and crisp white lines along the tops of the folds. The darkest part of the shadow appears next to the lightest area at the crest of the fold. The same rule applies for MATT FABRICS, but there is much less variation between the dark values in the interiors and the lighter values on the tops of the folds.

Top, a skirt made from a light fabric, indicated by the flowing pleats drawn with a curved fine line. Bottom, a skirt of a heavier fabric, possibly a gabardine, indicated by the heavier line weight and straighter folds.

garments/fabric
general points

(FABRIC ctd) HEAVYWEIGHT fabrics such as four-ply cashmere, silk brocade, heavy leather, corduroy, cable knit sweaters and others are drawn with wide folds and wide shadows.

GENERAL POINTS TO KEEP IN MIND WHEN DRAWING GARMENTS.
A number of points are common to drawing all types of clothes and should be constantly kept in mind:

1. The figure, particularly the female figure, is formed of curves, and has very few straight lines. Clothes tend to follow the form of the figure, bending around the figure in curves, and this is how they should be drawn.

2. In general, lines bend up above the waist and down below it.

3. It is essential to fit clothes to the figure: the center-front line of the figure and that of the clothing on top must be in exact alignment. This is especially noticeable with buttons, which, if centered, must sit precisely on the center-front line.

4. Princess lines—the style lines seen on the dress form—line up half way between the side seams and the center-front line of a garment, and fall from midway between the center-front and the sides of the shoulders over the bustline, and at the waist mid way between the center-front and the side of the hips. The princess line is an important indicator of where to place pockets, belt loops and seams in tailored garments.

5. When garments are symmetrical (and the majority are) then it is important to show the symmetry clearly in the garment. The figure itself is always symmetrical.

6. The bust and shoulder lines are parallel and should not be drawn at different angles.

7. Important details should not be obscured with a body appendage. Adapt the pose to the garment.

8. Do not outline everything with a heavy black line—it makes garments appear two-dimensional.

The bust and shoulder lines are parallel and should not be drawn at different angles.

Lines above the waist generally bend up, and below the waist, down. Compare the bracelet on the right arm and the belt at the waist.

Do not obscure important details with a body appendage. Adapt the pose to the garment. The bag is cleverly positioned so it will not obscure the intricate embroidery on the right leg.

The center-front of the clothing and figure must be in alignment. Note the zipper.

Garments (and the figure underneath) are symmetrical. Note the thighs and the legs of the pants.

Do not outline everything with a heavy black line—it makes garments appear two-dimensional. There is no black line around this silhouette.

The figure, particularly the female figure, is formed of curves, and has very few straight lines. Note the cuffs of the pants *curve* around the body.

Points to keep in mind when drawing garments.

skirts

SKIRTS

The first garments we will look at are skirts. Skirts are the simplest of garments to draw but display all the features that have to be clearly shown in good fashion drawing: the type of fabric used, how it is sewn together, how it folds and drapes (the direction in which it falls) and how it fits the figure.

A skirt can be thought of as a tube (and most of them are made as tubes) that circles around the waist, flows over the hip and covers the lower part of the body. Because a woman's hips are wider than the waist various constructional devices are used to eliminate the excess fullness of the fabric and make the garment fit the waist. These devices include seams, tucks, ease, gathers and pleats. If the design of the skirt requires that gathers, pleats or shirring (several rows of gathers) are included, then these details require more fabric and they will result in a skirt with a wider hemline. Straight skirts, where a relatively small amount of fullness has to be eliminated at the waist, are usually constructed with darts (v-shaped tucks) or shaped pieces of fabric joined by seams.

Numerous types of skirts exist, differentiated from each other by variations in silhouette and drape—length, fullness, position of the waist, tiering, finishing of the hem and differing construction in the body of the skirt. Included below are descriptions of how to draw three basic types of skirts: straight skirts, full skirts (without pleats) and pleated skirts.

In front view with the figure posed symmetrically, skirts have little drape. It is usual, then, to draw them on a variation of the S curve pose so the drape of the fabric can be seen. The explanations below are all based on that pose.

Skirts are drawn on the lower part of the figure; the top half is usually omitted, but a simple version of the rest of the figure can be included if so preferred.

Silhouette   Drape and fit   Details

Skirt lengths. From left, mini; above-the knee; knee; mid-calf; ankle-length; floor-length.

skirts/
straight skirts

STRAIGHT SKIRTS

Straight skirts have no fullness—the silhouette drops vertically down from the widest point of the hips, or in some cases even tapers back in towards the knees for a sheath-like fit. Straight skirts are drawn with the following steps:

1. Lightly draw in the lower part of the figure (the part covered by the skirt will be erased when the drawing is complete). Begin with the waistband, drawing it so it curves around the waist either up or down. (Do not draw the waistband as a horizontal line as this is not how it appears on the figure.) Belt loops and darts are always located on the princess lines and should be drawn in the correct location. Draw in any other detailing in the waist area such as shirring, pockets and belts. Darts and seams should be drawn at equal distances from the center-front line of the garment and curve to reflect the position of the figure underneath. The waistband usually has a fold in it.

2. Draw in the silhouette down to the widest point of the hip. Make sure the silhouette fits the underlying croquis at the hips. After the hips the figure becomes slimmer and the excess fabric drapes diagonally across the body towards the knee. Draw the silhouette down to the end of the skirt, whether at the thigh, the knee, the calf or the ankle, and draw the hem by bending a line around the figure at this point.

3. Like the waist, the hem is never drawn as a horizontal line but bends around the figure, (imagine it as an ellipse bending around the figure) following the curve of the waistline. If the horizontal waist and hip lines of the croquis were to be drawn in these would be parallel to each other and also to a horizontal line drawn across the hem.

4. Drape forms when the hip moves into an S curve, creating points of tension in the garment and giving rise to folds that stretch out from those points. Drape is seen at the widest part of the higher hip and falls to the knee on the same side of the garment. Study the series of drawings included here showing how drape forms in different types of skirts.

Straight skirt (short): Points of tension/where drape forms. Left, weight equally distributed, front view; center, S curve, front view, weight on left/front leg; right, S curve, three-quarter view, weight on left/front leg. Note in the S curve pose the fabric pulls from the raised hip.

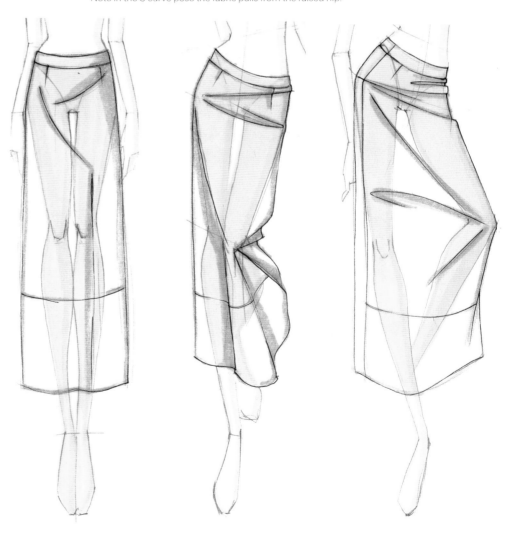

Straight skirt (long): Points of tension/where drape forms. Positions same as short skirt. The weight of the extra fabric creates more drape than a short skirt. Where the knee is against it, the fabric also pulls away from it.

skirts/ straight skirts

  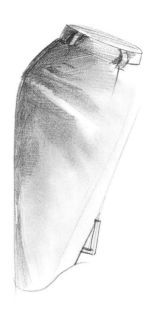

Drawing straight skirts. 1. Draw a simple silhouette with the weight on the left side.

2. Plot and begin to add areas of drape at the crotch with horizontal lines and diagonal lines down from the hip. Start to indicate the body under the gament with a light application of pencil. Darts are added, starting under the belt loops.

3. To finish off, fill in the folds using the side of the pencil. Note the shadows under the belt loops.

1. Dart on left; on right, modified sarong-wrap effect with gathers to a diagonal seam and button-over flap.

2. Waistband with belt loops.

3. Pleated skirt with decorative belts and buckles.

4. Waistband and tucks.

Ways the skirt is fitted to the waist.

Darts.

Seams.

Stitched-down pleats.

Inverted pleats.

Stitched-down inverted pleats.

Diagonal-paneled skirt.

Darts.

Princess seams.

117

skirts/
full skirts

FULL SKIRTS

Full skirts are made with several widths of fabric, either by (i) cutting in a circle with a circular hole for the waist, (ii) gathering or shirring the sewn fabric at the waist, or (iii) sewing together gores—tapered sections of fabric. Gored skirts can contain up to twenty or more gores. The description below is for full skirts that are gathered. Gored skirts are commented on in the next section along with other types of skirts.

1. Lightly draw in the bottom half of the figure and add a simple outline of the outer edge of the silhouette of the garment. The shape of the skirt is an important feature and must be drawn correctly before adding further details of the silhouette and the constructional and design details. Remember to visualize the hem as the front part of an ellipse, *curving* around the figure.

2. Begin to indicate the positions of the gathers in the body of the skirt. They all begin *at*, and not *below*, the waistband, where the fabric is "gathered" together. Do not make the gathers all the same length, and make the line lighter lower in the garment where the folds become less tight than nearer the waistband.

3. The gathers form folds at the hem of the skirt that have the appearance of cylinders, or cones, alternately facing out and then in. These cylindrical shapes will be of similar size, depending on the weight and stiffness of the fabric (or, sometimes, its motion—for example if a drawing is made of a skirt on a dancing figure). To plot the position of the folds at the hem it is useful to draw in a second line parallel to and above the hem and to draw the folds of the hem—the bottom parts of the cylinders—undulating between this line and the hemline.

4. Because a full skirt contains more fabric the figure is barely discernible under the garment (unless it is made of a transparent or semi-transparent fabric). As with straight skirts, with full skirts in the S curve pose there will be some drape on the side of the raised hip, and a subtle breaking of the fabric at the knee on that side if the skirt falls below the knee, but most of the drape in the skirt comes from the fall of

Full skirt: Points of tension/where drape forms. Full skirts flare out from the waist and then form vertical drape. The body defines the drape: drape forms from the knee when it touches the fabric, as seen in the S curve pose at the right.

Drawing full skirts. 1.
Draw a simple silhouette .

2. Define the gathers at the waist and the folds at the hem (draw a line parallel to the hem to plot the upper boundary of the folds.

3. Fill in the shadows along and under the folds of the drape.

skirts/
pleated skirts

the gathered fabric.

5. Lightweight fabric will form a large number of shallow folds at the hem; heavier and stiffer fabric will form a smaller number of deep folds.

PLEATED SKIRTS

Pleats are another way to control the fullness in full skirts as well as being an attractive and varied design feature in their own right. Pleats are folds inserted into the fabric at regular intervals. They are usually made flat by pressing or, in modern synthetic fabrics they can be permanently applied with a heat-setting process. Often the top part of the pleats are stitched down to give a a sleeker fit at the top of the skirt and enhance the way the pleats fall below (particularly with unpressed pleats that otherwise would not retain their shape). These are called *stitched-down* or *stitch-down pleats*.

There are numerous types of pleats. The techniques for drawing pleated skirts are the same as for all full skirts, but the pleats must be drawn carefully so they are clearly identifiable.

Pleated skirt. Points of tension/where drape forms. Pleated skirts are full skirts and the points of tension and drape lines are as shown in those diagrams.

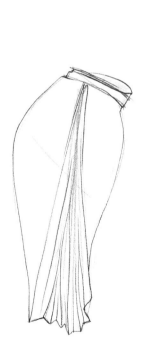

Skirt with stitched down inverted pleat and cluster pleats within.

Sunburst pleats.

pleated skirts

Wide knife (or side) pleats

Inverted pleat
(stitched down)

Kick pleat

Box pleats

Knife (or side) pleats

Stitched-down pleats

Mushroom pleats

Skirt with two ties of
mushroom pleats.

Unpressed pleats

Broomstick skirt. Not strictly a pleated skirt, a
broomstick skirt is made by tying the wet
skirt around a broomstick, producing a veri-
cally wrinkled effect when dry.

pleat variations

Unpressed pleats

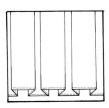

Box pleats

Pleated godet

Pleated godet

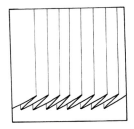

Tight knife pleats

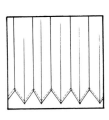

Accordion pleats

Unpressed, stitched-down pleats

skirts/gores and godets

GORED SKIRTS, GODETS

Gores are shaped sections of fabric that allow the waist of a skirt to be shaped without the use of tucks or gathers. The number of gores used to make up the skirt can range from four to over twenty. The shape of the gores at the hem can be varied to create different hemline silhouettes Godets are pieces of fabric, usually triangular or semi-circular, inserted into the hem of gored skirts at the seams to give a flounced effect.

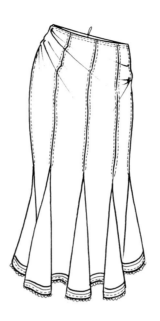

Gored skirt with set-in godets.

Gored skirt with asymmetrical yoke..

Gored skirt with set-in godets.

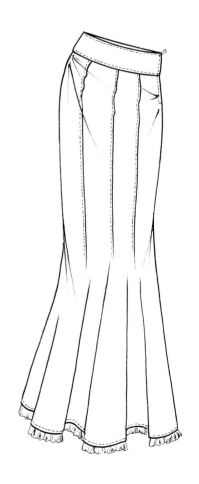

Trumpet skirt. This gored skirt is cut to flare out at the hem.

skirts/flounces/
tiers/exercises

FLOUNCES

Flounces are ruffles—strips of fabric gathered along one edge to form folds—that are attached to the hem of skirts. Flounces can be applied to both straight and full skirts; they are wider and often of a lighter fabric than the main body of the skirt, so add even more folds.

TIERED SKIRTS

Tiered skirts consist of tiers of fabric—often flounces—on a straight or flared skirt. Tiers are usually attached to an underskirt (though can be attached to each other) and usually overlap.

EXERCISES

1. Choose ten skirts of different types from photos in magazines. Trace the silhouettes practicing varying the line weight and nuancing the line in the silhouette.
2. Copy the same skirts but focus on reproducing the drape and folds accurately.
3. Draw (i) a straight skirt with an inverted pleat; (ii) an accordion-pleated skirt with a gathered waistline; (iii) a straight skirt with a flounce and (iv) a tiered skirt.

Flounce.

Flounce.

Simplified drawing of tiered skirt.

More detailed drawing of tiered skirt.

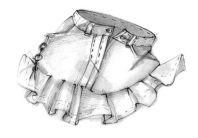

Jean-style skirt with flounce. Note the double top stitching typical of jeans and jean-style garments..

Tiered skirt. Note that each tier is sewn onto an underskirt, so fits *under* the tier above. Each tier requires a hem; note the hem stitching.

Prairie skirt.

123

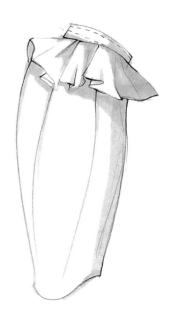

Gored skirt with flounce at waist.

Skirt gathered to fitted yoke.

Fitted yoke with full lower skirt.

Diagonal stitched-down pleats.

Sarong with tie.

Skirt with handkerchief hem.

A-line skirt with belt.

Bias-draped, gathered to side seam.

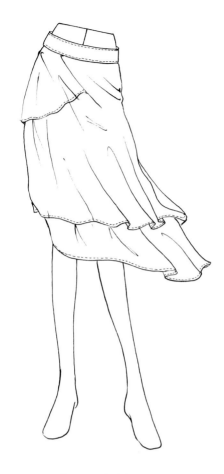

Asymmetrical tiers.

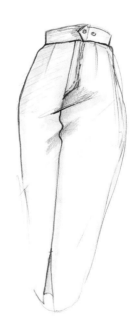

Jean-style skirt with inverted pleat.

Jean-style skirt, side view with asymmetrical seam.

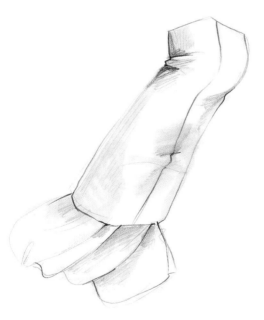

Straight skirt with bubble flounce.

skirts/various

Handkerchief hemmed

Skirt with scalloped hem.

Skirt with lace-trimmed hem.

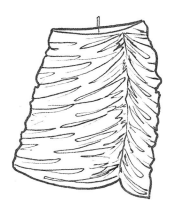

Ruched skirt.

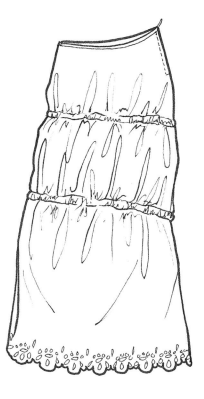

Three-section ruched skirt with lace-trimmed hem.

Short skirt with fringed hem.

Short skirt with tucked seams at hem.

Knee-length skirt with trapunto stitching.

Skirt with transparent lower section.

Skirt and blouse combination.

Skirts in combinations with blouse
and scarf and blouse and sweater.

sleeves/set-in/
raglan/kimono

Although there is a wide variety of
sleeve styles, most consist of one of
three types:
1. SET-IN SLEEVES, cut in one or two
pieces (in tailored jackets and coats two
pieces is more common) and attached
to the armhole with a seam around the
upper arm where it joins the shoulder.
2. RAGLAN SLEEVES, attached to the
bodice of the garment with a diagonal
seam or seams (up to three) that extends up to the collar.
3. KIMONO SLEEVES, which are cut in
one piece with the bodice of the garment and seamed above and below the
arm.

Sleeves can be straight and formal, as in
tailored garments, sometimes combined
with shoulder padding to give an exag-
geratedly geometric silhouette, or soft
and magnificent, with fullness and drape
both above and below the elbow.

The arm is one of the parts of the body
shaped like a cylinder, and sleeves,
which cover the arms, take a similar
form. It is important to keep this in mind
when drawing sleeves and to draw them
to appear three-dimensional, bending
around the arm. With eye level at the
middle of the sleeve-on-the-arm, close to
the elbow, sleeve hems appear to bend
upwards above the elbow and downwards below the elbow. Above the
elbow the sleeve rests along the upper
arm and excess fabric hangs below;
below the elbow the sleeve rests on the
inside edge of the arm from the elbow to
the wrist and excess fabric drapes
beneath.

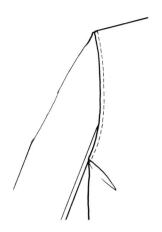

Set-in sleeve.

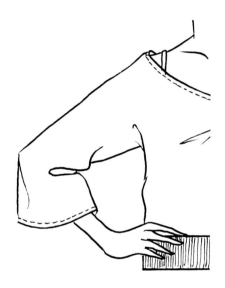

Kimono sleeve.

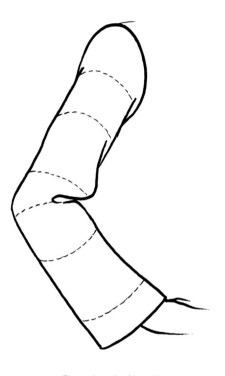

Sleeve lengths. Note the
upward curve of the sleeve
hems above the elbow and the
downward cuve below the
elbow.

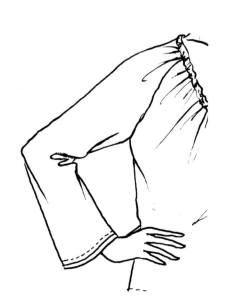

Raglan sleeve.

NARROW SLEEVES

The main differences in sleeves when drawing them are between narrow and full sleeves rather than the three types of sleeves.

1. First draw the arm with elbow bent and the wrist and hand slightly forward so that the detailing at the hem of the sleeve will be closest to the point of view.

2. With narrow fitted sleeves where the cap (the area of the sleeve where it fits into the armhole) sits at the point where the upper arm meets the shoulder (the usual position for tailored or more formal sleeves), first draw the cap, starting at the back of the shoulder, and then continue with a smooth, quick line to the elbow. The cap bends around the shoulder.

3. At the elbow the silhouette bulges out where the excess fabric that allows for ease of movement at this joint breaks. Draw this area nuancing the line to show where the fabric bends in and is in shadow (thicker line) and where it is straight and reflects the light (thinner line). The sleeve may be constructed from a drop shoulder and appear more relaxed, or a pad may be used that gives a sleeve a more architectural appearance. If the cap sits off the shoulder (a dropped shoulder sleeve), the cap is drawn as an upward curve around the upper arm below the shoulder.

4. Draw the other side of the arm starting just inside the first line showing the cap of the sleeve at the back of the shoulder, and continuing with a quick, smooth line to the wrist. The overlapping lines indicate the slight break in the fabric at the shoulder line where the body is present under the garment. With a dropped shoulder sleeve the line continues down from the lower-placed cap and there is no break in the fabric.

5. Add detailing. Sleeves end in hems or cuffs. Make sure to show hems and cuffs resting on the wrist—again, fabric is subject to the laws of gravity even when it bends. When seen front view with the arm hanging by the side cuffs slope up from the outer arm to the inner arm. The details of hems or cuffs should be drawn in last. Gathers, as with gathers at the cap at the other end of the sleeve, should be drawn straight out from the seam and hooked over at the end.

6. Add shading.

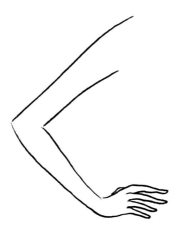

Drawing narrow sleeves. 1. Draw the arm with the elbow bent and wrist and hand slightly forward.

2. Draw the cap, starting at the back of the shoulder and continuing with a smooth, quick line to the elbow.

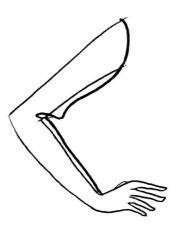

3. At the elbow the silhouette bulges to indicate the excess fabric required for ease of movement. Use a nuanced line here. Continue the line to the wrist.

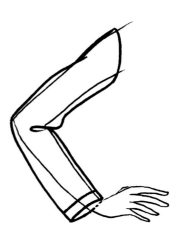

4. Draw the other side of the arm starting just inside the first line, and continuing with a quick, smooth line to the wrist. The overlapping lines indicate the slight break in the fabric at the shoulder line.

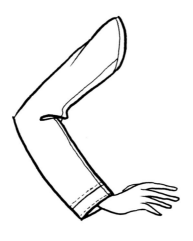

5. Add detailing.

6. Add shading.

sleeves/full/
exercises

FULL SLEEVES

1. Draw the arm with elbow bent so that the detailing at the hem of the sleeve will be clearly displayed.

2. For sleeves with fullness, start drawing the cap and the line of the inner side of the sleeve but stop the line where the drape of the fullness of the sleeve appears in front of it. Indicate this with a line that starts around the mid-upper arm, forms a wide fold and creases at the elbow. All these lines are curved, without angles, and are continuous and unbroken, showing the fabric's drape.

3., 4. Below the elbow, if there is fullness in the fabric the silhouette is fuller. If the garment is made of a stiff fabric the fullness will stand out from the arm underneath on both sides; if made of lightweight fabric the excess fabric falls only on the outer (lower) edge of the sleeve. Draw in the sihouette of the other side of the sleeve and indicate the position of the gathering at the cuff.

5. Make sure to show hems and cuffs resting on the wrist—fabric is subject to the laws of gravity even when it bends. When seen front view, with the arm hanging by the side, cuffs slope up from the outer arm to the inner arm.

6. The details of hems or cuffs should be drawn in last. Draw the gathers like petals, extending straight out from the seam and bending over at the end. They do not intersect.

Full sleeves can be gathered at the cap as well as the cuffs (puff and balloon sleeves are examples of this).

EXERCISES

1. Draw a blouse with six different types of sleeve.

2. Draw a full gathered sleeve (i) with a light fabric and (ii) with a heavier fabric. Show clearly the differences in the drape of the fabric when arm is bent.

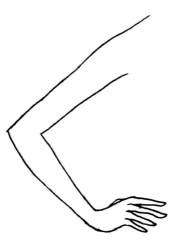

Drawing full sleeves. 1. Draw the arm with the elbow bent.

2. Start drawing the cap and the line of inner side of the sleeve but stop the line as the drape of the fullness of the sleeve appears in front of it, and indicate this with a line that starts around the mid-upper arm, forms a wide fold and creases at the elbow

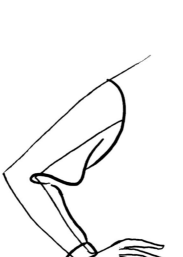

3. Continue below the elbow matching the silhouette to the amount of fullness in this area. Stiff fabrics stand out on either side of the arm; lighter fabrics will fall on the lower edge only.

4. Draw in the sihouette of the other side of the sleeve and indicate the position of the gathering at the cuff. Make sure to show the cuff resting on the wrist.

5. Add more detailing in the cuff area.

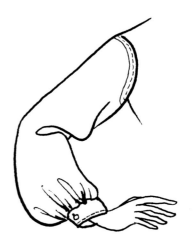

6. Finish off detailing and add shading.

sleeves/variations

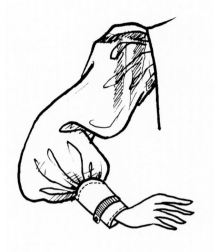

Gathers in sleeves, at caps and cuffs. 1.

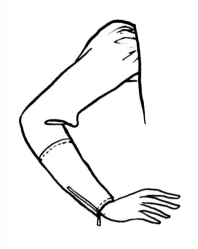

Gathers in sleeves, at caps and cuffs. 2.

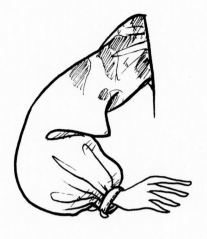

Gathers in sleeves, at caps and cuffs. 3.

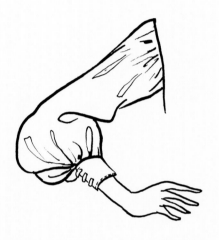

Gathers in sleeves, at caps and cuffs. 4.

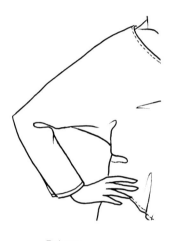

Dolman

Juliet

Set-in

Very short set-in

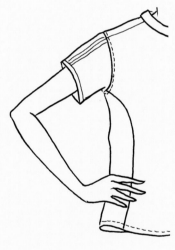

Short set-in

Set-in, flared, ruffle at cuff.

Short sleeve raglan

Dolman

131

Set-in

Circular

Puffed sleeve

Drop set-in bell

Balloon

Tulip

Raglan

Set-in bell

Saddle shoulder sleeve

Lantern

Raglan

Cap

sleeves/shaded, on-the-arm

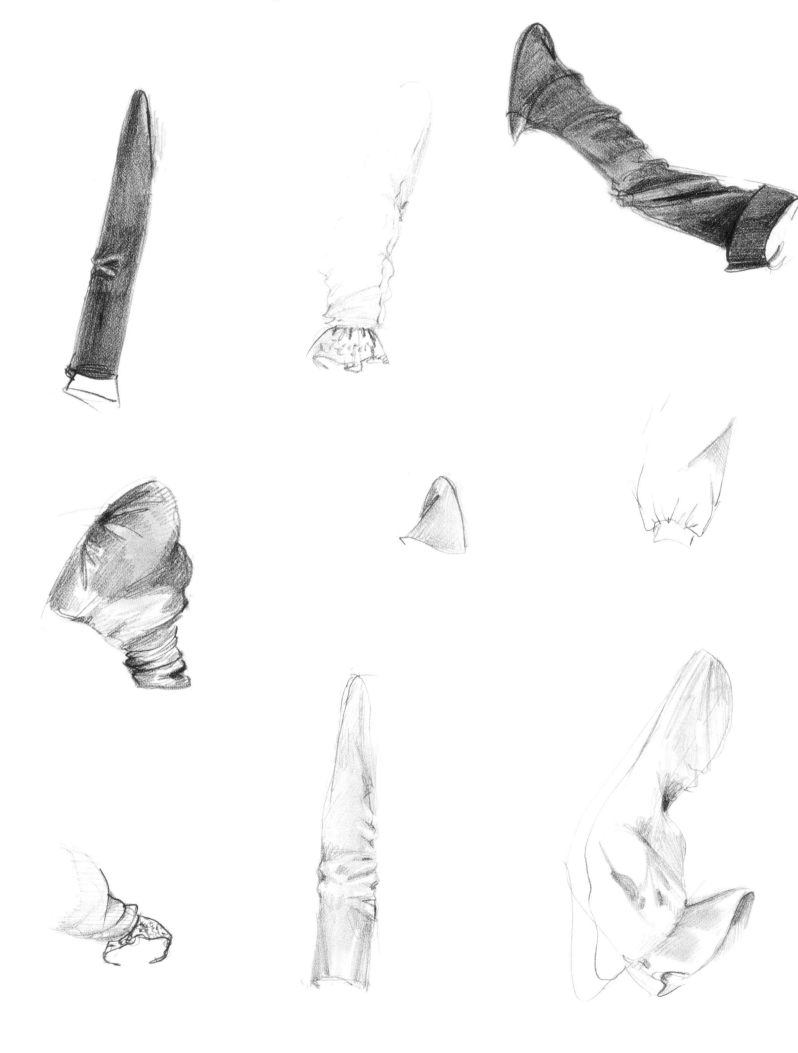

pants/general points

PANTS

Since women now engage in most activties that were previously restricted to men, they have, quite naturally, increasingly adopted the garment most suited to a large number of those activities: pants. Pants are practical, comfortable and stylish and are now worn on a wide variety of occasions ranging from formal evening and career wear to all manner of sports and casual wear.

Pants can be difficult to draw and care must be taken to make sure they look right. They can be thought of as being made up of six sections—the waist area, the hip/pelvis area, each of the top part of the legs from hip to knee and each of the bottom part of the legs from knee to ankle (or wherever the legs end) and care should be taken to ensure each section is correctly drawn. (The left and right leg are thought of separately as they are usually posed differently, so the drape of the fabric will be different.)

GENERAL POINTS TO KEEP IN MIND WHEN DRAWING PANTS

There are a number of other key points to be kept in mind when drawing pants:
(i) It is important to make sure that the center-front of the garment and the center-front of the body are aligned at all times so the pants are seen as properly fitting the figure.
(ii) If a zipper is included, then the flap covering the zipper must be drawn and positioned correctly: the zipper is always indepedent of the waistband; it ends at the bottom of the waistband and there is a snap or button at the waistband to allow access to the zipper. Zippers are almost always placed on seams, whether front, back or side, and it is important to show this seam continuing below the zipper.
(iii) Hems must be drawn in the correct position, according to the style of pant being drawn. They must also be seen to bend around the leg.
(iv) Details—and these have become increasingly varied and important styling elements—items such as pockets, pleats, belt loops, fly labels and bar tacks must be drawn correctly and in the correct position; they are often accompanied with top-stitching.

Silhouette

Drape and fit

Details

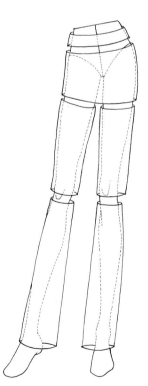

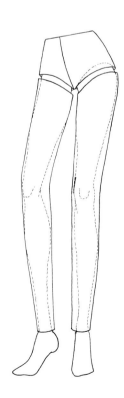

For drawing purposes pants can be thought of as comprised of six sections.

It is important to make sure that the center-front of the garment and the center-front of the body are aligned at all times so the pants are seen as properly fitting the figure.

When the leg bends, the pant breaks at the knee. Drape in pants appears in each leg and the waist/thigh section.

135

points of tension/ drawing pants

(v) The lines that define pants are mainly vertical. When drawing, it is easier to work from the top of the page downwards; this way one is always drawing on clean paper and the drawing is less likely to be smudged. It also seems intuitively easier to show the length of a pant leg that falls downwards by making downwards strokes.

(vi) In pant legs most of the drape appears at the knee where the garment is not as closely fitted to allow for movement of the joint. See Chapter Six: Fabrics for how to show drape in different fabrics.

DRAWING PANTS

To draw pants, begin by drawing the bottom half of the croquis. (For both pants and skirts the garments can, if so desired, also be drawn on the full croquis and paired with a simple t-shirt or top.) It is best to use a variation of an S curve pose when drawing pants, so that the drape can be clearly seen in the supporting leg. Choose a pose with the legs apart so the silhouette can be clearly seen.

1. Draw in the waistband as two parallel curves. Think of the waist as an elliptical shape extending round the back of the figure, with the part that is seen as the front part of that ellipse. It is usual to draw the waistband as upwardly sloping, as though the point of view was slightly below; if the pants are low-cut then the waistband can be drawn sloping down. If there is no waistband only one line is drawn. Note that there are folds and drape in almost all waistbands—only a small number contain internal construction that eliminates it.

2. Draw the silhouette of the hips and pelvis area of the pants. All pants have a center-front seam, and this should be drawn in lightly. Draw in the princess lines (as guidelines) midway between the center-front and the edge of the pants.

3. Draw in the inside edge of the support leg from the crotch to the ankle. This can be drawn as one line, stopping at the knee to indicate folds, (particularly for fabrics like denim which can have a lot of drape) and continuing to the ankle, or as two, with a small area of overlap at the knee to indicate the subtle break of a more classic cut and slightly stiffer fabric.

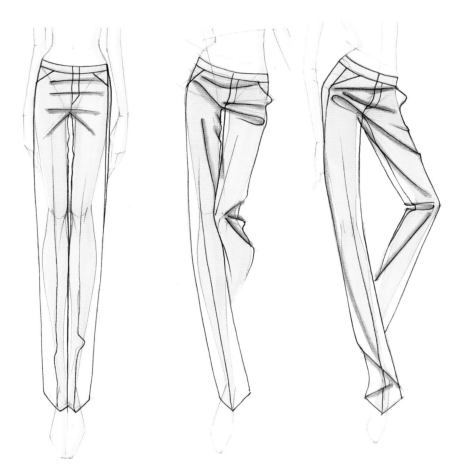

Straight-legged pants. Points of tension/where drape forms. Left, weight equally distributed, front view; center, S curve, front view, weight on left/front leg; right, S curve, three-quarter view, weight on left/front leg. Note in the S curve pose the fabric pulls from the raised hip.

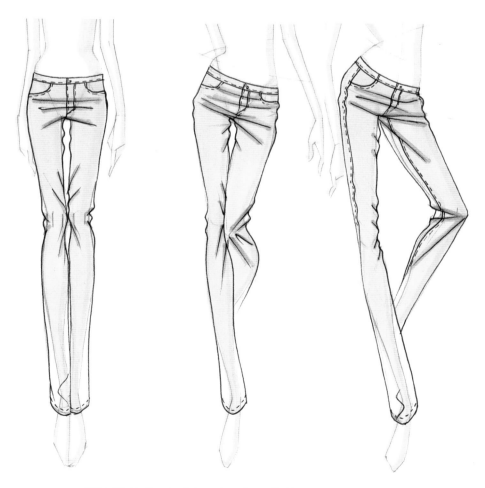

Jeans. Points of tension/where drape forms. Positions same as straight-legged pants above. Denim is a heavier fabric than that used in the pants above and forms wider, stiffer folds.

drawing pants/
various styles/exercise

4. Draw in the hemline of the support leg. For both legs, the hemline is a shallow curve that bends out from the foot. As when drawing the waistline, the shape is basically that of half an ellipse, varying according to the position of the leg and width of the pant leg. For wide-legged pants the hem can extend beyond the line of the hip; for average width pants the edge of the hem will fall almost directly beneath the hip line.

5. Draw in the other side of the support leg. If the hem is wide a fold of drape forms at the hip and falls diagonally across the leg to the outer edge of the ankle (in slimmer pants this drape line is less obvious).

6. Draw in the outside edge of the other leg from waist to ankle, again either with one line with a ripple at the waist to show folds of drape, or with two lines that overlap slightly in the knee area to show a more subtle break of the fabric. Draw in the hem as with the support leg, curving slightly towards the foot. Draw in the inside edge of the leg from the hem to the crotch as an almost straight line, without a break. With wider hems, a drape line is often seen forming around the knee area and falling diagonally to the inner ankle.

7. If pants are very long and the hem breaks over the shoe, a lot of drape will form in the bottom half of the leg below the knee. Depending on the cut and fit of the pants there will be more or less drape at the knee and crotch. Deep pockets can cause drape, as does a hand in the pocket.

8. If pants have a crease this will appear down the center-front and continue to the hems, which will appear more angular. If a pant has cuffs then these must be drawn to appear wider than the pant leg.

9. To draw a zipper correctly on classic women's pants it is placed to the left of the center seam directly beneath the waistband and is indicated by drawing in the stitching on the placket that covers it.

10. Avoid drawing a V at the crotch: drape at the crotch is indicated by a light line angling up from the point of the crotch.

EXERCISE
Draw 10 styles of pants clearly showing fit and drape.

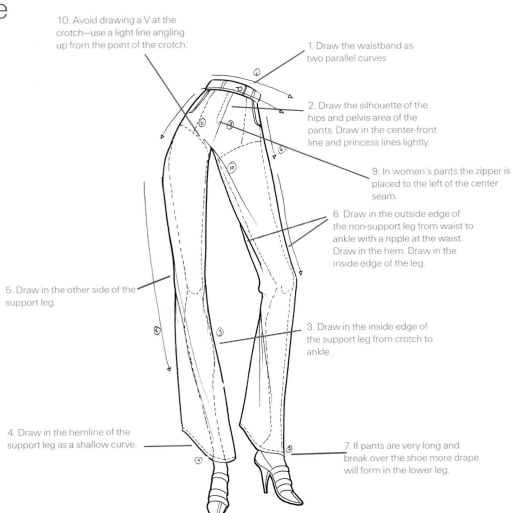

10. Avoid drawing a V at the crotch—use a light line angling up from the point of the crotch.

1. Draw the waistband as two parallel curves

2. Draw the silhouette of the hips and pelvis area of the pants. Draw in the center-front line and princess lines lightly.

9. In women's pants the zipper is placed to the left of the center seam.

6. Draw in the outside edge of the non-support leg from waist to ankle with a ripple at the waist. Draw in the hem. Draw in the inside edge of the leg.

5. Draw in the other side of the support leg.

3. Draw in the inside edge of the support leg from crotch to ankle.

4. Draw in the hemline of the support leg as a shallow curve.

7. If pants are very long and break over the shoe more drape will form in the lower leg.

Steps for drawing pants.

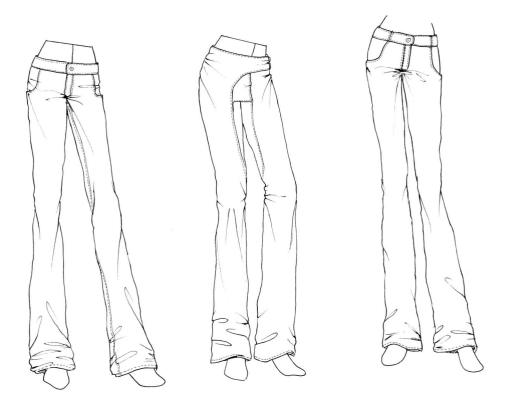

Various styles of pants and jeans. Women's *pants* usually have the zipper drawn on the left side; women's *jeans*, by contrast, styled after men's, usually have it drawn on the right. Note with extra long pants there is additional drape where the legs break over the shoes.

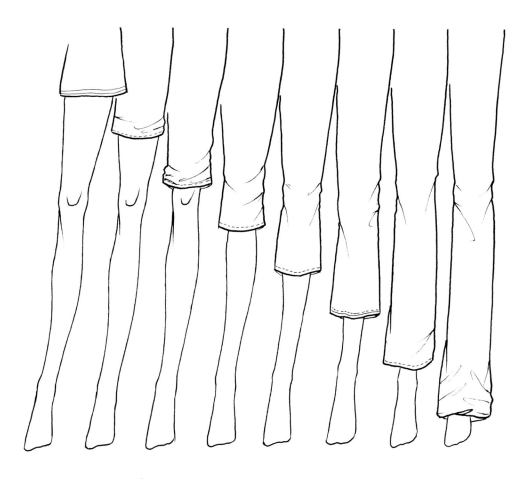

Pant lengths, from left: short shorts; mid-thigh; above-the-knee; knee; below-the-knee; mid-calf; above-the-ankle; floor.

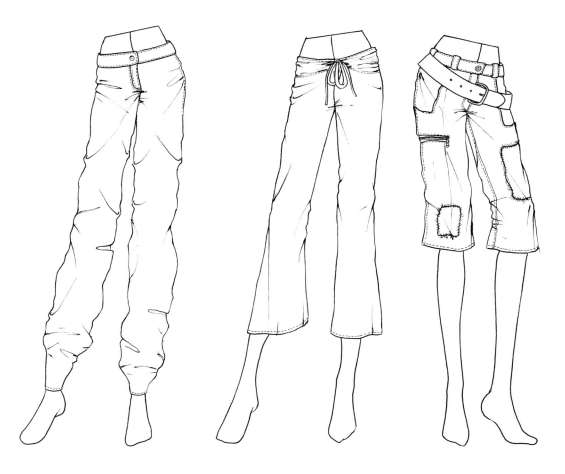

Different lengths and hem treatments, detailing.

jeans

Drawing classic five-pocket denim jeans.
1. Draw the silhouette and croquis. Note the double row of top-stitching is included right from the start. Without this important feature the garment will not look like jeans.

2. Indicate the drape at the thigh and knee using the side of the pencil.

3. Finish off the shading using a 2B pencil.

jeans/denim
(heavyweight fabric)

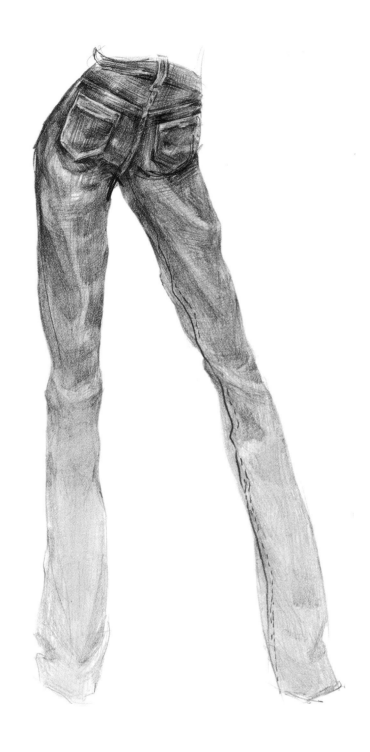

Denim jeans, three-quarter and back views. Denim is a thick, heavy-weight fabric that drapes in wide folds. Note in these drawings that everything—the cuffs, belts and legs—*bends* around the body.

pants/medium-weight fabric

Drawing pants of medium-weight fabric.
1. Draw the croquis and silhouette. The pants bend around the figure and the shift of the hip must be reflected in the diagonal drape it causes in the upper pelvis area and down the leg.

2. Draw in the folds as they drape to the knee and ankle. Note that in the front leg the hem touches the ankle at the left and the rest of it circles thte ankle.

3. Fill in the pants with shadows to show the soft drape and add the detailing. Avoid using heavy outlines.

pants/lightweight

1. Draw the croquis and silhouette. This is a walking pose, and the bent knee creates drape. Note the lower left leg, pointing backwards, is foreshortened. Make sure the "bumps" of the folds of the fabric show clearly in the silhouette of the side of the leg with most drape.

Drawing lightweight fabric pants. As they are lightweight these pants have the most drape of the three types shown in this section. On the left leg the fabric pulls to the knee; on the right, to the inner ankle.

2. Plot out the design of the drape, with multiple folds at the crotch, in the left leg from the hip to the knee, from the knee to the nakles and in the lower leg, and in the right leg pulling from the hip to the inner ankle.

3. Fill in the shadows that fall between each of the folds and the light on the surface of the folds. Note the shape of the pant cuffs.

Croquis with pants of different fabrics. Left, smooth finish medium-weight fabric (e.g. gabardine or polished cotton); center, transparent fabric (e.g. organza or ultra-lightweight cotton); right, lightweight fabric (e.g. lightweight cotton, linen). Note the variations in the drape of the three types of fabric and how the garments fit the body underneath.

Jodhpurs. This style of pant has excess fabric above the knee, around the hip and thigh. Shadows are used to show the position of the body under the garment in the hip and thigh areas. Note the tucks at the waistline and the tight fit from knee to ankle.

pants/contemporary poses

Poses for pants. Note that when drawing pants it is important to be able to see the silhouette clearly, so the legs should be kept apart and sometimes the leg bent to show the fit.

blouses/shirts/tops/ sweaters & knitted tops

BLOUSES, SHIRTS, TOPS, KNITTED SWEATERS/TOPS
BLOUSES are feminine garments constructed either with or without a collar and with or without buttoned fronts, They are usually lighter and of softer fabric than shirts (which are primarily mens-wear but have also been adopted by women). Blouses are generally drawn using more curves than shirts.

SHIRTS usually have more tailoring than blouses, often with long sleeves, sleeve plackets, cuffs, collar stands and collars, buttons and button bands/extensions. Because of the construction they contain shirts also generally have more straight lines than blouses. Illustrations of a number of different shirts for women are included in this section; for a detailed description of the different parts of a shirt and how to draw them see Chapter Seven: Men and Men's Clothing.

TOPS is the generic name for all garments worn on the upper body, so includes blouses and shirts, but usually refers to a less formal and less constructed garment (bustiers, corsets and camisoles being some obvious exceptions). Tops are often used in active sports (or adapted as casualwear from active sportswear), but are also worn as eveningwear, usually revealing a combination of arms, neck and chest and back.

KNITTED SWEATERS and KNITTED TOPS range from very tight-fitting to very loose-fitting. Knitted garments have elastic qualities: they stretch to allow limbs to enter and then resume their original form, closely fitting the body. Spandex and similar fabrics have increasingly been included in knitting yarns to allow more elasticity so that truly body-hugging fits can be achieved. When drawing sweaters, make sure to indicate the fit accurately and, if loose-fitting, show where the fullness is in the garment.
Knitted sweaters—as with other knitted garments—are constructed using a variety of methods, ranging from hand-knit to industrial knitting machines. How a sweater has been knit is clear when it is

Silhouette   Drape and fit   Details

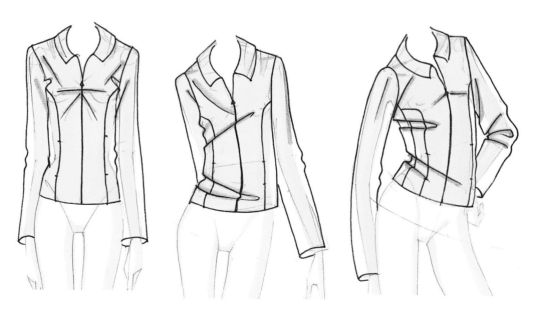

Blouses. Points of tension/where drape forms.
Left, torso straight—note the tension line at the bust; center, left shoulder down in typical S curve pose—note the tension points at the waist and diagonally from the bust as the bust slopes down; right, left shoulder down in S curve pose, three-quarter view with right arm bent and left away from body—tension points seen under armholes, at bend of right arm , at bust and at the waist on the left side where the body is compressed.

sweaters & knitted tops/exercises

handled and inspected, but does not usually show in a drawing unless it has been made with a relatively thick yarn that produces a chunky knit. If it is important that the stitch used in a knit be clearly seen, a separate magnified detail can be included with the drawing (*see* Chapter Five: Encyclopedia of Details for examples of knit stitches).

Besides the silhouette and detailing, the features of a knitted sweater or top that can be seen in a drawing are: (i) the different ways the hems, edges, sleeves and necklines are finished off—various types of ribbing, and rolled edges (because of the stretch of knits the constructional devices used to remove fullness in woven garments—tucks, seams and so on—are not required, and hems and edges are finished by changing the stitch/yarn/ pattern and knitting a ribbing or rolled, crotcheted or embroidered edge; (ii) the different textures and patterns—cables, diamonds or intricate jacquard-knit patterns—that are incorporated into the knit and (iii) if the sweater is knit with yarn made from a fiber with a distinctive appearance, such as mohair, angora or cashmere. Examples of these variations in sweaters are shown in the following pages.

EXERCISES
1. Draw twelve styles of tops on the croquis, including blouses, shirts, camisoles and tank tops. Legs do not have to be included. Include a variety of trim, top-stitching, appliqués, pockets, buttons and gathers.
2. Draw ten knitted tops using different types of wool or stitching and different ribbed finishes to sleeves and hems.

Variations of top silhouettes. These are knitted tops.

Blouse.

Blouse with ruffled neckline.

Corset.

Corset with ruched brassiere.

Blouse with cowl neckline.

Blouse with bertha collar.

Short-sleeved shirt.

tops/blouses

Asymmetrical top.

Double-breasted blouse.

Ruffle hemmed top.

Puff-sleeved top.

Twisted halter-neck top.

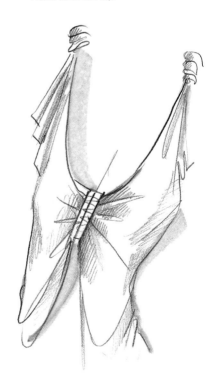

Sleeveless top gathered to center inset.

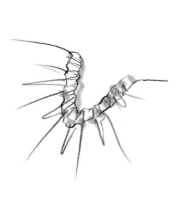

Gathering at neckline.

T-shirt.

Slip-style top

Blouse with short sleeves gathered at cuff.

Spaghetti-tie top with floral appliqué.

Sleeveless top gathered into empire waist below bust.

Blouse with fagoting and buttoned placket.

Sleeveless top with diagonal gathers below bust. .

Blouse with smocking on yoke and armband.

Flap front with tie.

Lace trim

Shirring

Embroidered cuff with tie.

Patch pocket with ruffles and tie.

Square pocket with inverted pleat and ruffles.

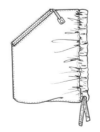

Zip pocket with gathers and tie.

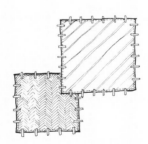

Appliqués with whip stitching.

Trim.

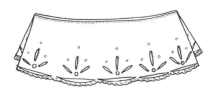

Eyelet trim.

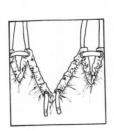

String ties.

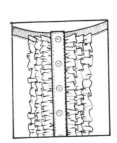

Ruffles

Padded zip pocket.

Ribbon trim with tie.

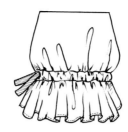

Cuff with casing.

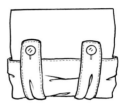

Button tab with cuff.

Scalloped lace trim.

Puff sleeve.

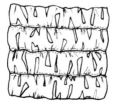

Ruching.

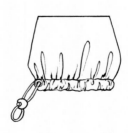

Cuff with button tab stop.

Herringbone trim.

Zip pocket with lacing and gathers.

Cuff with string tie.

Floral appliqué.

Ruffled cuff with scalloped edge.

Peter Pan collar with picot stitching.

Long point collar with
bow and top stitching.

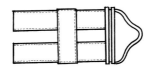

Buckle.

Beaded trim on puff sleeve.

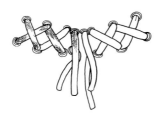

Lacing.

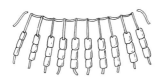

Beaded trim.

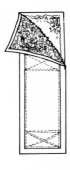

Velcro closure.

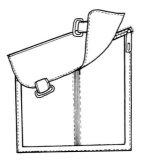

Square patch pocket
with zip and strap.

Center zip pocket

Tabbed laced pocket

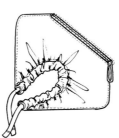

Zip drawcord pocket

Diagonal rib-knit sweater

Rib-knit sweater and skirt combination.

Argyll (also spelt Argyle) sweater.

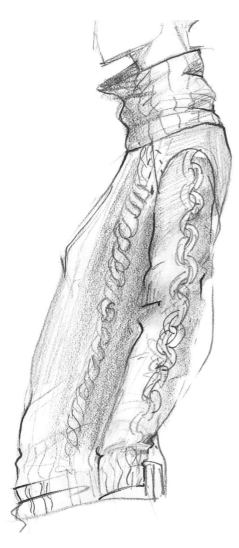

Cable sweater with turtle neck.

Slipover with cable stitching over
tailored shirt. Flat shown upper left.

Popcorn-stitched cardi-
gan over bow blouse.

Silk-knit sweater with zipper under denim top.

Left, rib-knit wool sweater; right, striped merino wool turtleneck sweater. Flats shown upper left and right.

knitted sweaters

Cashmere bolero sweater with
three-quarter length sleeves.
Flat shown upper right.

Cable-stitched wool sweater.
Flat shown above.

Knitted wool sweater with
satin trim. Flat shown left.

knitted sweaters

Alpaca and angora wool sweater.

Metallic-knit sweater with oversized collar.

Merino wool sweater set.

All these sweaters were drawn using the side of the pencil to create soft folds common to all wool knits. There are no hard edges at the silhouette—only in the detailing—and everything is shaded to soften the overall effect. The metallic knit sweater has a wider range of values to emphasize the shine on the yarn.

cuff/hem treatments
for knitted garments

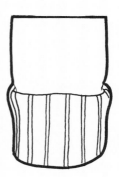

Double-ribbed cuff, folded over.

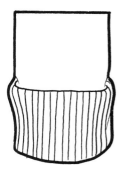

Single-ribbed cuff, folded over.

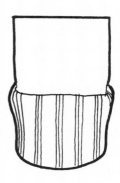

Triple-ribbed cuff, folded over.

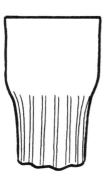

Single-ribbed cuff, unfolded.

Fringed cuff.

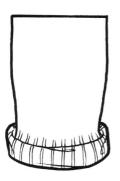

Double-ribbed cuff, folded over.

Because of the way knitted garments stretch they are finished differently to woven garments. The constructional devices needed to remove fullness in woven garments—tucks, seams and so on—are not required, and hems and edges are finished by changing the stitch and/or yarn and/or pattern and knitting a ribbing or rolled, crotcheted or embroidered edge.

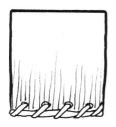

Whip stitch.

crochet-knit poncho

Building up the detailed shading of a crochet-knit poncho. Flat shown upper right.

dresses/ general points

DRESSES

Although dresses are one-piece garments, there is little difference in drawing them from the way a top and skirt are drawn. Dresses are usually the most feminine and sensuous of garments, with fabric draping next to the body for the full length of the figure. They often are made with large quantities of fabric, which usually implies copious amounts of drape. The fabric and drape is a large part of the appeal of the dress, and a pose should be chosen that shows them off to best effect: often an "in-motion" pose with numerous diagonals will be best for achieving this.

There is a wide variety of dress silhouettes, ranging from tight "sheaths" that fit tightly to the curves of the body, to, at the other extreme, forms that are almost completely independent of the shape of the body underneath. For dresses that do not fit the body closely, it is nevertheless important to know exactly where the figure is under the garment, and to sketch in the pose of the croquis before drawing the dress. Unless the position of the body under the dress is known, the parts that emerge from the top, sleeves and bottom of the dress cannot be accurately positioned, and the drawing looks incorrect.

For dresses the pose is often also an indicator of the market the garment is designed for: for example, a dress for a younger woman might be shown with a pose where the legs are apart. Choose a pose that shows off the best features of the garment, and if it contains a large quantity of fabric use the full page to do it full justice.

GENERAL POINTS TO KEEP IN MIND WHEN DRAWING DRESSES

1. Be attentive to scale and silhouette. Belts often create a slim area close to the body and, when pulled tight at the waist, create a soft silhouette in the upper torso.
2. All parts of a dress have to be drawn as curving around the figure underneath. Draw the neckline around the neck, the armholes around the arms and the hem around the legs.

Although dresses often *cover up* a large portion of the body it is nevertheless important to know the position of the figure underneath. Unless the position of the figure under the dress is known, the parts that emerge from the top, sleeves and bottom of the dress cannot be accurately positioned and the silhouette of the dress itself cannot be correctly positioned, so the drawing appears incorrect. It is often helpful to lightly sketch in the croquis before drawing the dress.

Silhouette

Drape and fit.

Details.

dresses

3. All hems bend around the bottom of the figure; collars bend around the neck and sleeves bend around the arms.

4. Wedding dresses and evening gowns require a full sweep and curve of the hem which can dip down at the back of the figure, in the front of the figure or perhaps off to the side. Where fabric extends along the ground it drapes horizontally rather than vertically when on the body.

5. No matter how long a hem is, it is often a good idea to show the shoe protruding underneath—it can make the drawing more realistic by providing a point of reference for the eye, and can make the drawing look graceful.

6. Tailored dresses are drawn with crisp sharp lines and straight folds.

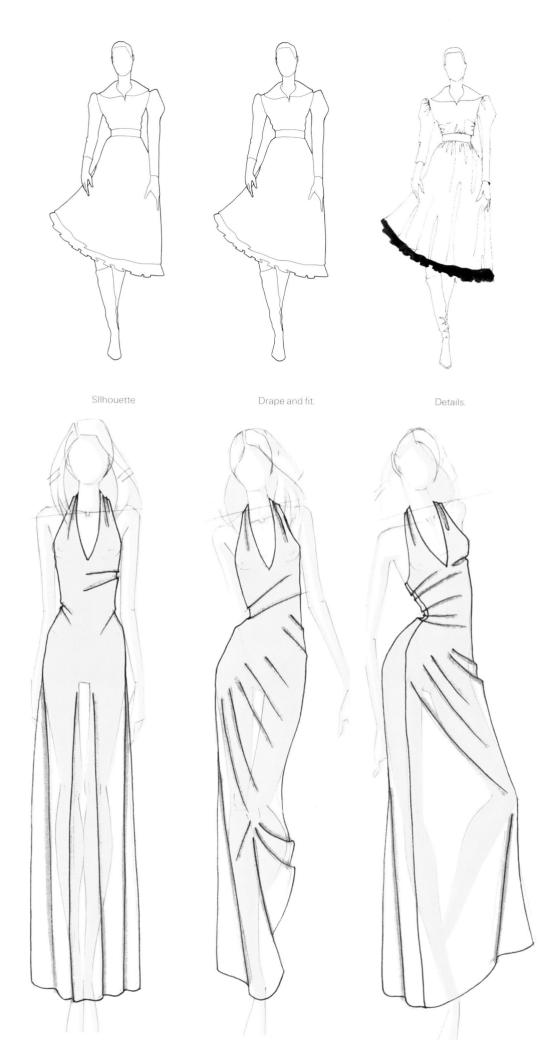

Silhouette   Drape and fit.   Details.

Dress. Points of tension/where drape forms.
Left, front view, dress drapes into long, vertical folds; center, S curve pose, front view, drape radiates from raised hip on left and across bodice; right, S curve, three-quarter view.

dresses/batiste
evening gown/exercises

7. As mentioned, dresses are the garments that usually contain most fabric, and as a result they also usually contain the most folds and drape. Design features are often incorporated specifically to show off the fabric and drape, and include such details as pleats, gathers, shirring, cowls (at front and back and on sleeves), deeply plunging necklines and backs and other features that highlight the fabric. (When dresses incorporate these design features the fabric of the dress is also often cut on the bias—on the diagonal—so it stretches more than when it is cut "on grain"—when the cross and lengthwise threads are at right angles to each other.) These design features are as a rule vital to the overall appearance of the garment and should be accurately rendered using techniques to show clearly the fabric type and the detailed way it folds and drapes. Refer to Chapter Six: Fabrics to see how to render different types of drape and different fabrics.

EXERCISES
1. Draw (i) a cocktail dress, (ii) an evening gown and (iii) a wedding dress. Include with each accessories chosen from Chapter Three: Accessories.
2. Draw (i) a dress with gathers, (ii) a fitted dress and (iii) an Empire-waisted dress.

This sleeveless cotton batiste evening dress is constructed in sections, with gathers to and trim at each sectional seam, a flounce at the hem and knotted into a bow at the bustline.

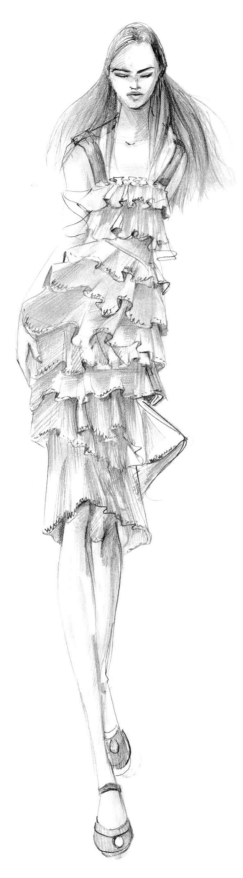

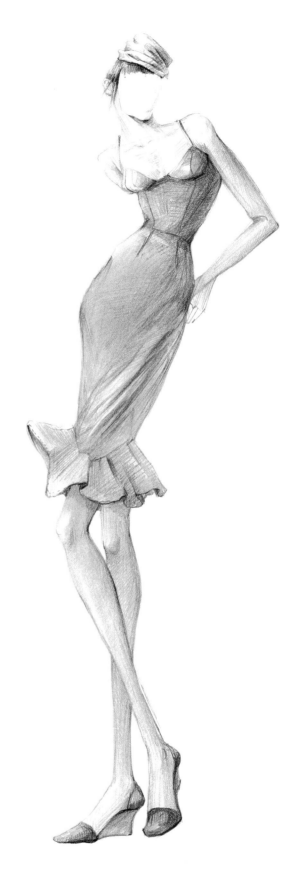

Rayon-knit tiered dress with numerous ruffles.

Double-weight silk charmeuse dress. This fabric is heavier than that of the dress on the left, so the drape of the folds is wider.

dresses/various

Left, satin stretch crepe; middle, four-ply satin silk-faced crepe with beaded neckline; right, lighweight silk twill. Step 1. Draw the croquis. Step 2. Define the drape and begin to build up the shading on the garments. (Continued on next page.)

(*Continued*) Step3. Finish off the shading and add details. The satin stretch crepe has a slight sheen and is drawn with a more even application of shading than the fabrics of the other dresses. The satin silk-faced crepe is shinier and has more contrast of value; its folds are medium-sized. The lightweight silk twill clings to the torso and around the legs.

dresses/transparent/
polyester-knit

Left, transparent lightweight-tulle dress with mohair mini cape. The dress is drawn almost completely with fine straight lines, curving in the folds at the hem. The beads on the surface of the fabric are drawn as semi-circles with dark semi-circular shadows next to them.
Right, polyester-knit top and poly-knit skirt, with tie in same fabric as top. The silhouette was drawn and fine lines used to show the fluid drape of the folds. Light shadows were applied to each of the small folds using the side of the pencil. A light touch is required to express the lightness of the fabric.

dresses/silk chiffon/
wool challis

Left, silk chiffon dress with two-ply crepe de chine straps. The silk chiffon is gossamer light and makes an interesting contrast with the fabric of the dress on the right, which is also very lightweight but has more body, so forms wider folds.
Right, wool challis dress and jacket.

Double satin-faced silk organza evening gown with beaded top. This fabric forms voluminous, soft-edged folds and is drawn with soft nuanced lines and shading. The trim at the neckline, under the bustline and at the waistline is more defined than the rest of the garment.

tailored garments/
drawing tailored jackets

TAILORED GARMENTS

A tailored garment is a garment with a shape of its own, largely independent of the figure underneath. It is distinguished by sleek lines, with no hint of the underlying construction, precise fit without the apperance of stiffness, hidden seams and hems and exquisite quality and finish of all details. The shape of a tailored garment is achieved by molding the fabric using specialized hand-sewing and pressing techniques, using interfacing and other inner fabrics for shaping and support.

Tailored garments are often thought of as a limited number of types, comprising jackets, suits, coats and other formal-wear, but in fact most types of garments, including tops, blouses, sleepwear, casualwear worn in the home (such as coats and robes) and underwear can be tailored. Tailored garments are also those garments that require tailoring in certain areas to provide shape and structure that the fabric alone cannot provide, for example, a roll collar on a thin summer dress.

DRAWING TAILORED JACKETS

The jacket is the classic tailored garment. Coats can be thought of as long jackets and are drawn in a similar fashion.

1. First draw the basic shape of the garment at the shoulders, waist and hips. Draw in the center-front line. Decide how low the jacket opening will be and where the topmost button will be placed. The placement of the first button is a major determinant of fit and silhouette, and can be placed at the bustline, above the bustline or below the bustline, even as far down as the waist or below. Position the top button on the center-front line.

2. There is no set sequence for drawing in the different parts of the garment, but as with pants it is often easier to work from the top downwards to avoid smudging the drawing. It is usually best, though, first to draw in the opening of the jacket and the roll line (where the overlapping lapel on the left curves

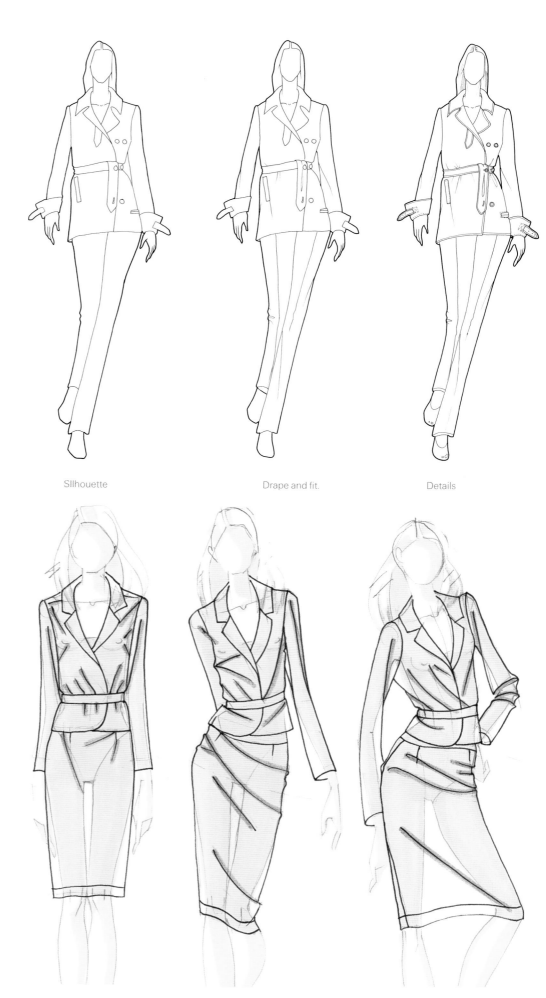

Silhouette   Drape and fit.   Details

Tailored jacket with belt. Points of tension/where drape forms .Left, front view, belt creates folds as it gathers in the excess fabric; center, S curve pose, front view, drape shifts to left of jacket as shoulder and hip compress; right, S curve, three-quarter view.

170

tailored garments/ drawing tailored jackets

round the first button) as the collar and lapels are placed in relation to this. The button is placed on the center-front line and the buttonhole is to its left. Be precise in the placement of the button as this determines the appearance of the front of the jacket. Start by drawing in the collar where it bends around the back of the neck, making sure it curves upwards.

3. Continue drawing the collar on both sides as it fall onto and then rolls out across the shoulder and then returns to the notch—the point where it joins the lapel. Continue from the notch to draw in the lapels. It is easiest to draw in the left lapel (the overlapping lapel in women's garments) first, drawing in the outer edge curving around the top button and then turning and joining the front body of the jacket. Be precise when determining the width of the lapel—lapel width is an important design element—and how far it extends towards the armhole, as well as the relative sizes of the collar and lapel (another important design element). Make sure the gorges (the seams between the collar and the lapels) are the same length and are drawn in lightly. The lapels are almost symmetrical— one ends in a button and the other a buttonhole— except that the left tucks over the right at the roll line .

4. Draw in the sleeves in the armholes, falling, if the arm is straight, in a very straight line (characteristic of tailored sleeves). When the arm hangs by the side the cap of the sleeve is barely noticeable, but when bent (as is the left arm in the drawings here) the cap is very noticeable. The hems of the sleeves bend around the arm, so appear curved. If the arms hang straight the wrist sits in the middle of each sleeve; if the arms are bent the sleeves drape from the wrist.

5. Refine the silhouette of the garment, showing the degree of padding in the shoulders (or unpadded shoulders, as the case may be), the cut of the jacket at the front, the fit at the sides and the vents—if any— in the sleeves. Finish the drawing by adding the details—buttons, buttonholes, pockets, top-stitching, darts and seams, trim and so on. Tailored garments

Drawing tailored jackets. (Steps refer to points in text).
Step 1. Draw the basic silhouette of the jacket . Draw in the center-front line and place the top button at the desired position on this line.

Step2–4. Work from top down drawing the back of the collar to the shoulder and then to the notch, continuing to draw in the lapels. Draw lapels and collar accurately and symmetrically.Left lapel tucks over right. Draw in sleeves.

Step 5, 6. When arm is straight the cap of the sleeve does not show; when bent it is clearly visible. Refine the silhouette, add details and shading at the collar, under the lapels , under buttons and at the opening of the jacket.

The top button must be accurately placed on the center-front line—it is a major determinant of fit and silhouette. Note the sleeve bends around the arm.

Be precise when determining the width of the lapel—an important design element. Make sure the gorges (the seams between the collar and the lapel) are the same length.

With tailored jackets, when the sleeve hangs by the side the cap is hardly visible; when the arm is bent the cap is clearly visible.. Princess lines are important in tailoring construction and should be accurately indicated.

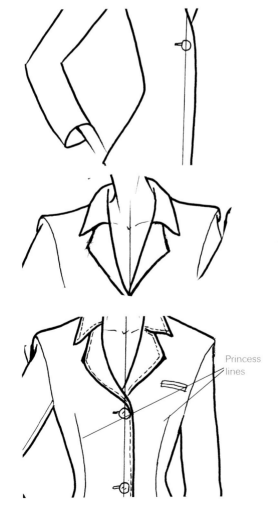

Princess lines

tailored garments/ general points/buttons/belts

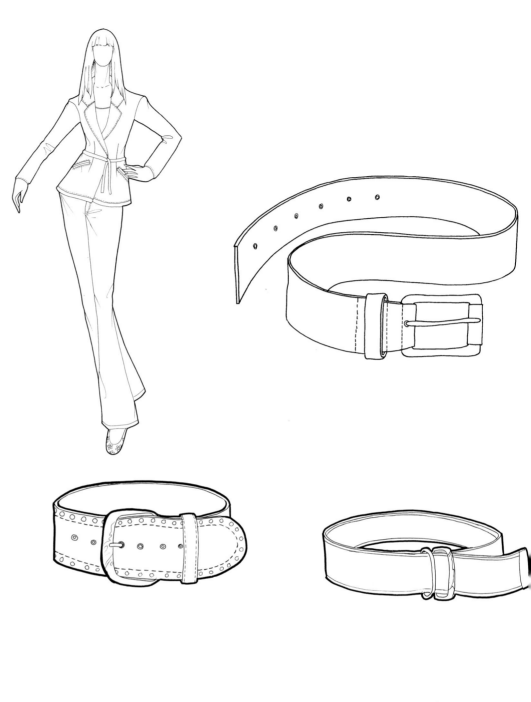

are made with precision, and details should be drawn in also with precision. 6. Add shading at the collar as it bends into the notch, under the bottom half of the lapels and along the bottom part of the opening of the jacket to indicate the thickness of the fabric and give the garment a three-dimensional appearance.

GENERAL POINTS TO KEEP IN MIND FOR DRAWING TAILORED GARMENTS. Tailored garments are made with precision and attention to detail, which is responsible for a large part of their overall appearance. It is important to respect this attention to detail when drawing these garments to capture the clean and crisp lines and detailing. Openings, hems, seams, darts and the shape and lengths of sleeves, collars, lapels and the main body of the garment must all be accurate.

BUTTONS must be evenly spaced vertically and if the garment is double-breasted the two lines of buttons must also be placed at equal distances from the center-front line and in horizontal alignment with each other. Pay attention to the type of button and buttonhole being drawn.

Remember that jackets are, except for the area where the lapels cross, almost completely symmetrical, and the strong lines created by tailoring accentuate this and make it more noticeable if they are not drawn with complete symmetry.

When jackets are drawn over a garment—a blouse or shirt, for example—it is advisable to draw the undergarment first, making sure the collar is abovethe shoulder line, and then to draw the collar of the jacket overlapping it.

Do not draw a line under the bustline with tailored jackets. Most tailored jackets smooth out the bustline rather than accentuate it.

Belts and buckles.

tailored garments/jackets/ belts & sashes/exercises

BELTS AND SASHES are frequently an important feature of tailored jackets: They are usually integral to the intended silhouette of the garment, gathering any fullness of fabric to a slim, figure-flattering waist, as well as often being attractive design details. If a belt *is* an important design detail in a jacket then it should be drawn with care. There are numerous types of belts-sand sashes. Belts can be straight or contoured to follow the curves of the body and have a variety of fastenings, including prong and eyelet with a buckle, snaps, hooks and eyes and clasp buckles. Except where the fastening is positioned off-center, make sure the buckles, knots or other fastening devices sit symmetrically on the center-front line.

EXERCISES
1. Draw a tailored jacket with (i) a notched collar, (ii) a shawl collar, and then draw a double-breasted jacket with no collar. (Refer to the drawings overleaf, the section on collars and necklines later in this chapter and Chapter Five: Encyclopedia of Details for examples of these types of collars.)
2. Draw five jackets with different silhouettes and of different lengths.Choose a skirt or pair of pants to go with each jacket.

Contemporary jacket styles.

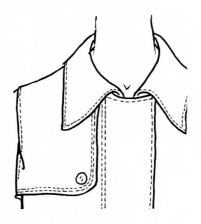

Buttoned down
yoke and fly front.

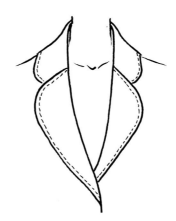

Clover leaf lapel

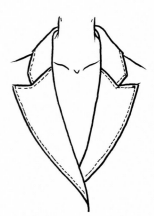

Semi-peaked lapel

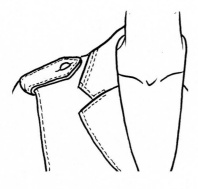

Epaulette

Notched lapel

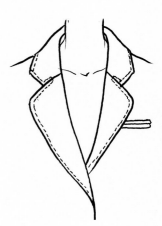

Clover leaf lapel
with slit pocket

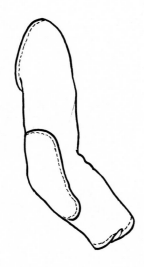

Sleeve patch

Belted cuff

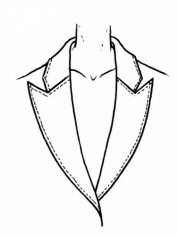

Peaked lapel

Buttonholes—top, key-
hole; bottom, bound.

tailored jackets/
leather/fitted/relaxed

Leather jacket. Garments made out of skins require more seams than others because only the small, good parts of the pelts can be used, and to cover the larger expanses of the jacket these have to be pieced together. The cap of the sleeve is rigid and the tailoring lines are straighter than for textile fabrics.

A contrast in tailoring styles: The suit on the left has more internal structure, so the jacket has more body of its own, as is clearly seen in the wide lapel and the silhouette of the hem of the jacket. This is indicated in the drawing with the use of thicker, darker and straighter lines. The jacket on the right has less construction below the shoulderline and the fabric has more drape.

tailored vest/jacket

Left, tailored vest; right, tailored jacket with fur collar. Although they are made to fit the body, the shape of tailored garments is the result of their internal construction rather than the presence of the body underneath. This means that the interaction between clothes and the body underneath is less than for untailored garments, particularly in the areas of the garment with most construction—shoulders, collars and lapels, and cuffs.

tailored garments

Belted tailored garments. Belts pull in the silhouette at the waist, creating a "blouson" effect where the excess fabric sits above the belt. Note on the coat on the right the collar frames the face and reaches almost to the chin; the neck is not visible. Collars are often drawn incorrectly, sitting too low, with the neck sticking out too far.

Tailored coats. Left, princess coat with mandarin collar; right, coat with fur collar. Note in the princess coat the princess style lines are clearly indicated; the coat fits the torso to the hip and then flares out..

tailored garments/
various jacket silhouettes

tailored coats

Left, princess coat. Make sure the princess lines fall correctly from the armhole to the hem, following the lines of the body underneath. Right, three-quarter length car coat with asymmetrical button closure. Note that shadows are emphasized under the collar, buttons, belt and flap to indicate the depth of these features.

tailored coats

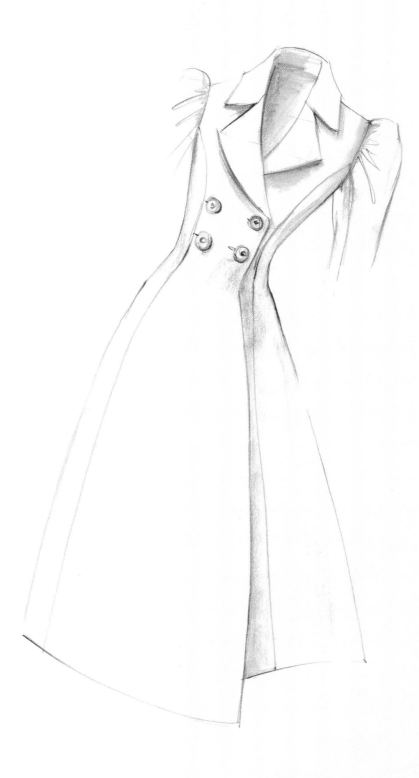

Left, trench coat with epaulettes and large buttoned patch pockets. Use ample shading to show that the details are sitting out from the main body of the garment. Right, double-breasted princess coat. With all coats and jackets, make sure the lapels and collars are equidistant to the center-front line. Buttons sit on the center-front line or, as in the case of the princess coat on the right, which is double-breasted, are equidistant from it.

tailored coat

Wool plaid coat with fur collar and fur trim at cuffs and sleeves. The plaid pattern is first planned out by defining the major horizontal and vertical stripes and then inserting the details with lines and narrower bands. The fur is drawn mainly with the sid e of the pencil to show the softness of the folds. Note the individual fibers of the fur outlined at the silhouette of the collar and cuffs.

tailored coat

Fur coat. Note the size of the individual pelts used in drawing fur coats: in this coat they are smaller (probably a mink). They are drawn with the side of the pencil to indicate the softness of the fur. The belt is tied into a knot, slimmer than the rest of the belt, and then flares out into triangles on either side.

active sportswear

Active sportswear has become an increasingly important clothing category, worn both when practicing the sport it is designed for and also as casualwear. It used to be the case that clothing for professional athletes differed from that designed for amateurs: for performance garments function had often to be favored over design. Nowadays, though, new fabrics and materials have allowed function and design to come together and the exact garments worn by professionals can be sported by all: the stylish jacket or t-shirt worn on casual occasions will often embody professional standard performance characteristics of insulation, breathability, moisture-wicking, support and protection, while at the same time being comfortable-to-wear and often ultra lightweight.

Active sportswear clothing is, for sports not requiring protective padding, usually designed to fit close to the body, with a bias towards making the body appear sleek and athletic, especially for those who miss the occasional workout.

1. Active sportswear is drawn with many seams. Seams are introduced to create stronger areas where the fabric is subject to repeated stress and also to get thick fabric (fabric for active sportswear is often thick—e.g. denim, leather, corduroy) to lie flat. Seams are often indicated by showing top-stitching. More padding is employed and layering is used to keep the body warm when the body begins to cool down. Snaps, elastic and velcro are often used in addition to buttons and laces for ease of access.

2. Because the construction materials are often man-made, the silhouettes of active sportswear are usually clear and crisp. Draw them using a clean, clear, sharp line that bends around the body.

3. Use a young, active fashion pose that represents a typical movement in the sport, or a relaxed, "off-court" pose. It is often helpful to include one of the main accessories of the sport—for example, a tennis raquet, skis or snowboard—in order to clearly identify the exact type of garments.

4. Accessories—gloves, hats, goggles and others— are commonly included as an important part of the outfit for function, protection and style. Accessories can be witty, functional or very sexy.

Top, skateboarding; bottom, roller-blading. When drawing active sportswear it is most effective to use a pose that expresses the movement of the sport, with lots of diagonals and foreshortened limbs in different planes. Including a piece of the equipment used in the sport as an accessory gives a clear indication of what the sport is that the clothes are designed for. Note that clothes for active sportswear have lots of seams.

active sportswear

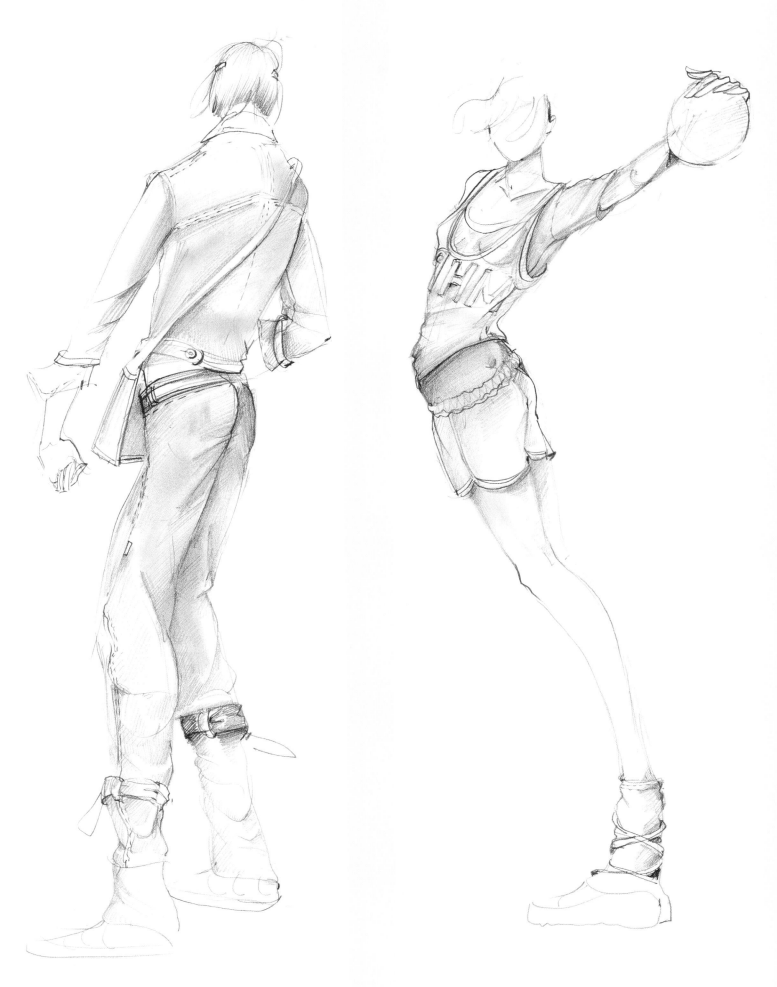

Poses for active sportswear should be youthful with lots of movement.

With swimwear it is important to make sure that the center-front line of the clothing matches up with the center-front of the figure: the position of the figure is clearly apparent and any mismatch will be clearly visible.

sleepwear/swimwear/ lingerie/exercises

SLEEPWEAR/ SWIMWEAR/LINGERIE
Garments in these categories are made in a variety of styles and fabrics but are mostly designed to fit close to the figure. These types of garments are usually small, and often designed purposely to reveal the figure, so it is important that the figure is drawn well and shaded correctly so its dimensionality can be clearly seen and the garment fully understood. Care should be taken also to draw the fabric so it can be immediately recognized—whether it is silk, cotton, lace or another. Poses should be youthful, fun and sassy.

EXERCISES
1. (Active sportswear). Copy ten figures engaged in three different active sports from the sports section of a newspaper or a sports magazine.
2. Draw clothes for a sport that requires minimum protection (e.g tennis) and one that requires maximum protection (e.g.skateboarding).
3. (Sleep/swimwear). Choose two sets of sleepwear, two swimsuits and two sets of lingerie from magazines. Copy, drawing in the croquis on each.

Drawing lingerie requires a very light touch—most of the fabrics used are gossamer light and many are transparent. Poses should be fresh, perky and sexy.

sleepwear/swimwear/
lingerie

When drawing swimwear it is important to ensure that garments line up with the bodies underneath—that the center-fronts of both are closely matched up. The garments fit very close to the body so their lines must closely follow the body's curves. Note also that hats, whatever they are worn with, as seen here, sit firmly on the head, coming down to just above eye level, and also follow the curve of the head.

necklines and collars

NECKLINES AND COLLARS

Necklines and collars are common to a range of garments—dresses, blouses, shirts, tops, jackets, robes, capes and coats. They have been left to the end of this chapter because, although not always the largest part of a garment, they are almost always prominent and are often tricky to draw, sitting as they do in close relation to the head and neck and often seen in three-quarter and other angled views.

The area around the neck of a garment can be finished either by attaching a collar—a separate detail with varying degrees of construction and complexity—or finishing off the garment into a simpler opening for the neck, often combined with the garment's principal closure at the front or the back, and referred to simply as its NECKLINE. Necklines are finished using facing, topstitching or a variety of types of binding that follow the edge of the neck of the garment itself.

Necklines are symmetrical (with the exception, of course, of the small proportion of necklines that have asymmetrical construction) and encircle the neck. Necklines vary in shape and extension and can be placed at varying distances below—or above—the base of the neck, both at the front and the back of the garment, so they can, at the extremes, either be close to the neck or fall over the shoulders and drop down almost to the bust-line in front, and to the waist or below behind.

When drawing necklines—in all views—they must be carefully aligned with the center-front of the body, as they are conspicuous, and the garment is symmetrical about this point. To make sure the alignment and curvature of the neckline around the body is correct the base of the neck should be lightly sketched in as an ellipse and the center-front line marked in. It is difficult accurately to draw the neckline curving around the body with a single line gesture—foreshortening and the exact curvature of the line can be tricky— so draw it in two halves, starting at the back, curving over the shoulder and ending at the center-front line, then repeating on the other side. Unless it happens to be one that falls at the back, a neckline will most commonly appear higher at the back of the neck than

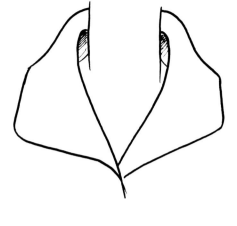

Collars are usually symmetrical and encircle the neck.

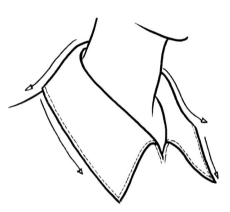

Rolled collars extend from the neckline up the back of the neck and then "roll" over; the line of the roll being higher at the back than the sides and front.

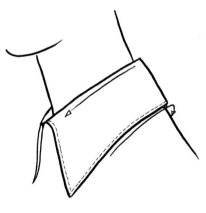

Side view of rolled collar. The silhouette of the collar slopes down from the back of the neck to the front.

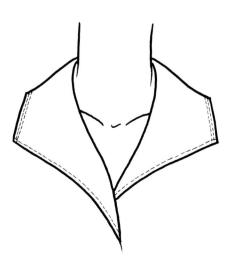

Collars are made in all shapes and sizes. Make sure the points of the collar—where it turns back towards the center-front—line up.

necklines and collars/exercise

the front. Nuance the line, making it thicker as it curves over the shoulder to indicate shadow and the three-dimensional shape of the body; otherwise keep the line smooth and steady.

COLLARS are important, prominent style features of garments—clear indicators of the quality of the workmanship—so must be drawn accurately to convey their intended effect. Collars frame the neck and vary in type according to their shape and where they sit in relation to the edge of the neck of the garment and the neck itself.

There are four basic types of collars: FLAT, ROLLED, STANDING and DRAPED. FLAT COLLARS lie flat on the neck of the garment, so there is practically no difference between the shape of the collar and that of the garment at the neck.
ROLLED COLLARS are tailored collars—molded to extend up the neckline and then rolling over onto the neck of the garment. The shape is achieved by attaching the upper collar to an under collar, sometimes with interfacing inserted between the two. The under collar and interfacing (if the collar is well constructed) do not show, nor do any seams at the finished edges. Rolled collars where the collar and lapels are cut as one piece are known as SHAWL COLLARS. Shawl collars are commonly found on robes and wraps, held together with a belt or sash instead of buttons or other closures.

The line of the high point of the collar, as it circles around the neck, is called the ROLL LINE, or ROLL. The roll line rises at the back of the collar as it extends further up the back of the neck. When drawing rolled collars the roll must be even and smooth as it extends around the neck. STANDING COLLARS are of many different types, constructed to stand straight up from the neck like a band around the neck; if the fabric turns down it does so almost without roll. Men's tailored shirts usually have standing collars. DRAPED COLLARS—cowls are examples— are made with excess fabric, usually cut on the bias so it falls folds as it falls away from the neckline, either in front or behind.

EXERCISE
Draw a blouse with six different collars.

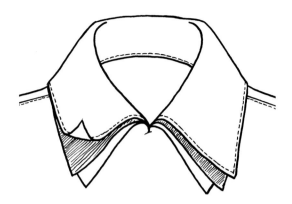

Tailored rolled collars are made with an upper collar and lower collar and often a layer of inter-lining between. When drawn, only the upper collar is seen.

The *roll line* is the "ridge" of the collar as it circles the neck. It is higher at the back.

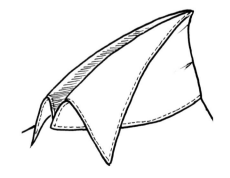

Roll collars stand up at the back of the neck. This collar has been constructed with a high stand.

necklines and collars

Different collars and necklines
See Chapter Five: Encyclopedia of
Details for a large variety of different
collars and neckline treatments.

Color adds a new dimension of information to a fashion drawing. To be able to draw well in color, though, it is best first to master how to use line and shading in black and white so that the silhouette, drape and fit ,and details of a garment can be presented in a clear, accurate and attractive way.

chapter three:
accessories

drawing accessories/
hats

Accessories are items of fashion worn or
carried in addition to the primary articles
of clothing. They include such items as
hats, gloves, jewelry, bags, umbrellas,
shoes, scarves and bows, belts,
watches, socks, nylons, eyeglasses.
Today the range of accessories is wider
than ever because of the numerous gad-
gets of the modern age—cell phones,
pagers, sophisticated watches, laptop
computers, hand-held electronic
devices, cameras, binoculars, video-
cams, tape recorders, roller skates,
skateboards. Accessories used to be
made from a limited choice of materials.
Today they are made from a far greater
range, both naturally occurring and man-
made, including plastics, nylon, rubber,
metals, papers, leathers and animal
skins.

When drawing accessories first pay
attention to the material they are made
from. If the accessory is made from a
solid material, e.g. metal, plastic, glass,
wood or gemstone, it should be drawn
with a crisp, clean outline. Use a very
sharp pencil point or thin ink line.
When drawing cut gems (diamonds,
sapphires, rubies, emeralds) be sure to
leave a tiny separation at the corners
where the different facets meet. This
gives the illusion of reflection and shine.
Draw pearls with a tiny highlight and a
dark area where each individual pearl is
connected to its neighbor. Be sure that
all jewelry appears to go around the
body.

HATS
Hats come in many shapes and forms
and have many different functions; they
can be decorative, protective or part of a
uniform. Hats are also made from a large
variety of materials. The hat must fit
around the head, with the rim usually
extending down the forehead, often as
far as the eyebrows. Since hats actually
change the scale of our heads, they are a
significant and important accessory.
Don't let hats levitate, they cannot float
in space.

Hat with veil

Jockey/horseriding

Feather

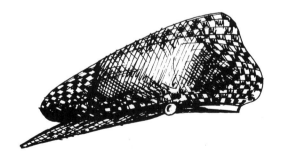

Newsboy/casquette

Cloche

hats

Crochet/knit hat

Beret

Fedora

Cossack

"Garbo" hat/ capeline

Tam-O´-Shanter

Hunting cap

Motorcycle helmet

Turban

Straw hat

watches/gloves bows and shawls

GLOVES

Gloves are often made of plastic, fur, fabric, leather or are knitted. They add volume to the hand so must be drawn with care and an elegant line to avoid a bulky sausage-like shape. You can taper the fingers and wrist to enhance the beauty of the drawing. Remember to add stitching, especially round the thumb.

BOWS AND SHAWLS

Begin with a simple butterfly shape consisting of two triangles touching in the center (refer to Encyclopedia of Details). Add the knot , which bends around the center of the two triangles and often has a little fold. Bring the ties or streamers out of the sides of the knot. Remember the streamers cannot come out of the center of the knot. This is a do-not do! Shade with a soft pencil or ink wash. Drawing the streamers in a soft scarf or bow requires more curves and fluid lines as if the wind has softly whisked the scarf into the air.

Shawls require a large amount of fabric and are often drawn framing the head and shoulders. To show the luxury and fullness of the drape, use sweeping, voluminous lines. Shade with wide, soft tones. Add fringe and pattern as desired.

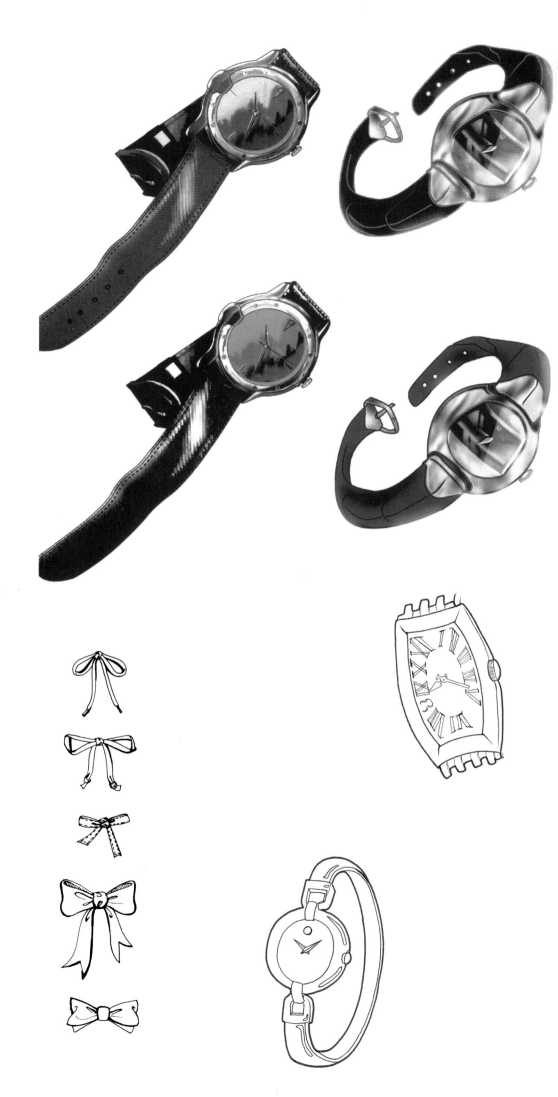

bags and jewelry/ exercise

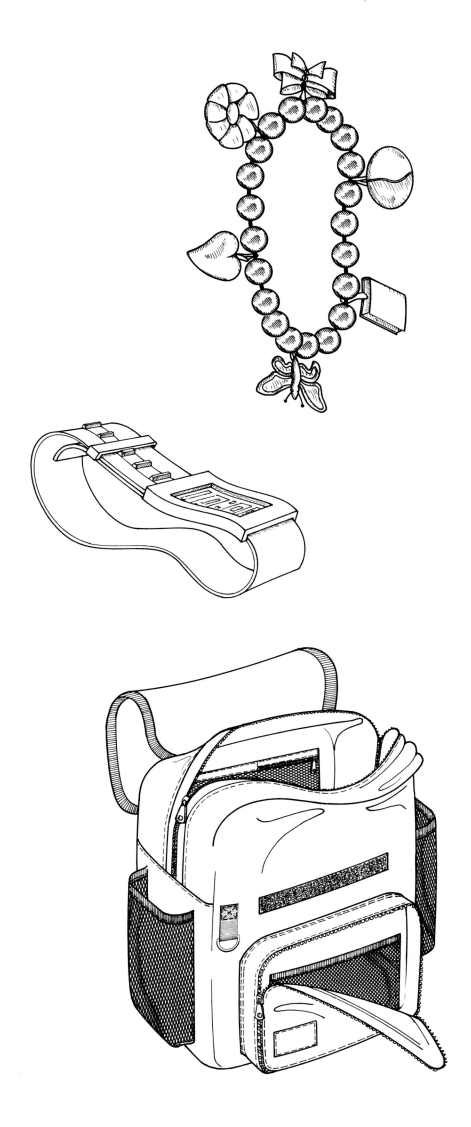

BAGS
The best angle from which to draw a bag to show its design details to the best effect is the three-quarter view. Start with a cube or cylinder, whichever is closest in shape (refer to Chapter One for how to draw these three-dimensionally); add shading and design details.

JEWELRY, BRACELETS AND WATCHES
When drawing these items, think about simple ovals. A bracelet may be drawn using two parallel ovals, connected at the ends. Shading is darker in the interior of the bracelet. Add additional elements such as beads or indentations using a dark tone. Watches must be drawn with care so that the face and the frame of the watch remain distinct. Surface reflections may be drawn by adding an even tone of pencil. To add the appearance of a reflection on the face of a watch, use a sharp eraser, such as a pink pearl, quickly make a streak across the drawing. This gives the illusion of reflected light.

A variety of drawing techniques are used in this section of the book: pencil, pen and ink and computer-generated drawings. This is to show how ideas about accessories can be expressed in a number of different ways and that some accessories are best drawn with a particular technique: Accessories made out of plastic or man-made materials with hard edges can often be best expressed using a computer-generated drawing; fine, hand-made accessories, like Hermes bags or Tiffany jewelry are usually best drawn by hand.

EXERCISE
Begin by drawing twenty ovals. Divide a piece of paper into four sections. Choose four favorite accessories from your wardrobe. Draw each of these accessories carefully, paying attention to the materials they are constructed from and how shadows form on them and light is reflected. Work slowly and with great precision so you will have a piece good enough for your portfolio.

bag and necklace

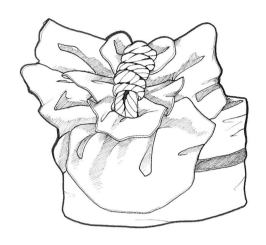

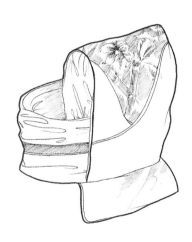

bags/belt/hairclip/gloves

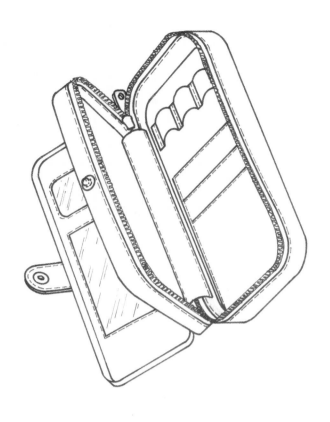

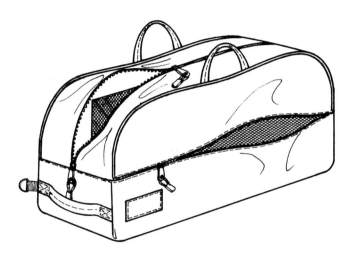

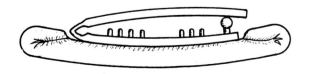

gloves

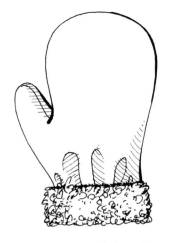

Mitten with fur cuff

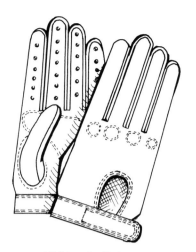

Walking /golf glove

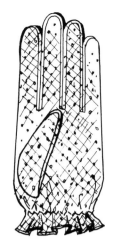

Lace glove with elastic wrist

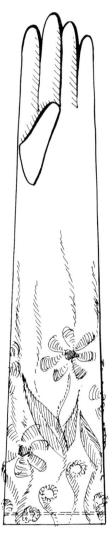

Arm length with embroidery

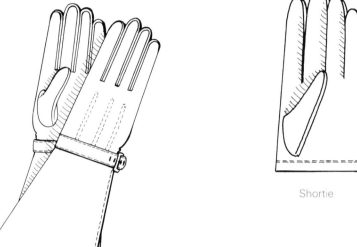

Gauntlet

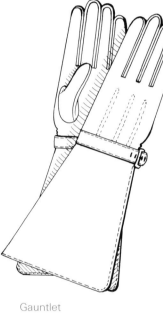

Shortie

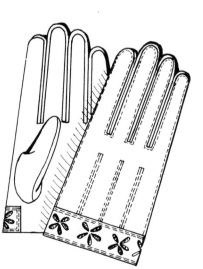

Slip-on with burn out flower design

Knit glove with rib cuff and jacquard inset

Opera glove with trim

Fingerless sports/workout glove

Oxfords

Work boots

Backless/slip-on pump

Ankle strap/ D'Orsay

1950s Roland Jourdan
pump (elongated toe)

Spectator pump

Delicate pump

Jester

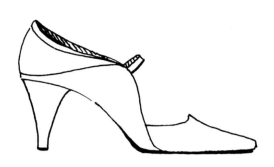

Mary Jane pump

Golf shoe

Saddle shoe

Birkenstock sandals

Chopines (17th c.
Venetian lady's shoe)

Ballet shoe

Clog

Sports shoe

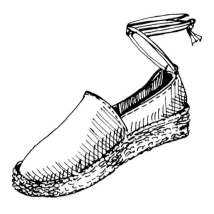

Espadrille with ankle tie

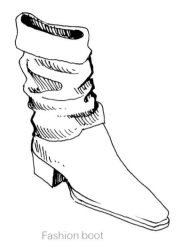

Fashion boot

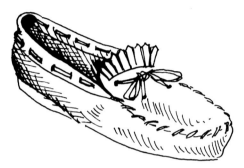

Moccasin

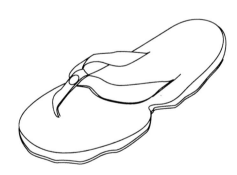

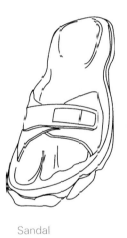

Sandal

Flip-flop sandal

Ski boots

shoes/high heels/sneakers/
cowboy boots

High heels

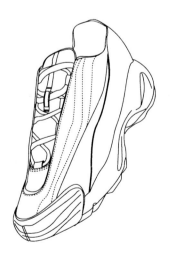

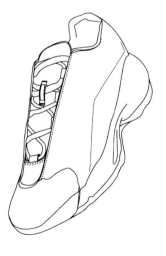

Sneakers

Cowboy boots

Sneakers

Ski boots

Flip-flops

Sandals

chapter four:
flats

flats

FLATS

Flats are two-dimensional drawings of garments with all proportions and measurements made exactly to scale, like architectural blueprint drawings. In flats the garments are drawn alone, without the figure. When accompanied by the vital measurements and details of a garment flats are known as "specs" (short for specifications) and provide a definition exact enough to allow a garment to be constructed. These flats are known as "production flats".

Flats are usually complements, rather than substitutes, for concept drawings of garments: For a completely new design for a garment it is important to know the intended mood, fit and drape of a garment, and these aspects are best shown in a concept drawing. Where new designs are evolutions of, or are closely related to existing garments, however, and the look and feel of the garment are well known, flats alone often can communicate all the information required. This is especially so for active sportswear garments, where silhouettes, fit and drape are usually familiar, and new designs are often simply changes of superficial detailing.

Because flats are scale drawings used directly in the construction of garments they must reflect actual body proportions—a length equivalent to eight heads— rather than the idealized proportions of the nine-head fashion croquis. The croquis template used for flats is also fuller-figured than the slim nine-heads croquis.

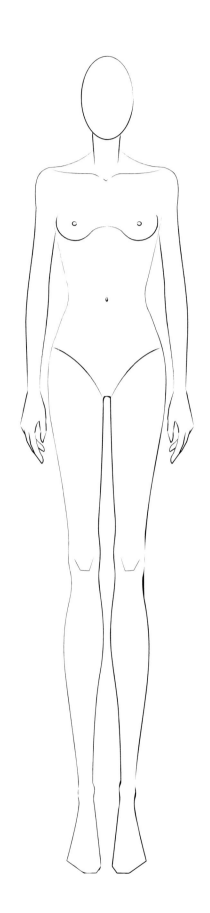

The original nine heads croquis used in concept drawings.

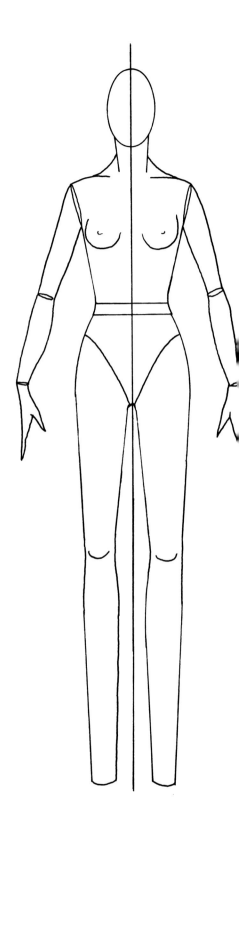

The template for flats based on the eight heads figure. Besides being shorter it is fuller than the nine heads figure.

precision of line/ materials for drawing flats

PRECISION OF LINE

In concept drawings lines can be free and expressive, and artistic license can frequently be taken: although proportions and details must be accurate, conveying exact quantitative information is often not as important as conveying mood and overall appearance. In concept drawing lines are also frequently nuanced—their thickness and weight varied— to indicate shading and fabric type. This is not the case with flats: lines used in flats have to be precise, smooth and with no jagged edges or wobbles so that the exact shape of the garment is made crystal clear. Flats, particularly when learning to draw them, are first drawn in pencil, but the final presentation is made using a fine point ink pen that produces a smooth, even line.

When drawing flats, any tool or device that helps produce better drawings can and should be used: rulers help in drawing straight lines and French curves help in drawing smooth curves. While making full use of these tools, it is also useful to develop the ability to draw lines freehand from an early stage; this will make the process of drawing flats quicker and easier. A good exercise to develop this skill is to fill a page with dots and practice joining them with as straight a line as possible using a single fluid movement of the wrist without pausing partway. Practice drawing curves freehand by copying curves produced with a French curve and tracing over garment outlines.

In concept drawing lines can be free and expressive and are frequently nuanced. Garments are often shaded using dense flat applications of pencil. These techniques contrast strongly with the precise use of line required when drawing flats.

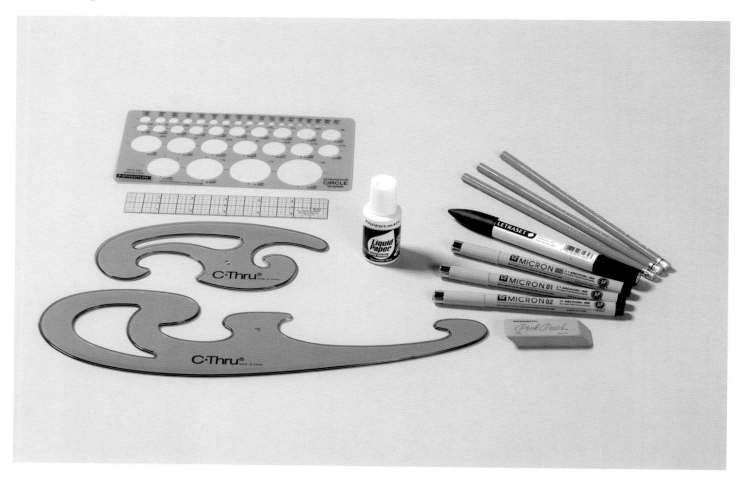

Materials for drawing flats.

PENS: .005 for silhouettes
          .003 for detailing
          .05   for shadow on buttons,
          pockets, collars etc.
PENCIL : 2H lead pencil
PAPER :   Layout or copy paper
          Tracing Paper
MARKER   (for shading)–10% Cool grey
RULER: 6" Transparent plastic
FRENCH CURVE
ERASER
WHITE-OUT CORRECTING FLUID
PENCIL SHARPENER (Electric sharpeners are best)

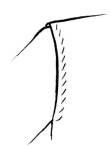

Marks used on knitted garm-
nets to show where parts of
the garment are sewn to the
main body.

Usual lineweight for drawing
flats, made with a .005 pen.

Saddle stitching, made with a
.03 pen for the horizontal line
and .005 pen for the stitches.

Blind stitching, made with a
.005 pen.

Top stitching, made with a
.005 pen.

Usual lineweight for shading
flats, made with a .03 pen.

Double-needle top stitch,
made with a .005 pen.

Lineweight and use of line when drawing flats.

templates/knitwear/
bodysuit/general points

DRAWING FLATS: TEMPLATES

Flats are based on the actual proportions of the figure. The eight-head *croquis* that is the basis for flats can be used as a guide, placed directly underneath the flats being drawn, to ensure the proportions are correct. Rather than working with the croquis, though, it is more usual to work with *templates* based on the eight head figure and made for different garment types. In this chapter these templates are used as the starting points for the explanations of how to draw flats for a number of basic garments. The templates included here are examples of near-generic garments. In the garment industry, particularly for sportswear, templates are developed in-house, and new designs worked out quickly and easily using the templates derived from existing garments.

GENERAL POINTS TO KEEP IN MIND WHEN DRAWING FLATS

There are a number of characteristics common to all flats, as well as techniques and helpful tips that should be considered when beginning to learn to draw flats, and indeed kept in mind whenever drawing flats. These are:
1. Flats are symmetrical: the left and right sides match exactly, except in those cases where the garment contains an asymmetrical design element. One method to ensure symmetrical flats is to draw one side of the garment up to the center-front line, trace over that drawing, flip it over and trace again to give a mirror image for the other side (see "flipover flats below)
2. As mentioned, flats are eight heads, reflecting real proportions. All proportions are the same as the nine-head figure but the legs are shortened by one head. Flats appear slightly wider and larger than garments drawn on a nine-head figure.
3. Flats should be first drawn in pencil (always use a very sharp pencil) and then inked in when correct. French curves and rulers should always be used.

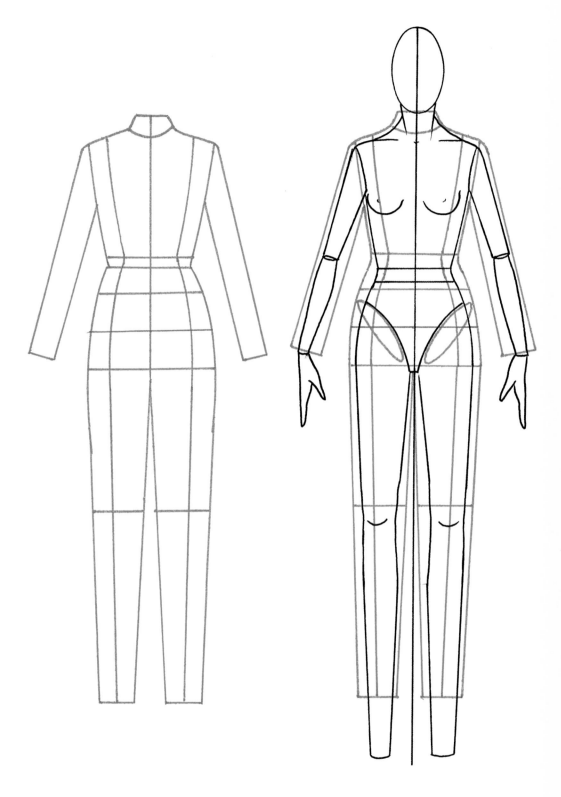

Bodysuit/knitwear template.

Bodysuit/knitwear template over 8 head croquis.

how to draw
skirt/pant flats

4. Especially when beginning to draw flats, sketch on top of the eight head croquis template or one of the basic garment templates included in this chapter. *Always* indicate the center-front line and make sure measurements are symmetrical on either side of that line.

5. All seams and other constructional details must be included in flats, drawn to the scale of the garment. For garments with sleeves, arms are shown away from the body so the silhouette of the sleeve can be clearly seen. If sleeves contain details on the underside, one or both arms can be shown bent at a 45° angle so the detail is revealed.

SPECS

Methods for measuring specifications for the garments described in this chapter is included in an appendix at the end of the book.

PANTS

Flats for pants should be drawn with the legs about shoulder-width apart so the silhouette of the legs can be clearly seen. The template shown in the illustration is taken from the full-body template for flats and is for relatively close-fitting pants but can be used to develop any number of variations. The fit in the waist and hip area is close, and fullness in the legs of the pants can be varied by changing the line of the outer edge below the lower hip line; the inseam remains near-vertical for all shapes of pants.

SKIRTS

The skirt silhouette is almost the same as that of pants with the obvious difference that skirts do not have legs. The flat is drawn by indicating the position of the hem and then finishing the silhouette by joining the hem to the pants template where the fullness starts, at the lower hip line, as with pants (unless the skirt is gathered at the waist, in which case the fullness starts at the waist). A breakdown for drawing skirt flats is shown at right.

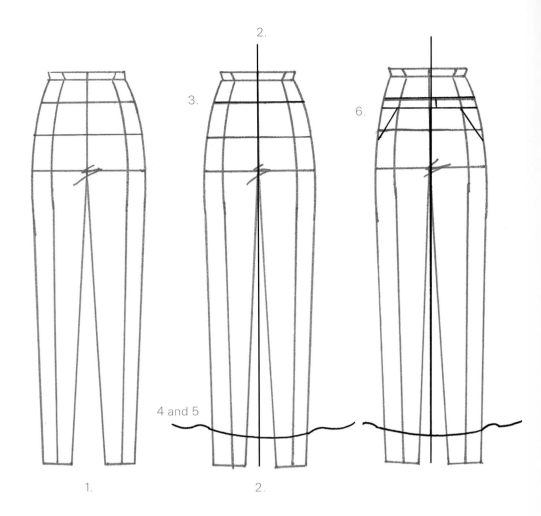

Drawing skirt and pant flats.
1. Start with the skirt/pant flat template.
2. Establish the axis/center-front line.
3. Determine position of waist (options :high waist/on waist/natural (just below)/high hip (hipsters)/low hip (low riders.)
4. Decide on the length of the garment.
5. Decide on the fullness of the garment. The fuller the skirt the more curves it will have at the hem. How far down does the fullness start?
6. Determine the width of the waistband and indicate the position of the pockets.

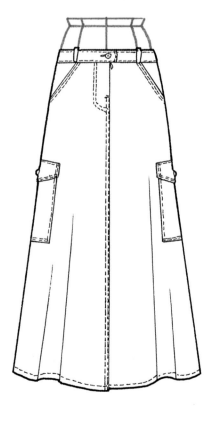

7. Flesh in waistband styling. Draw in pockets. Draw in the center seam and princess seams if necessary. Indicate the position of the zipper pull and the stitching of the zipper seam.

8. Add details (for example, double needle stitching; zippers; shading; hem treatments; belt loops, buttons/buttonholes).

pant and skirt lengths/
pant and skirt widths

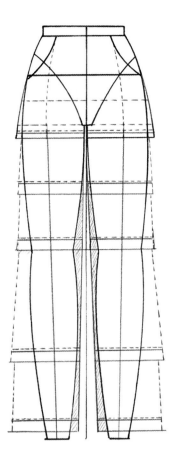

Pant lengths.

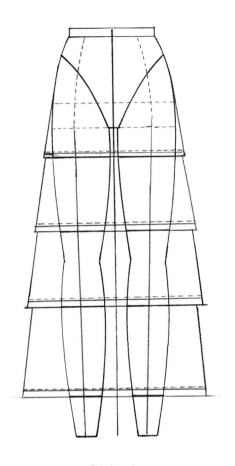

Skirt lengths.

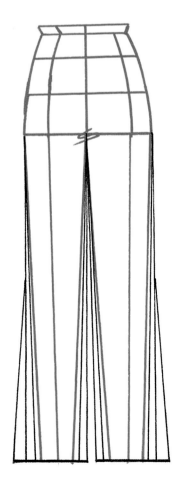

Pant widths.

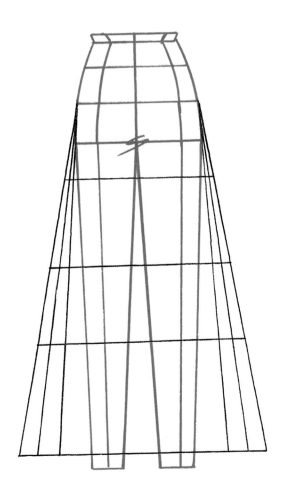

Skirt widths.

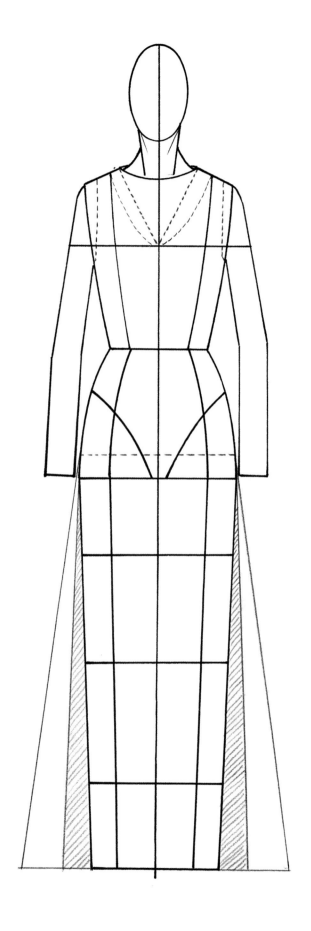
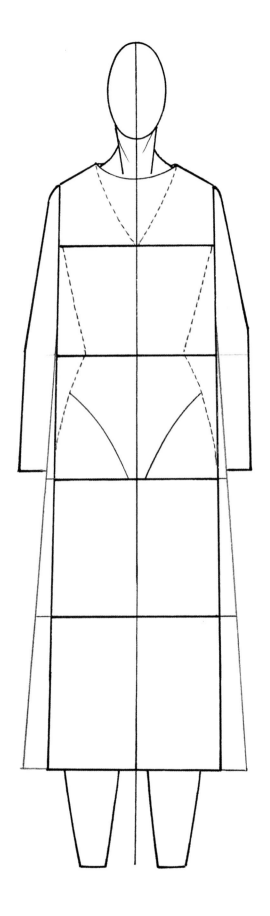

how to draw fitted garment flats

1. Draw in the center-front line. Draw in the collar opening to the wrap point Define the length and indicate the armhole/sleeve adjustment.

2. Flesh in the "shell" of body and the ties.

3. Add drape.

4. Add shading/ stitching details/ indicate construction at back of the neck.

how to draw tailored jacket flats

1— Establish center-front and position of buttons. If single breasted the buttons will be on the center-front line. Space evenly by marking the center of each button.

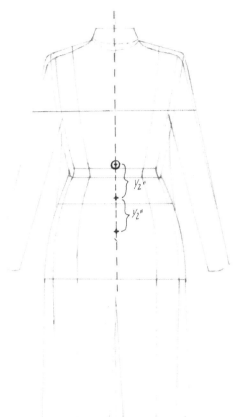

2— Draw in the opening of the jacket by extending lines from the center front to the break-points of the collar on each side.
— Add buttons
— Add the roll of the collar, hugging the neck, and drawing a slightly curved line from the neck to the break point.
— Repeat on the other side. Note: that this line will extend to the imaginary break point on the other side of the jacket. If this is done correctly the ends of the collar rolls will be at center front.
— Establish the finished length of the coat.
—Make allowance for the thickness of the shoulder pads (incorporate into the croquis)

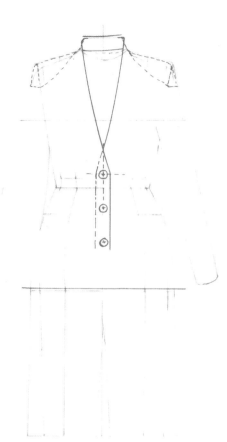

3— Establish the lapel—below the collar—first, then add the collar shape.

4— Pencil in the internal details of the jacket i.e., welts, princess seams etc.

5— Establish the hem line shape at front and pencil in. Again measure from center-front to check symmetry.

6— Add in the "shell" of the jacket.
— Ink in details & add buttonholes (usually keyhole on tailored jackets).
—Add top stitching (if any)
— Add lining details (if any)
— Add shading to give depth under the collar, lapel & back.

Note: Tailored jackets generally have two-piece sleeves. Do not forget to show the seams.

fitted dress/square jacket templates
positions for showing sleeves

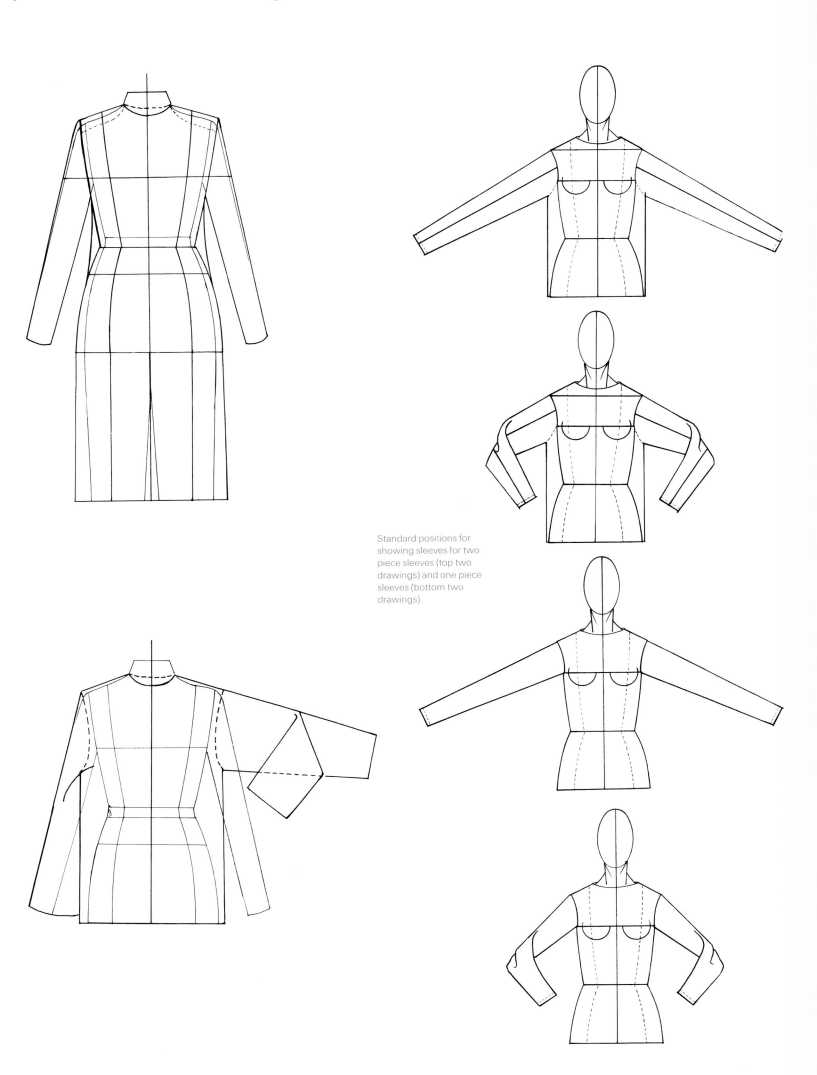

Standard positions for showing sleeves for two piece sleeves (top two drawings) and one piece sleeves (bottom two drawings).

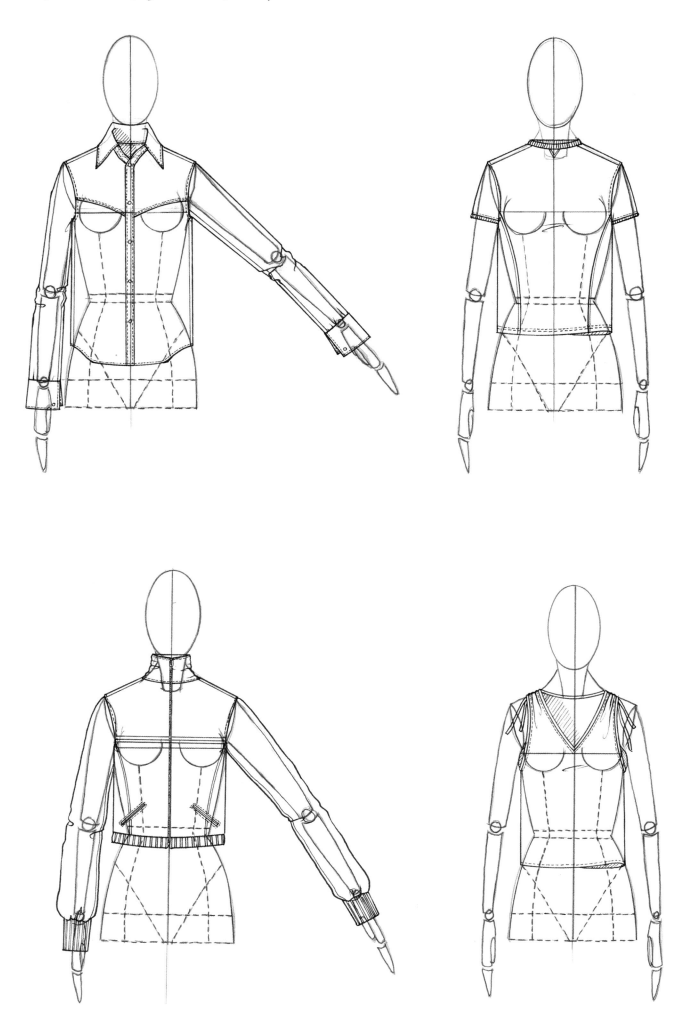

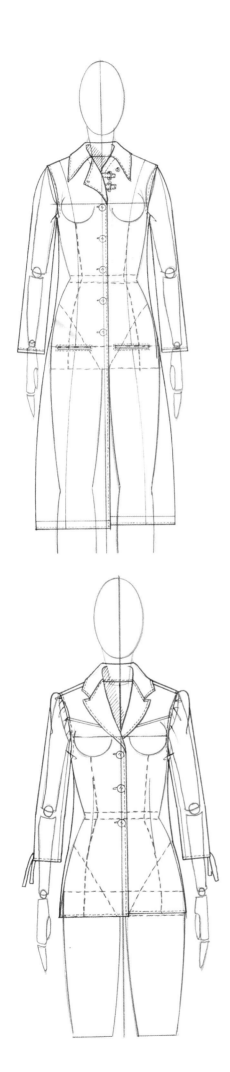

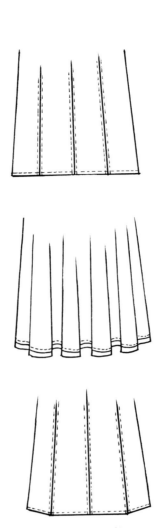

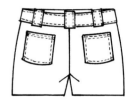

Skirt Do's and Do not Do's. The middle drawing is correct, the other two are incorrect. Where hems end in folds these should be drawn as cylinders: attempts at shorthand two-dimensional graphic representations will often be misinterpreted as seams.

Pant Do's and Do not Do's. Top two drawings are correct; bottom two are incorrect. The break in pants can be shown by a squiggle or horizontal line but not by "frown" or "smile" V-lines.

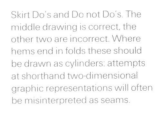

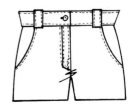

Do not Do. Waistbands must be drawn with square edges.

Pant waistlines. Top, correct; bottom ,Do not Do. Gathers at the waist must be drawn to show the fullness of the fabric or will be misinterpreted as flat bands.

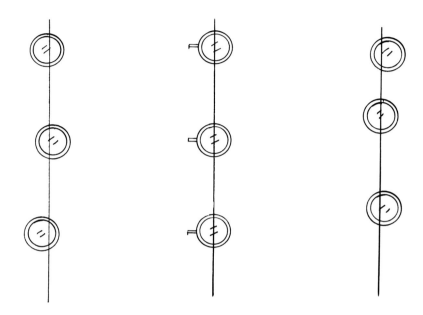

Button Do's and Do not Do's. Left and right are incorrect, center is correct.
Buttons must be drawn on the center-front line and equally spaced. When the
buttons have buttonholes the buttonholes should always be drawn. Buttons can
be an important fashion feature and the drawing should show their detailing.

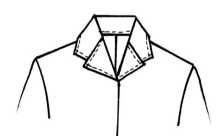

Collar Do's and Do not Do's. Left, correct; middle and right, incorrect. The
edge of the collar and roll line meet at the silhouette of the shoulder of the
garment (the drawings on the right suggest that angles have been introduced into the shape of the collar). The curve of the collar around the back
of the neck should be indicated and the top and bottom lines of the band
should be parallel.

flipover flaps

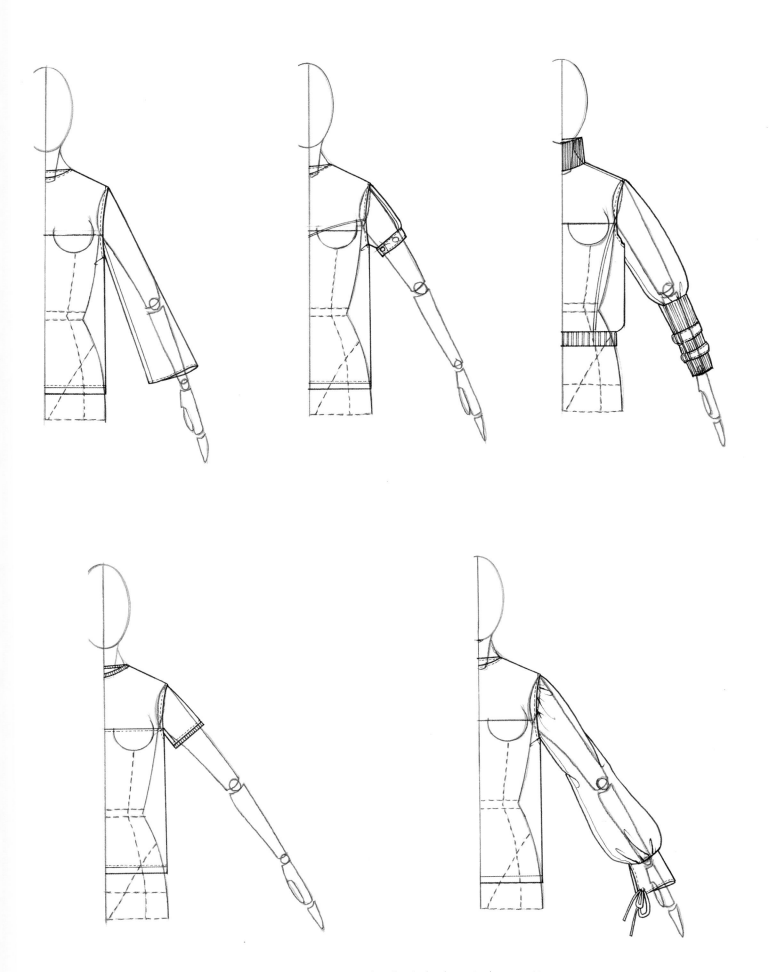

Flipover flats. A common way to draw flats is, drawing on tracing paper, to draw half the flat, fold the drawn half under the paper so it becomes its mirror image, trace over that onto the other half of the paper and open out the paper with the complete flat. This technique can save time and ensures the flat will be symmetrical about the center-front line.

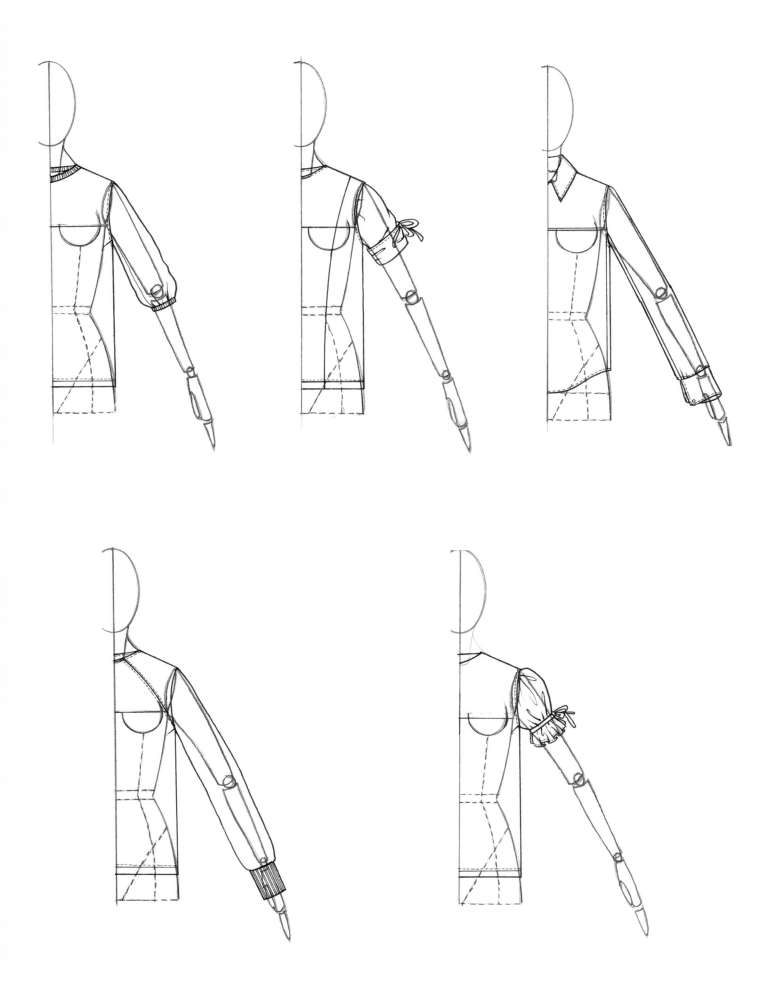

freehand flats

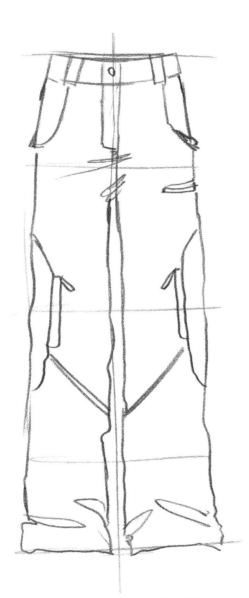
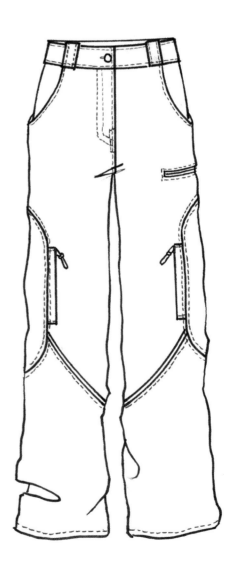

Freehand flats. With experience it is possible to sketch flats "freehand" with pencil without drawing in the template and with little use of rulers and curves. The sketches are then inked in and tightened up to produce the final flat, as shown in these illustrations.

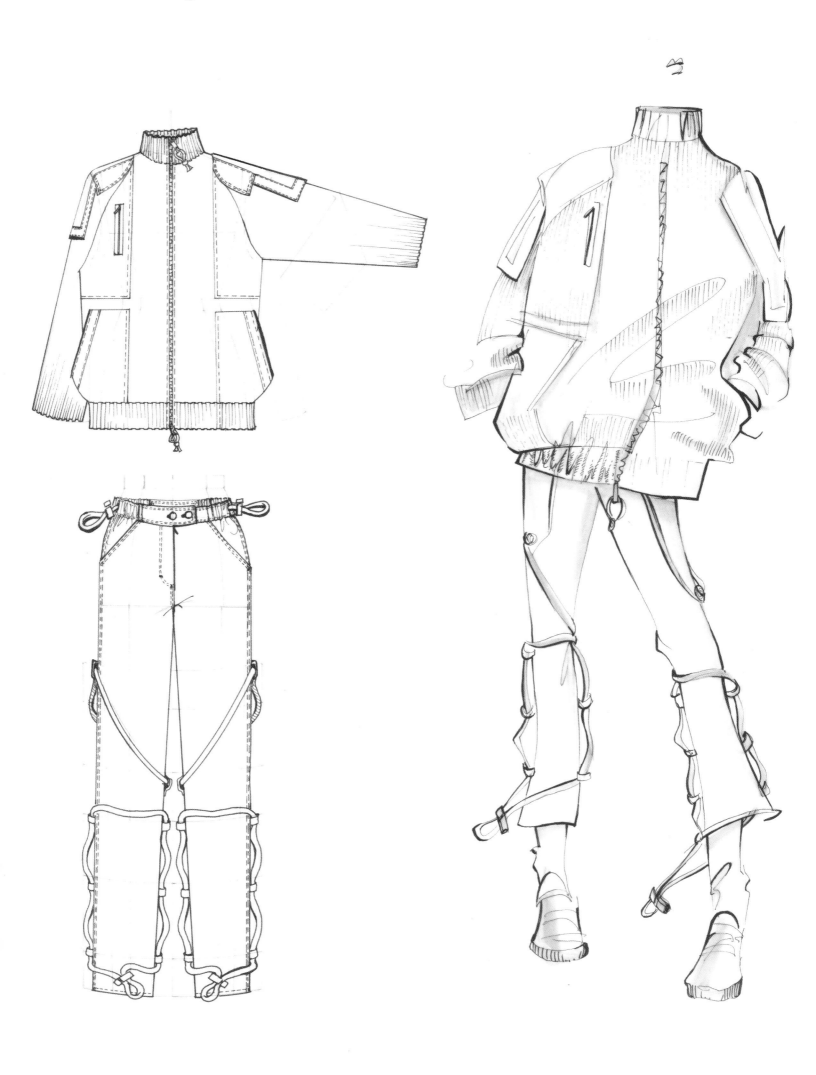

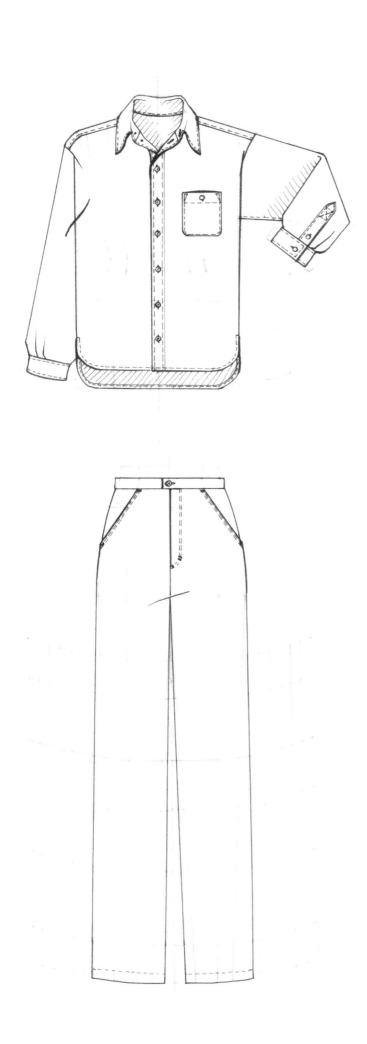

chapter five:
encyclopedia
of details

fashion details/ collars

A large part of the process of designing new fashion involves creating variations from garments that already exist. This is done by combining the different elements of fashion in new ways, using new fabrics and colors and altering shapes and proportions. In most cases all the individual details of a new fashion garment are familiar and instantly recognizable to the fashion expert but are now presented in a fresh and unique new design combination.

Fashion details—known also as construction details (though some details are purely decorative)—are the different ways that the different parts of fashion garments can be made. Together the body of details forms a visual vocabulary from which the designer can freely choose and combine into new designs, both in the process of drawing new designs and in the actual construction of the new garment. When learning to design fashion it is most important to become familiar with a wide range of fashion details, to root them deeply in the memory so they are instantly recognized and can immediately spring into the imagination when a new design is being conceived.

This chapter is a mini encyclopaedia of (mainly) modern fashion details (many of the details have in fact existed for several centuries or more, but are still in common use and are regarded as "classics"). It can be used as a reference guide (all the different details are listed in the main index) or as a source of inspiration when working on new designs. The details have been drawn as accurately as possible mostly in two-dimensional flat-style form, but they can be used as references to create accurate three-dimensional concept drawings also. Careful note should be made of the way that line weight is used in the drawings to convey information about different types of details and the different parts of those details. Line weight is used here to indicate a number of different variables, including fabric type, weight and thickness and garment construction.

Funnel

Square

Shirt—basic rolled collar

Round roll-back & buttoned

Cowl—stand style— high

Button-down collar

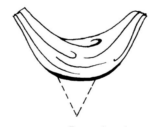

Draped neck

Stand-up/banded collar

Fichu-tie front

Turtleneck

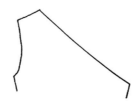

One shoulder

Mandarin

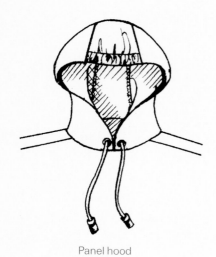

Panel hood

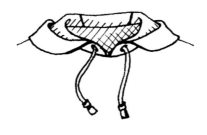

Hooded—drawstring

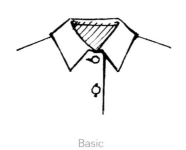

Basic

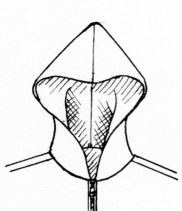

Panel hood/zipper

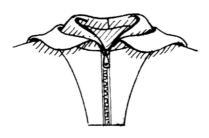

Hooded—zipper

Round zipper/bobber

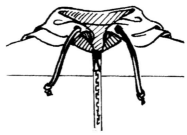

Hooded—drawstring & zipper

Peter Pan

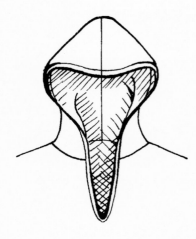

Panel hood/neck opening

Double-breasted notch

Polo

collars

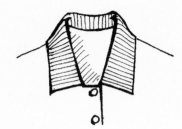

Ribbed

Sweetheart

Round—basic

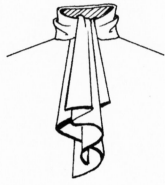

Stock tie

Round—jewel

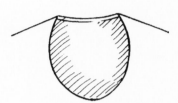

Scoop—basic

Wing—Chelsea

Round—bound/banded

V-neck

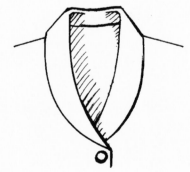

Shawl

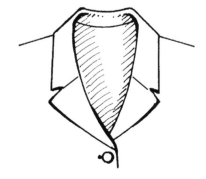

Notched

Boat/bateau

collars

High rib with
railroad stitch

Funnel with
invisible zip

Off neck

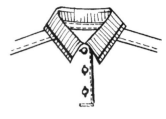

Polo with tipped collar
& back neck taping

Turtle with knit neck

Mock turtleneck with
railroad zip cover

French turtle—clean

Boat neck—faced

Peter Pan with
picot trim

Bertha with zip back

Pilgrim with button loop

Puritan with button loop

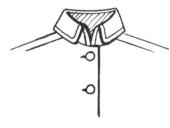

Convertible collar/high stand

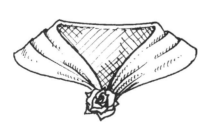

Fichu with rosette

Scarf/ascot

Stole collar

Notched Bertha

Buster Brown (Bertha)

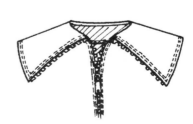

Zip-up Bertha

Bertha with knotted end

collars/openings

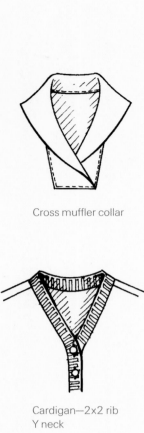

Cross muffler collar

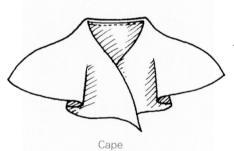

Cowl

bottle

Roll with cover stitch

Cardigan—2x2 rib
Y neck

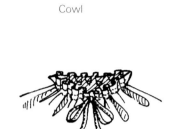

Drawstring

Convertible collar

Wing

Sailor

Mandarin with edge-
stitch

Cape

Chinese with frog

Bow

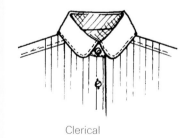

Clerical

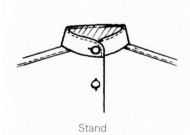

Stand

Tab

Cascade

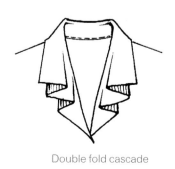

Double fold cascade

Tie front

Capelet—basic

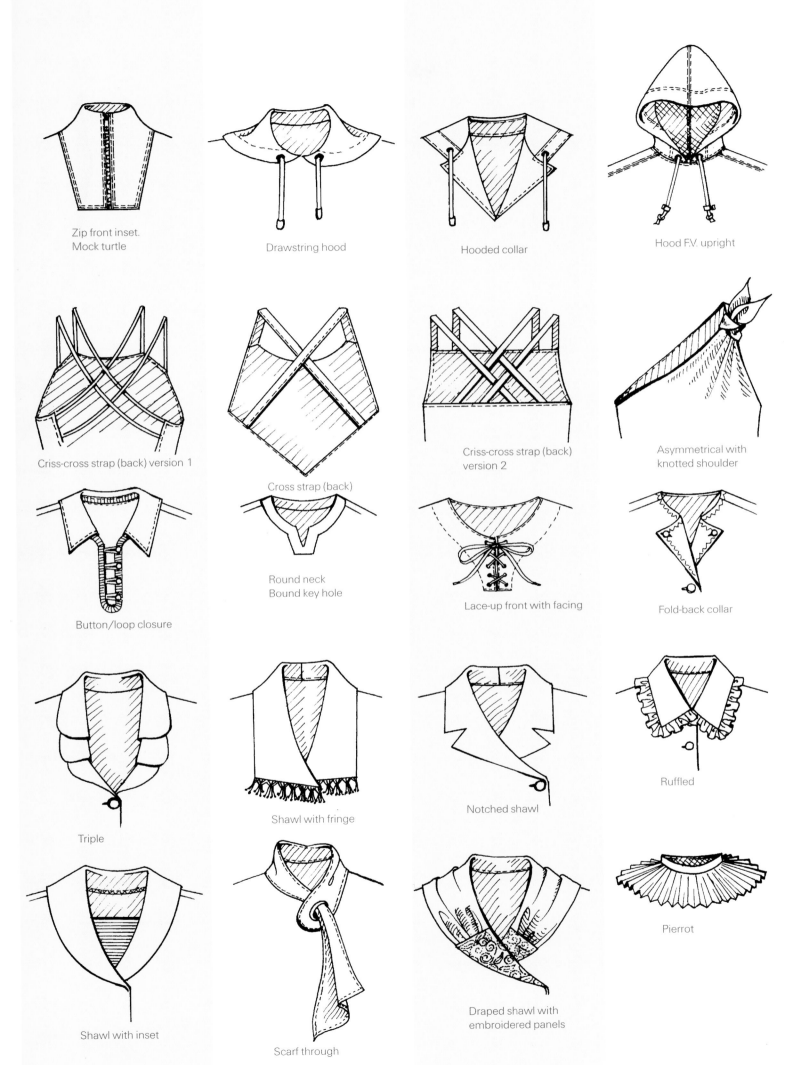

Zip front inset.
Mock turtle

Drawstring hood

Hooded collar

Hood F.V. upright

Criss-cross strap (back) version 1

Cross strap (back)

Criss-cross strap (back) version 2

Asymmetrical with knotted shoulder

Button/loop closure

Round neck
Bound key hole

Lace-up front with facing

Fold-back collar

Triple

Shawl with fringe

Notched shawl

Ruffled

Shawl with inset

Scarf through

Draped shawl with embroidered panels

Pierrot

Wide hood with
blanket stitch (front)

Wide hood with blanket
stitch (back)

Alternate back view—
hood

Roll back shawl collar

Bound armholes
with embroidery

Spaghetti straps with
beading

Knotted shoulders

Center front ring

Snap front with twill tape
& back neck

Chanel-style round neck

Button over collar

Zip front stand collar

Wing—Chelsea

Round with shell stitch

Square sailor with braid

Shawl sailor with braid

Flounce V-neck

Off-the-shoulder double
flounce

Cowl stand/turtle

Rounded Chelsea

collars

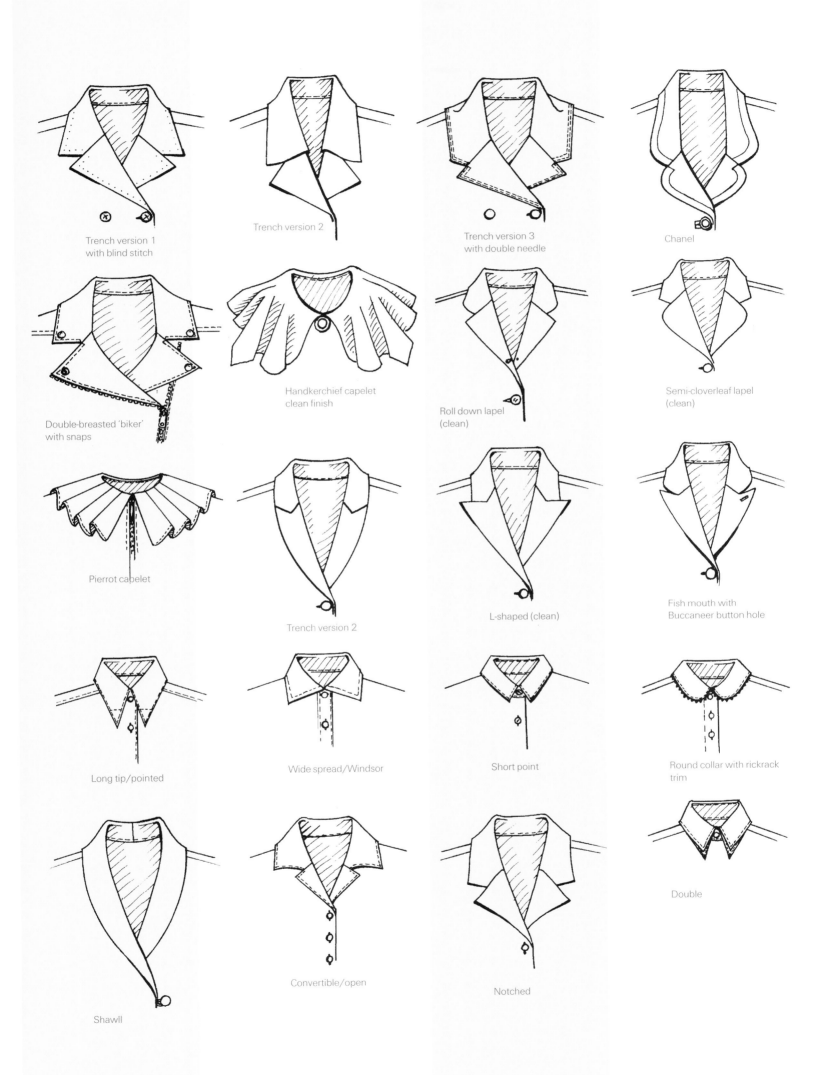

Trench version 1
with blind stitch

Trench version 2

Trench version 3
with double needle

Chanel

Double-breasted 'biker'
with snaps

Handkerchief capelet
clean finish

Roll down lapel
(clean)

Semi-cloverleaf lapel
(clean)

Pierrot capelet

Trench version 2

L-shaped (clean)

Fish mouth with
Buccaneer button hole

Long tip/pointed

Wide spread/Windsor

Short point

Round collar with rickrack
trim

Shawll

Convertible/open

Notched

Double

collars

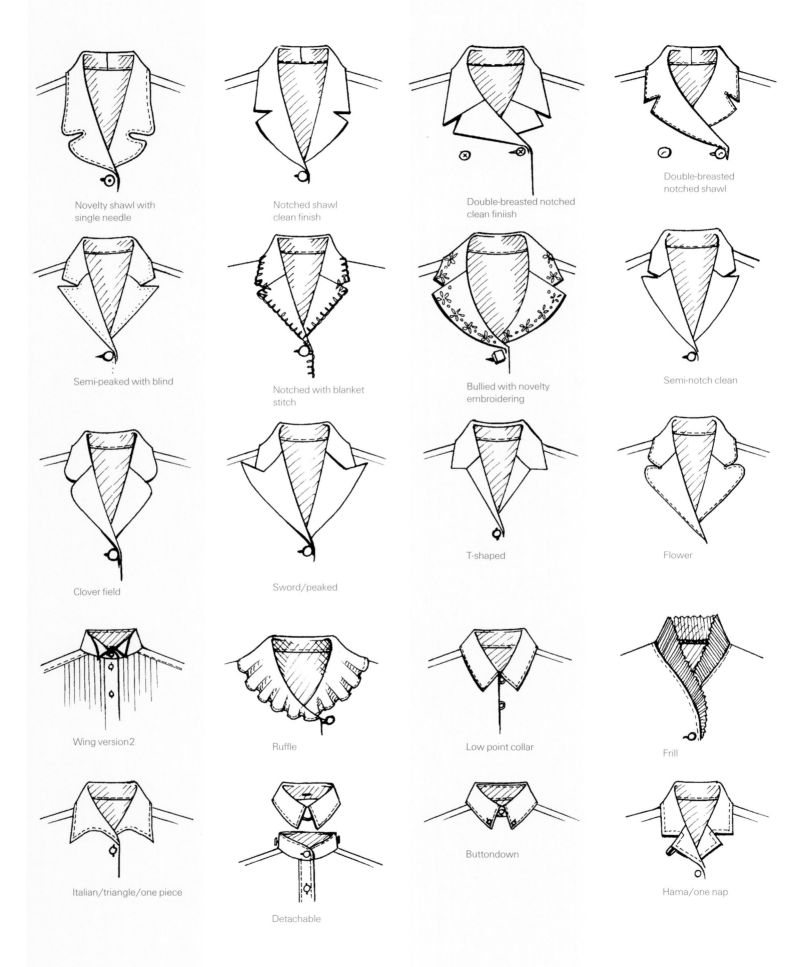

Novelty shawl with single needle

Notched shawl clean finish

Double-breasted notched clean finiish

Double-breasted notched shawl

Semi-peaked with blind

Notched with blanket stitch

Bullied with novelty embroidering

Semi-notch clean

Clover field

Sword/peaked

T-shaped

Flower

Wing version2

Ruffle

Low point collar

Frill

Italian/triangle/one piece

Detachable

Buttondown

Hama/one nap

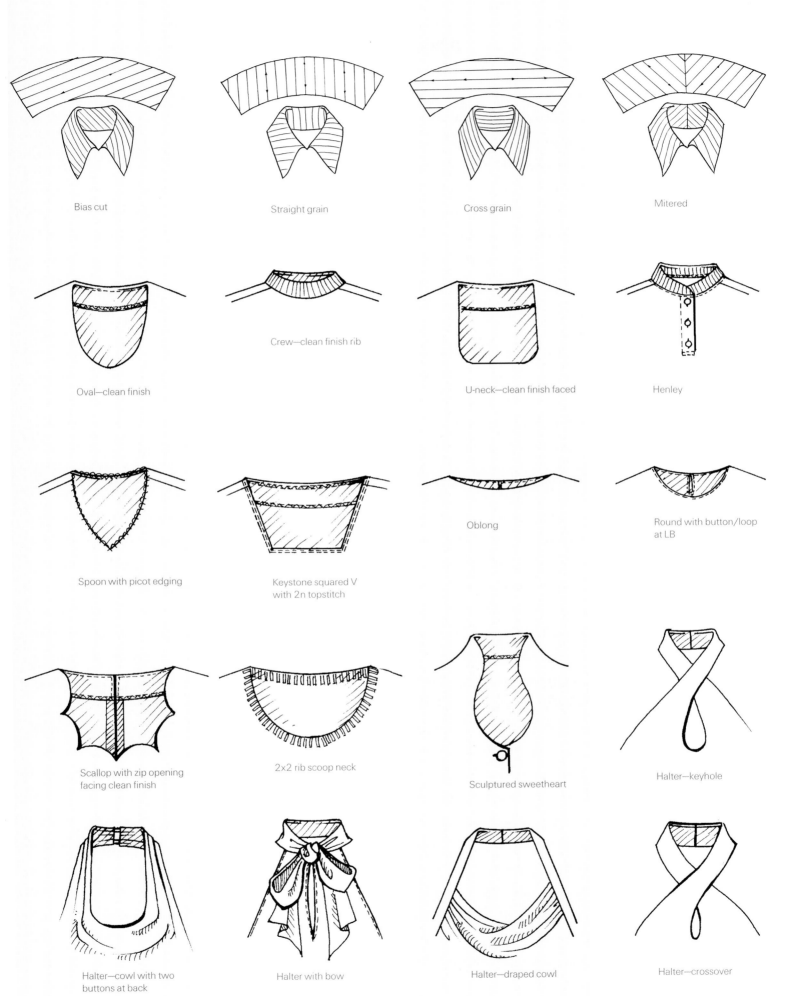

Bias cut

Straight grain

Cross grain

Mitered

Oval—clean finish

Crew—clean finish rib

U-neck—clean finish faced

Henley

Spoon with picot edging

Keystone squared V
with 2n topstitch

Oblong

Round with button/loop
at LB

Scallop with zip opening
facing clean finish

2x2 rib scoop neck

Sculptured sweetheart

Halter—keyhole

Halter—cowl with two
buttons at back

Halter with bow

Halter—draped cowl

Halter—crossover

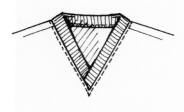

Cross over V

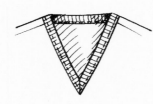

Deep V

Regular V

V-shaped crew

Keyhole version 1

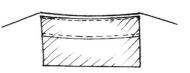

Square with facing
clean finish

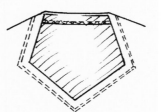

Diamond with 2n topstitch

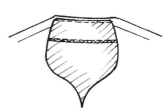

Heart with facing
clean finish

Keyhole version 2
with novelty stitch

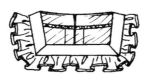

Square with flounced
Merrow edge

Halter-cut out shoulder

Sweetheart

Halter with tie at back

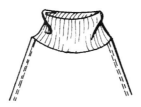

Halter-rib turtleneck

Halter—twisted

Halter—piped square front

skirts

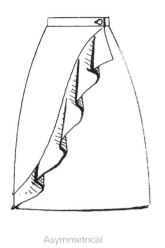

Asymmetrical

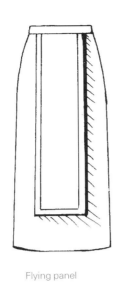

Flying panel

Granny

Culottes

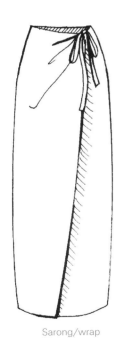

Sarong/wrap

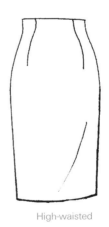

Yoke skirt

High-waisted

Handkerchief hem

lingerie

Half underwire bra

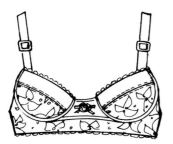

Full underwire bra

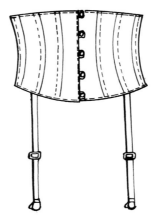

French cinch guepiere

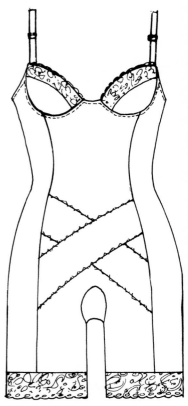

Full body summer

Panty girdle

High cut control brief

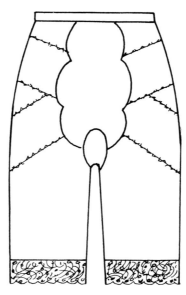

Knee length panty girdle

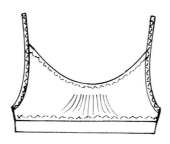

'Seamless' bra

High cut brief

Sports bra with racer back

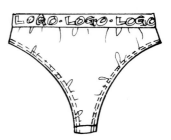

Sport thong front view

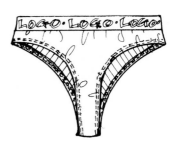

Sport thong back view

Standard 4 dart

French dart

Armseye darts

Center front seam parts

H dart princess

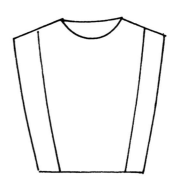

Princess seams

Armseye princess seams

Princess seams

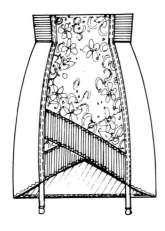

Panty girdle

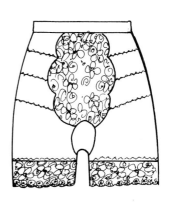

Flaired

Mini with side slit

Full flaired

Fitted at waist

Invested pleat

Full flaired mini

A-line

Knife pleat

Belted

skirts

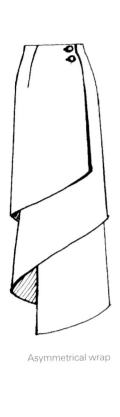

A line

Dirndl

Draped

Asymmetrical wrap

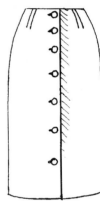

Button front

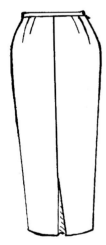

Miniskirt

Fly front micro mini

Peg top skirt

Prairie

Slit skirt

pants

Culottes

Gaucho pants

Jodhpurs

Knickers

Boxer shorts

Pajama/lounge

5 pocket jeans

Hip huggers

Sabrina/Capri

Tuxedo pants

Cargo pants

Daisy Dukes/cut-offs

Hotpants

Board shorts

Bike pants

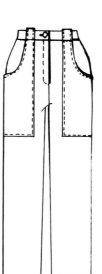

Bush pants

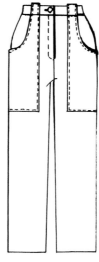

Shorts

pants

Tapered pants/cigarette

Bell bottoms

Stovepipe/straight leg with wide waist

Sweatpants

Sailor pants

Harem pants

Stirrup pants

Zoave/Sarroyed pants

Paper bag waist

Palazzo pants

Suspender trousers

Wide leg

Running shorts

Pantaloons

Bloomers

waistlines

Unisex 5 pocket jean with
2n & bartacks

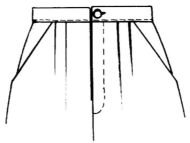

Unisex 2 pleat zip front
with slash pockets

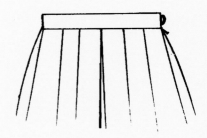

Pleated with set on waist
band—side seam zip/ button
opening

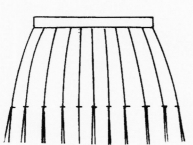

Pleated with back opening

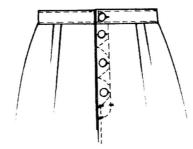

Button front pant

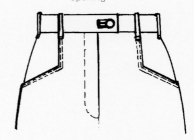

Belt loops, welt buttonholes
and novelty slash pockets

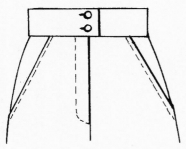

Wide waistband with 2-button
closure and slash pockets

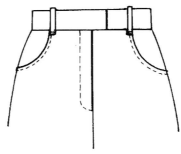

Wide waistband with belt
loops and bar/hook closure
and rounded pockets

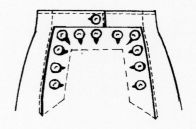

Sailor front 12 button opening

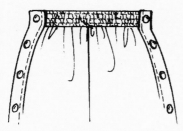

Elastic waist surge set
with"tearaway" side seam
snap closure

Faced waist with bow knot
at front

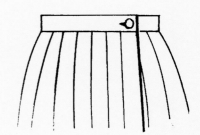

Asymmetrical button closure

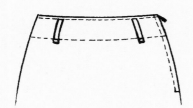

Faced natural waistline with
railroad side zipper

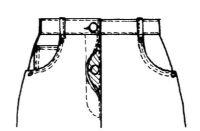

Womens 5 pocket jean with
button fly and rivet details

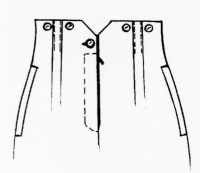

High-waisted 2 pleat pant with
single on seam welt pockets

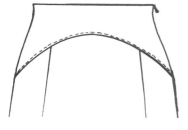

Invisible spider and yoke set

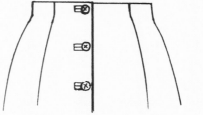

Half elastic waist with zip front and novelty pockets

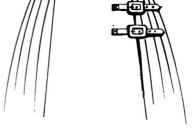

Kilt style with buckle side closure

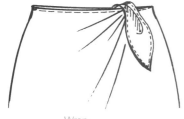

Wrap

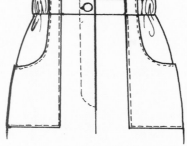

Fitted high waist with button closure

Flat front pant with bound waist and button side closure

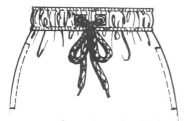

Set on drawstring elastic waistband with on seam pockets

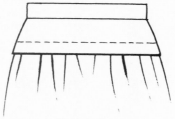

Pleated yoke

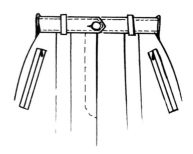

2 pleat pant with double welt zipper pockets and belt loops

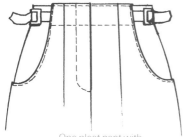

One pleat pant with side tabs

Natural faced waistline with button draped detail

High waist with skinny belt tied at center front and belt loops

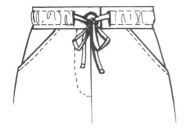

Button front waist band with drawcord and slash pockets

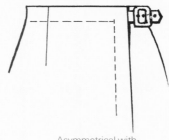

Asymmetrical with buckle side closure

Novelty belting

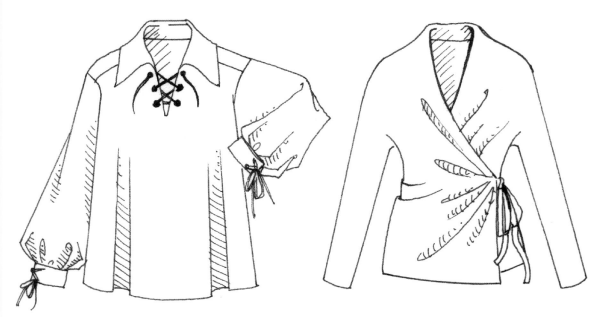

Poet/pirate style

Wrap around surplice

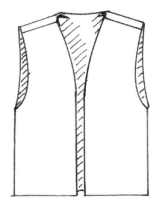

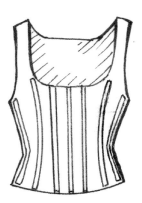

Straight vest

Boned bustier

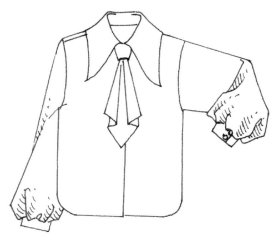

Tie front

Fitted with puff sleeves

Fitted ruffle-front blouse

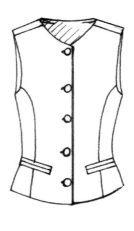

Fitted princess vest

L/S tunic with cowll neck and
fully fashioned arm well

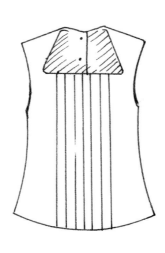

Sleeveless with front tuck
detail

Basic unisex 1 pocket shirt

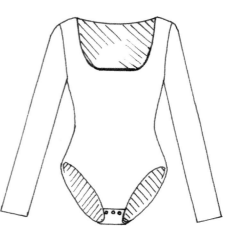

L/S bodysuit with open neckline

Dress shirt with pleated front

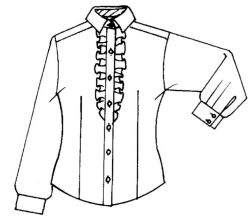

Fitted ruffle front

Shirt with hidden placket

With snap front

Bishop's sleeves and fold
backcuffs

Peplum and bell sleeves

Basic short-sleeved polo

Basic short-sleeved
pocket t

tops

With pin tuck front

shirt

Military style

Western style

Short sleeve—basic button down

Hidden placket

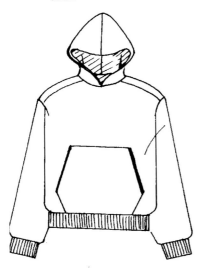

Hooded sweatshirt with kangaroo pocket

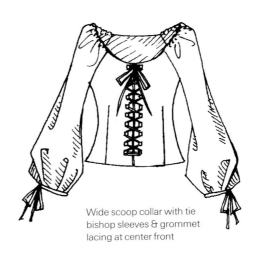

Wide scoop collar with tie bishop sleeves & grommet lacing at center front

jacket styles

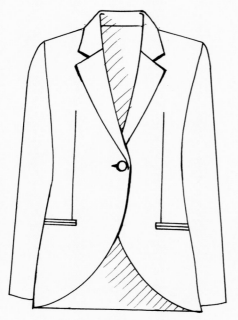

Single-breasted cutaway. Single button.

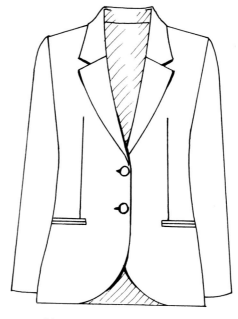

2 button single-breasted. Round hem.

2 button roll-down single-breasted with regular front hem.

3 button single-breasted with regular front hem.

6 button double-breasted with square hem

4 button double-breasted

jacket styles

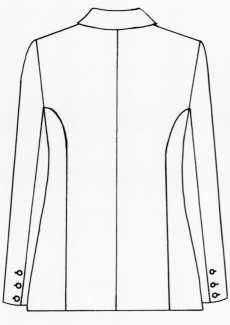

No vent

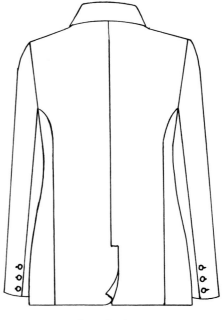

Center hook vent

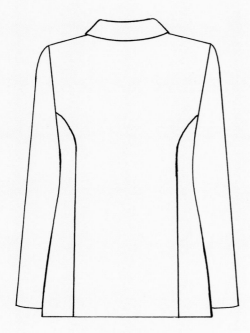

One piece back

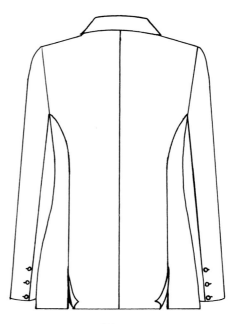

Side vents

jackets

Stadium jumper/
letterman's jacket

Zip front bomber with
tipped ribbing

Tie locken or wraparound

Nehru

Biker jacket

Riding jacket

jackets

Denim jean

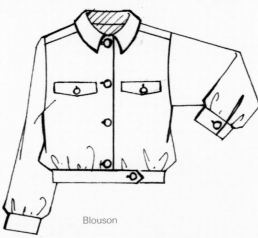
Blouson

Safari

Tuxedo/smoking jacket

Spencer

Chanel style

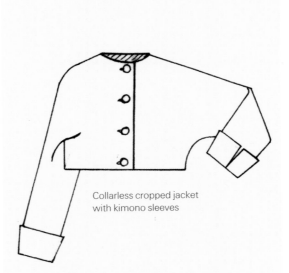
Collarless cropped jacket
with kimono sleeves

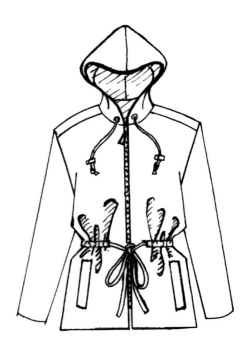
Hooded anorak

Trench coat

Cape

Chesterfield

coats

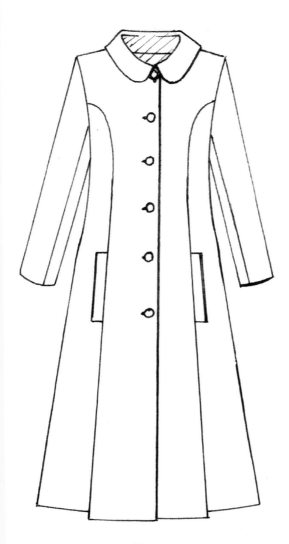

Princess

Duffle

Pea coat

Double-breasted

sleeves

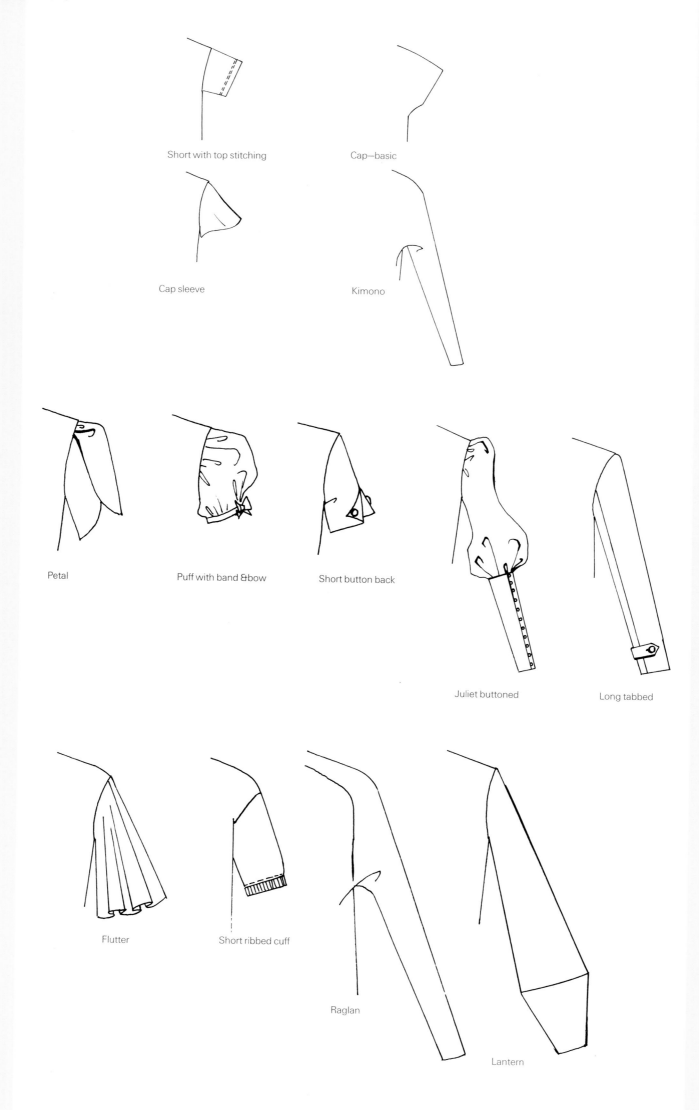

Short with top stitching

Cap—basic

Cap sleeve

Kimono

Petal

Puff with band &bow

Short button back

Juliet buttoned

Long tabbed

Flutter

Short ribbed cuff

Raglan

Lantern

sleeves

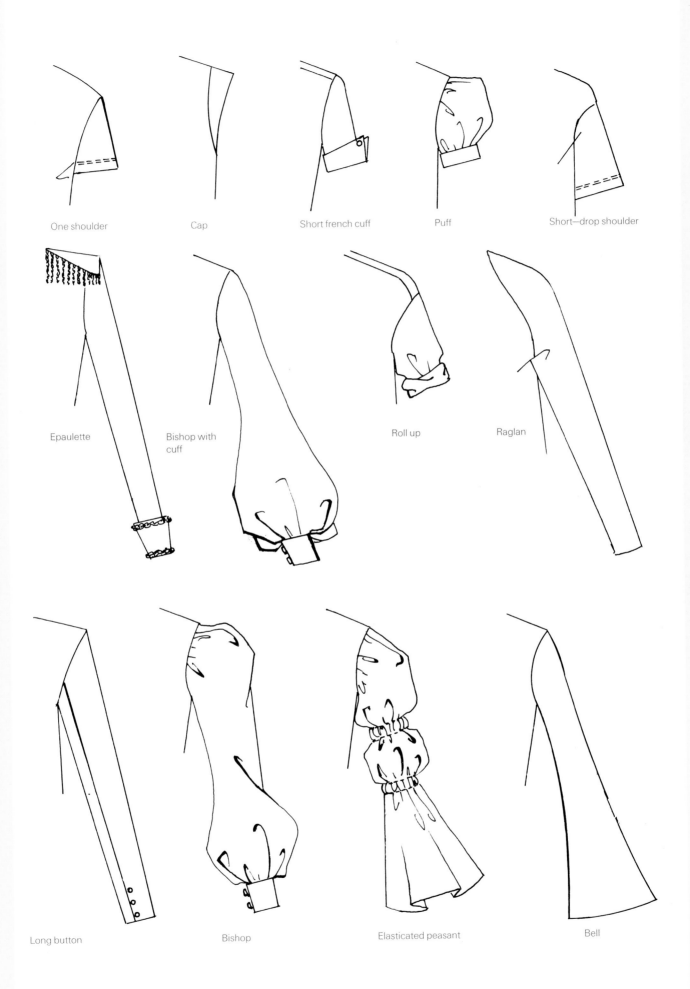

One shoulder

Cap

Short french cuff

Puff

Short—drop shoulder

Epaulette

Bishop with cuff

Roll up

Raglan

Long button

Bishop

Elasticated peasant

Bell

Gladiator sandal

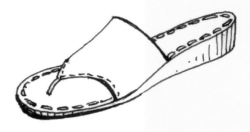

Thong sandal

Galosh/arctic boot

Cowboy boot

Pants boot

Pacboot

shoes

Ice skate

Rollerskate

Water moccasin

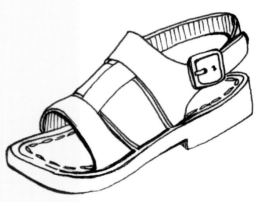

Dress sandal

Platform mule

Roller skate

shoes

George boot

Jodhpur boot

Squaw boot

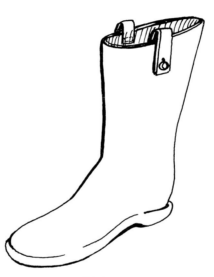

Wellington boot

Half boot

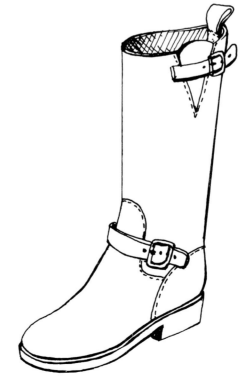

Engineer's boot

Clark pumps

shoes

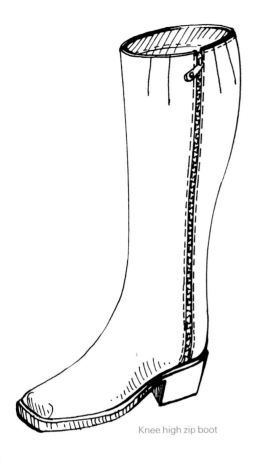

Knee high zip boot

Ankle strap pump
closed toe

Charles David pump

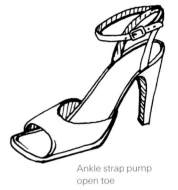

Ankle strap pump
open toe

Slingback platform sandal

Raised sandal

Mule

Wedge

eyeglasses

Wellington

Aviator

Oxford/Lexington

Oval/Ben Franklin/Granny

Queen

Square

Half moon

Bevelled

Foxy

Pentagon

Boston

Round/Lloyd

Half/reading glasses

Flip up

Pince nez

eyeglasses

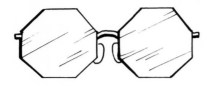

Octagon

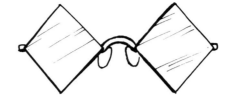

Harlequin

Tear Drop

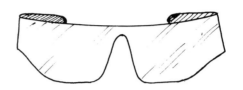

Wrap

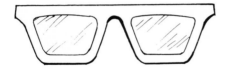

Flat top

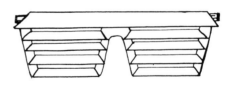

Lounge

John Lennon

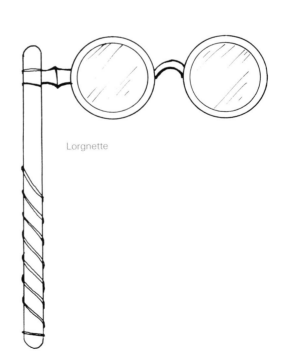

Lorgnette

Monacle

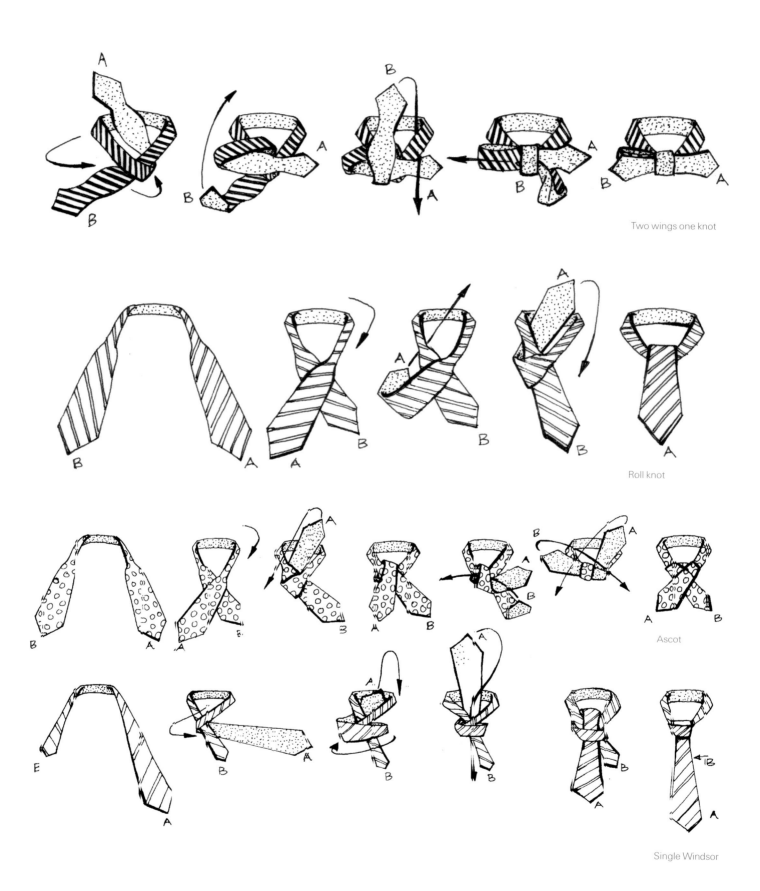

Two wings one knot

Roll knot

Ascot

Single Windsor

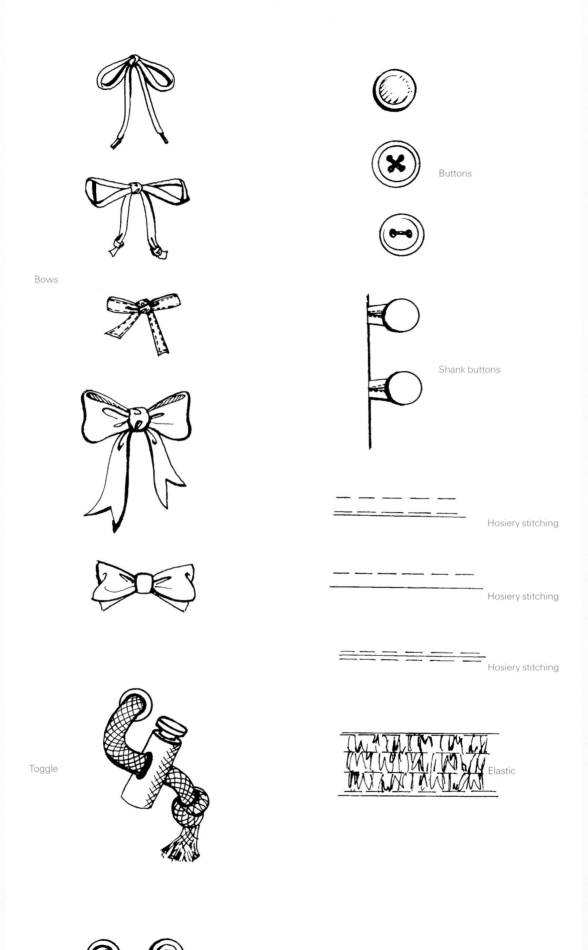

Bows

Toggle

Frog

Buttons

Shank buttons

Hosiery stitching

Hosiery stitching

Hosiery stitching

Elastic

stitches

Top side	Underside		Top side	Underside

SN chain stitch

SN blindstitch

SN saddle stitch

SN modern saddle stitch

SN lock stitch

SN zig-zag lockstitch

Two thread chainstitch

Cording for permanent crease

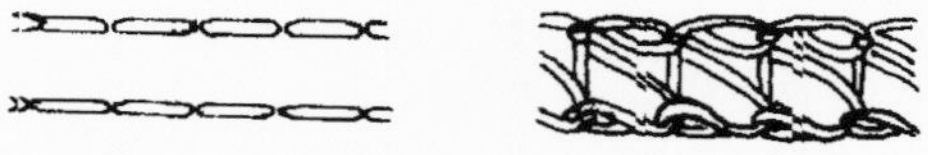

Converse stitch

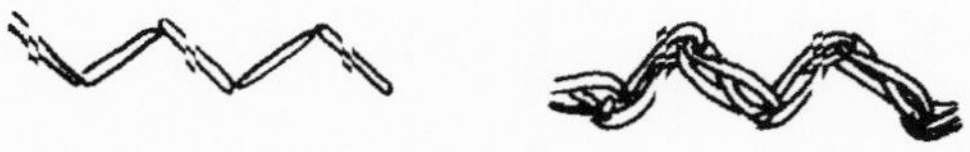

Zig-Zag chainstitch

Modified multi zig-zag chainstitch

Four thread safety

Five thread safety

Six thread safety

Two needle cover

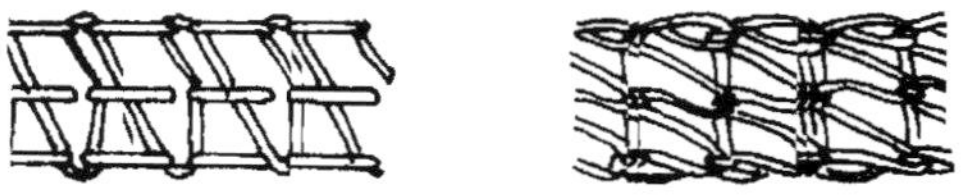

Three needle cover

Four needle cover

Serge pearl on edge

Serge stitch

Mock safety

Hosiery stitch

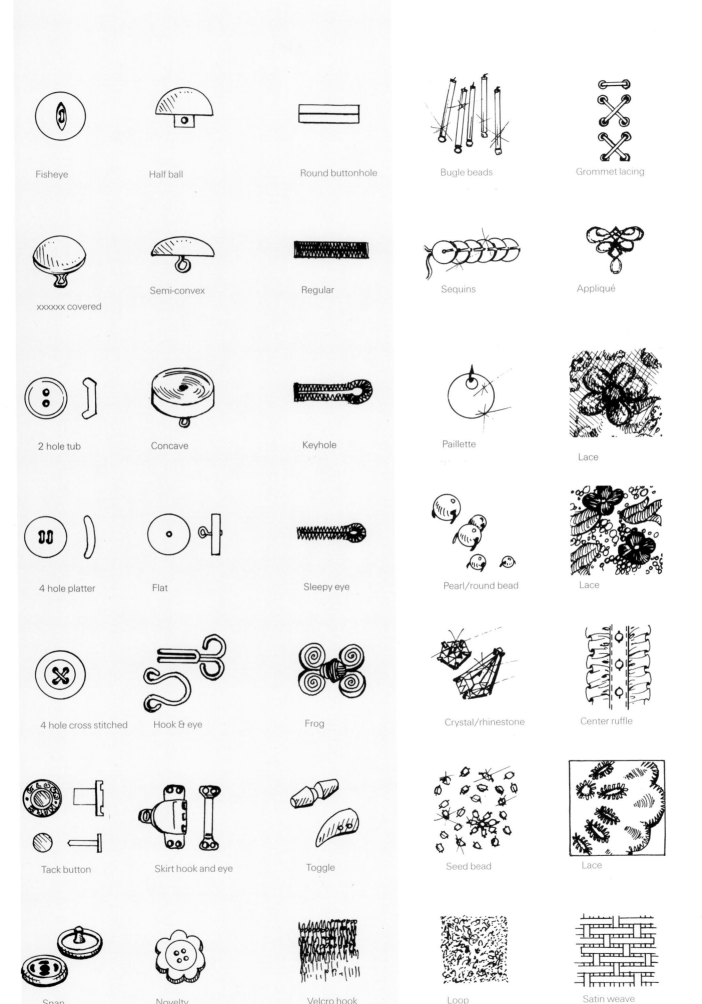

Fisheye

Half ball

Round buttonhole

Bugle beads

Grommet lacing

roses

xxxxxx covered

Semi-convex

Regular

Sequins

Appliqué

Appliqué

2 hole tub

Concave

Keyhole

Paillette

Lace

Bow

4 hole platter

Flat

Sleepy eye

Pearl/round bead

Lace

Bow 2

4 hole cross stitched

Hook & eye

Frog

Crystal/rhinestone

Center ruffle

Quilting

Tack button

Skirt hook and eye

Toggle

Seed bead

Lace

Brocade

Snap

Novelty

Velcro hook

Loop

Satin weave

Twill weave

Doctor's bag

Tote

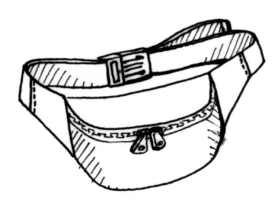

Fanny pack

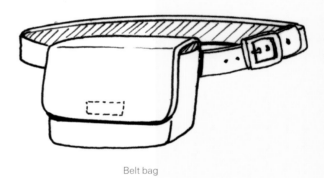

Belt bag

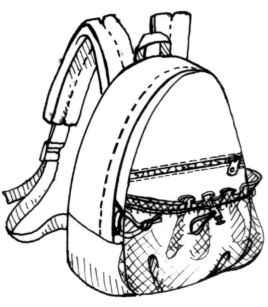

Backpack

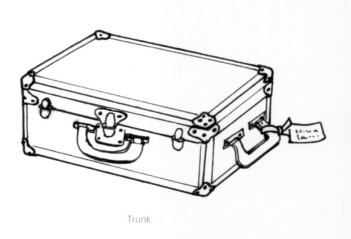

Trunk

bags

Envelope bag

Clutch purse

Lunch box

Square tote

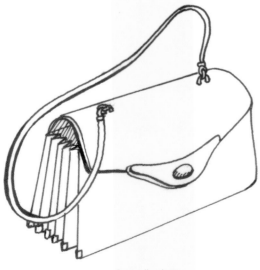

Accordion bag

Straw bag

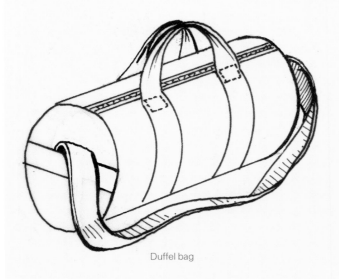

Duffel bag

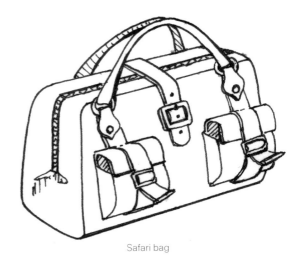

Safari bag

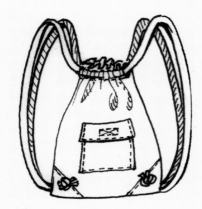

Knapsack/sack pack

Coin bag

Squaw bag

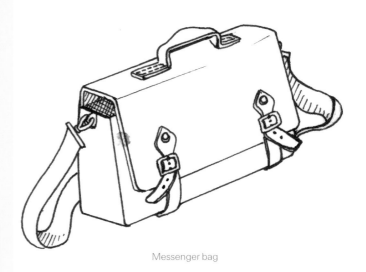

Messenger bag

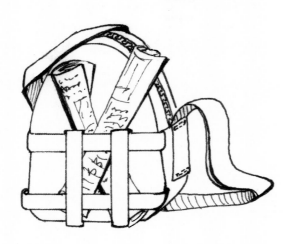

Newspaper bag

Bracelet bag

Suitcase

Dallas bag

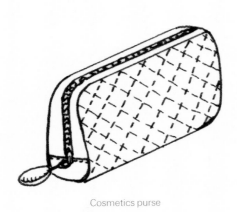

Cosmetics purse

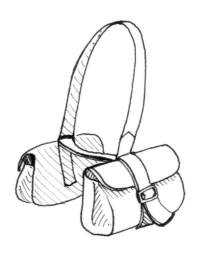

Saddle bags

fabric/folds

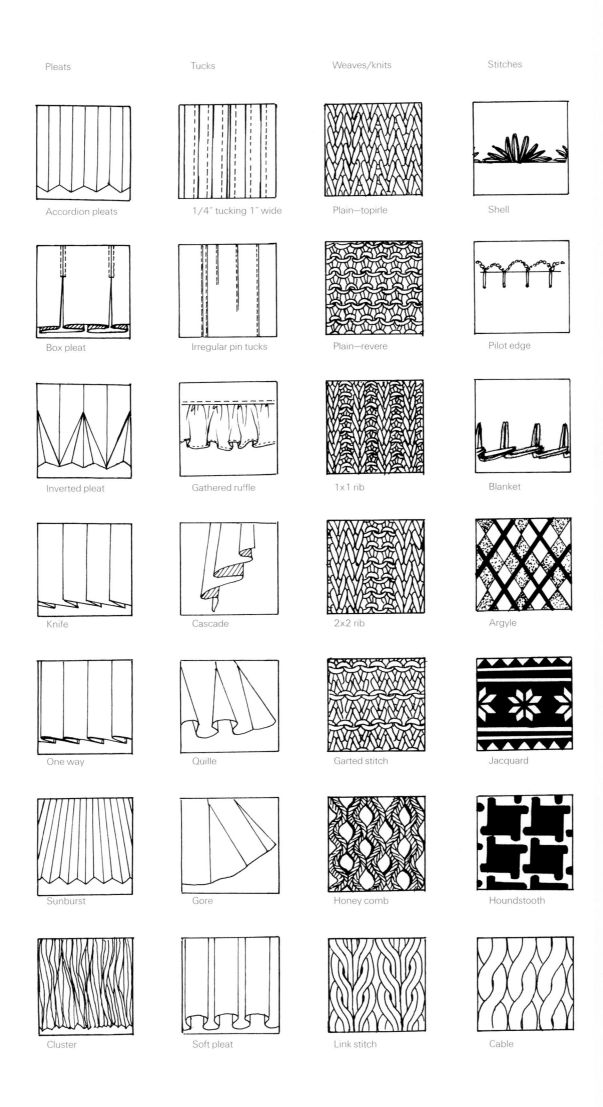

Pleats

Accordion pleats

Box pleat

Inverted pleat

Knife

One way

Sunburst

Cluster

Tucks

1/4" tucking 1" wide

Irregular pin tucks

Gathered ruffle

Cascade

Quille

Gore

Soft pleat

Weaves/knits

Plain—topirle

Plain—revere

1 x 1 rib

2x2 rib

Garted stitch

Honey comb

Link stitch

Stitches

Shell

Pilot edge

Blanket

Argyle

Jacquard

Houndstooth

Cable

Garter

Bulky chunky yarn

Plain weave

Crochet

Sport yarn

Popcorn stitch

Cable

Cable

Micro rib

Crocodile

Zebra

Terry cloth

Short fur

Leopard

Houndstooth

Long fur

Silk

Lace

Sequins

Animal print

Bouclé

pockets

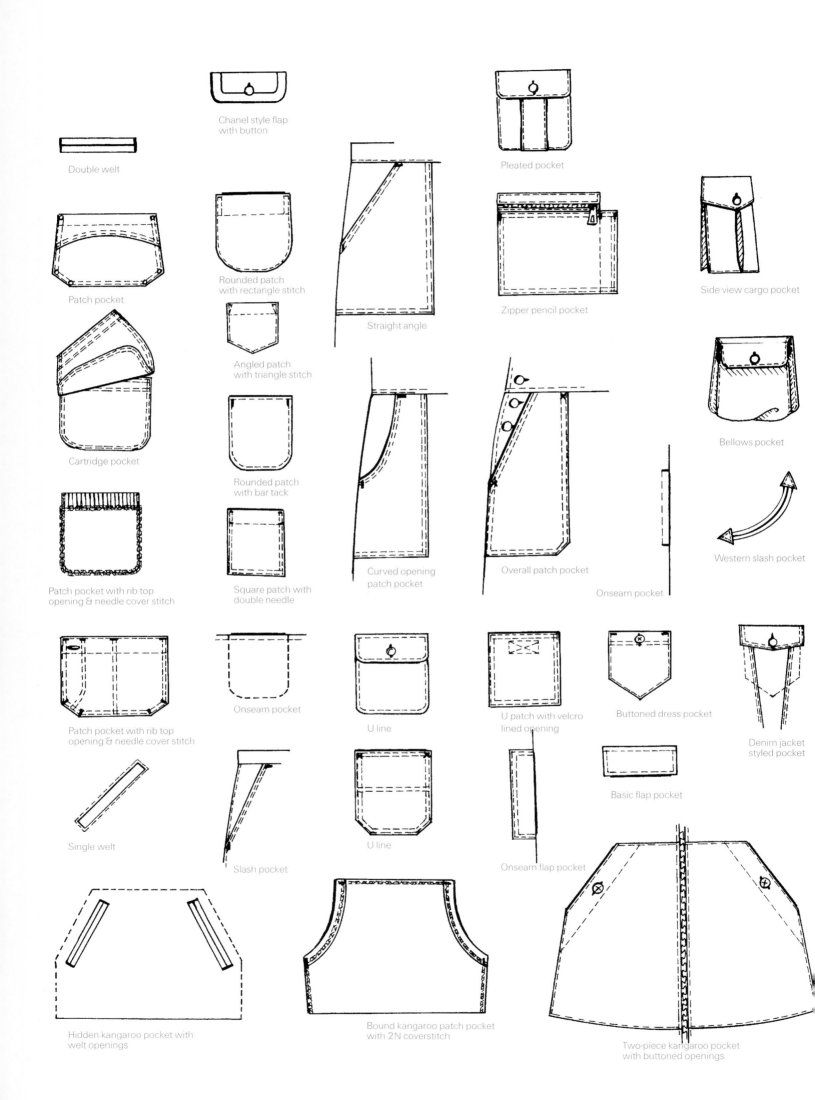

Double welt

Chanel style flap with button

Pleated pocket

Patch pocket

Rounded patch with rectangle stitch

Straight angle

Zipper pencil pocket

Side view cargo pocket

Cartridge pocket

Angled patch with triangle stitch

Rounded patch with bar tack

Curved opening patch pocket

Overall patch pocket

Onseam pocket

Bellows pocket

Western slash pocket

Patch pocket with rib top opening & needle cover stitch

Square patch with double needle

Patch pocket with rib top opening & needle cover stitch

Onseam pocket

U line

U patch with velcro lined opening

Buttoned dress pocket

Denim jacket styled pocket

Single welt

Slash pocket

U line

Onseam flap pocket

Basic flap pocket

Hidden kangaroo pocket with welt openings

Bound kangaroo patch pocket with 2N coverstitch

Two-piece kangaroo pocket with buttoned openings

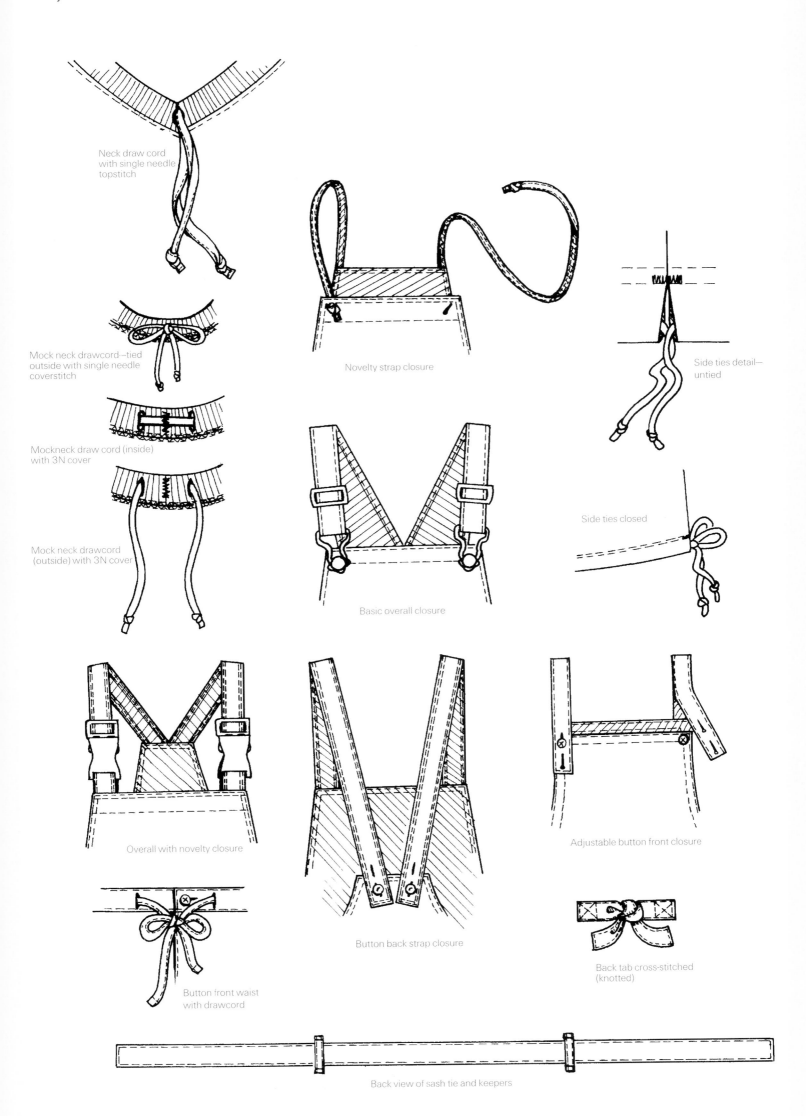

Neck draw cord with single needle topstitch

Mock neck drawcord—tied outside with single needle coverstitch

Mockneck draw cord (inside) with 3N cover

Mock neck drawcord (outside) with 3N cover

Novelty strap closure

Basic overall closure

Side ties detail— untied

Side ties closed

Overall with novelty closure

Button back strap closure

Adjustable button front closure

Button front waist with drawcord

Back tab cross-stitched (knotted)

Back view of sash tie and keepers

Fur

Barrel coat

Down jacket

Poncho

Quilted jacket

Barn jacket (casual)

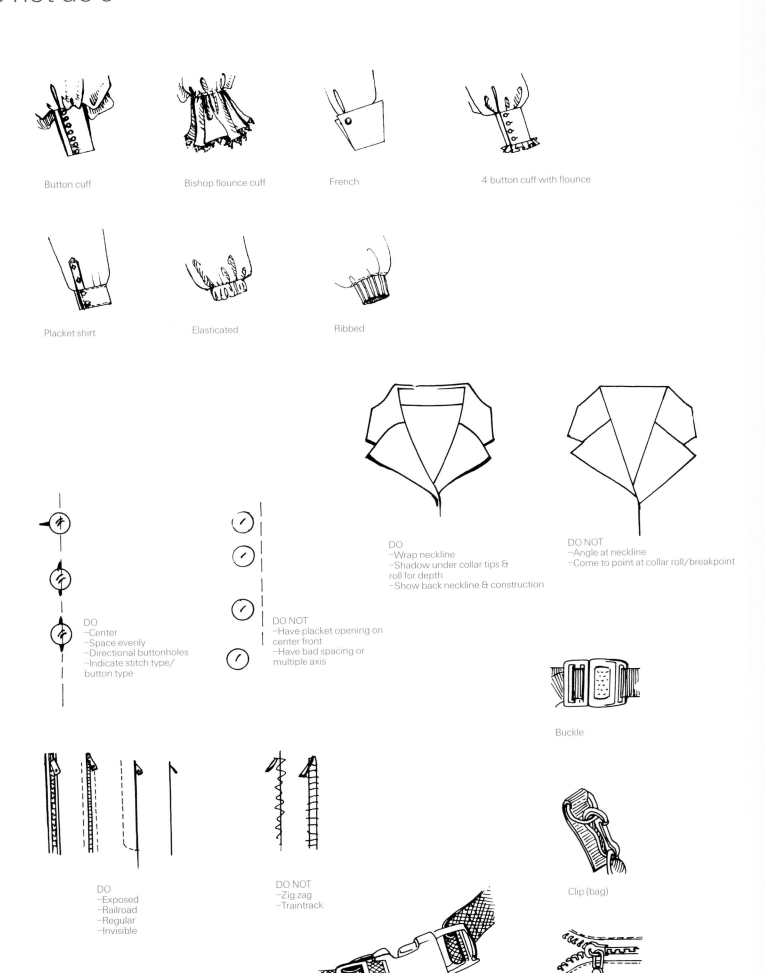

Button cuff

Bishop flounce cuff

French

4 button cuff with flounce

Placket shirt

Elasticated

Ribbed

DO
–Center
–Space evenly
–Directional buttonholes
–Indicate stitch type/
button type

DO NOT
–Have placket opening on
center front
–Have bad spacing or
multiple axis

DO
–Wrap neckline
–Shadow under collar tips &
roll for depth
–Show back neckline & construction

DO NOT
–Angle at neckline
–Come to point at collar roll/breakpoint

Buckle

DO
–Exposed
–Railroad
–Regular
–Invisible

DO NOT
–Zig zag
–Traintrack

Clip (bag)

Parachute clip

Zipper

chapter six:
how to draw fabrics

drawing fabrics/ fabric on the body

DRAWING FABRICS

This chapter completes the range of techniques we have learnt for accurately representing the defining features of a garment—silhouette, drape and fit and details—by showing how we can achieve similar standards of accuracy and realism in our depiction of the other defining feature, the fabric.

A drawing of a garment in which we can see at once and with a high degree of certainty what fabric the garment is made of is a highly effective fashion drawing. Such a drawing makes us feel (assuming of course that the garments are well drawn in all other respects) an immediate familiarity with the garments, an instinctive understanding of how it will feel, fit, drape and look; we will instantly form a clear idea of what markets, occasions and age ranges it is designed for and are free to switch our attention to the finer points of design and construction. Drawings like these can take a little longer to produce (though surprisingly less than might be thought) but in terms of the accuracy and immediacy of the information they convey they can be considered as being well worth any extra effort.

There are two aspects to drawing fabrics so they appear realistic and immediately recognizable. One is the accurate rendering of the actual surface appearance of the fabric. Leaving aside color, the surface appearance consists of, predominantly, (i) the surface texture (which depends on the size of fiber, yarn, weave, composition or natural texture of the fabric) and (ii) how light is reflected from the surface (whether it is shiny or matt or perhaps has a sheen). The second aspect of drawing fabrics is the accurate depiction of how the fabric folds and drapes on the body. Color is obviously a distinguishing feature of fabrics, but it is important to know how to represent the other visual aspects before adding color to a drawing; remember, color can improve a good drawing but can make a poor drawing look terrible, and color is not

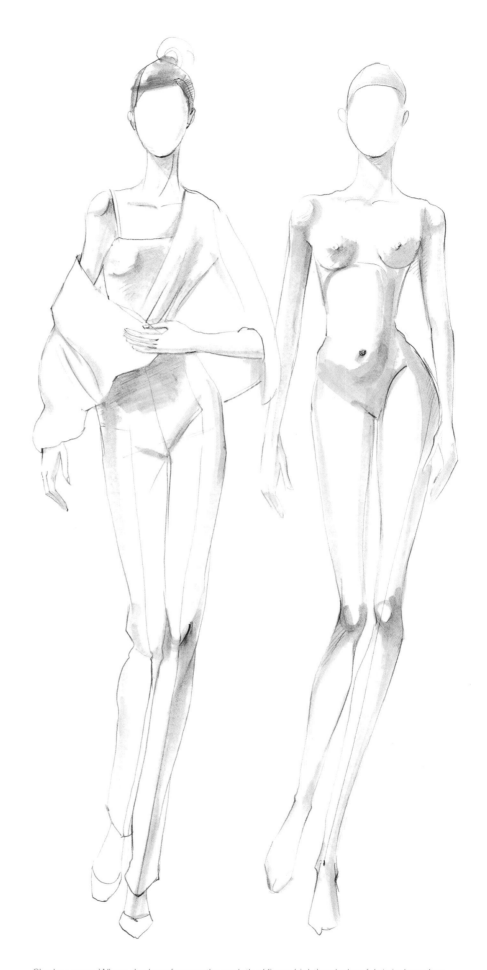

Shadow maps. Where shadows form on the unclothed figure (right) and when fabric is draped on the figure (left). Fabric draped close to the body forms shadows in the same way as they form on the unclothed body. Where the fabric fits loosely on the figure it forms folds and drape which create deeper shadows in the folds with light areas on the tops of the folds and a gradual change of the value of the shadow betweeen.

fabric on the body/
shading fabric/value scale

that helpful as additional information if the fabric type itself cannot be identified. The tools used in drawing to capture these two aspects of the appearance of fabrics are, as in the other parts of fashion drawing, line and value.

This chapter begins by examing the relation between construction and drape—how drape is formed by garment construction, and how to shade it c orrectly. Then the characteristics of different fabrics and how they are drawn is covered. Value—the degree of light and dark—is an important factor in a drawing. The value range used in drawings is usually indicated next to the drawing.

FABRIC ON THE BODY

In fashion drawing we are interested in giving a realistic impression of how clothes will look when worn *on the figure*. In order to do this it is necessary to understand the shading of the *body* under the fabric and then to understand the shading of the *fabric* in the parts where it fits and where it falls away from the body. The drawings overleaf show these two sets of shadows.

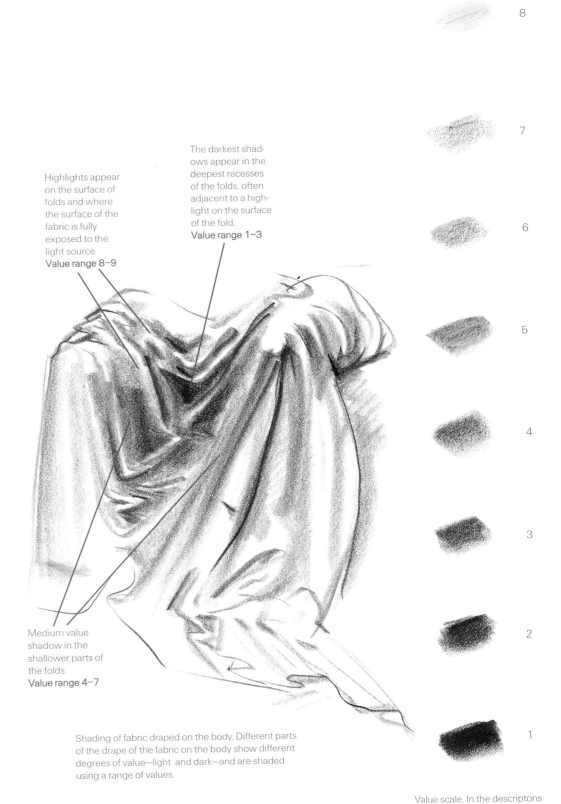

Highlights appear on the surface of folds and where the surface of the fabric is fully exposed to the light source.
Value range 8–9

The darkest shadows appear in the deepest recesses of the folds, often adjacent to a highlight on the surface of the fold.
Value range 1–3

Medium value shadow in the shallower parts of the folds.
Value range 4–7

Shading of fabric draped on the body. Different parts of the drape of the fabric on the body show different degrees of value—light and dark—and are shaded using a range of values.

9

8

7

6

5

4

3

2

1

Value scale. In the descriptons of shading fabrics included in this chapter reference is made to a **value range.** This refers to the value—the darkness or lightness—of the shading to be used. The numbers refer approximately to the values shown above, with 9 the white of the paper and 1 close to black.

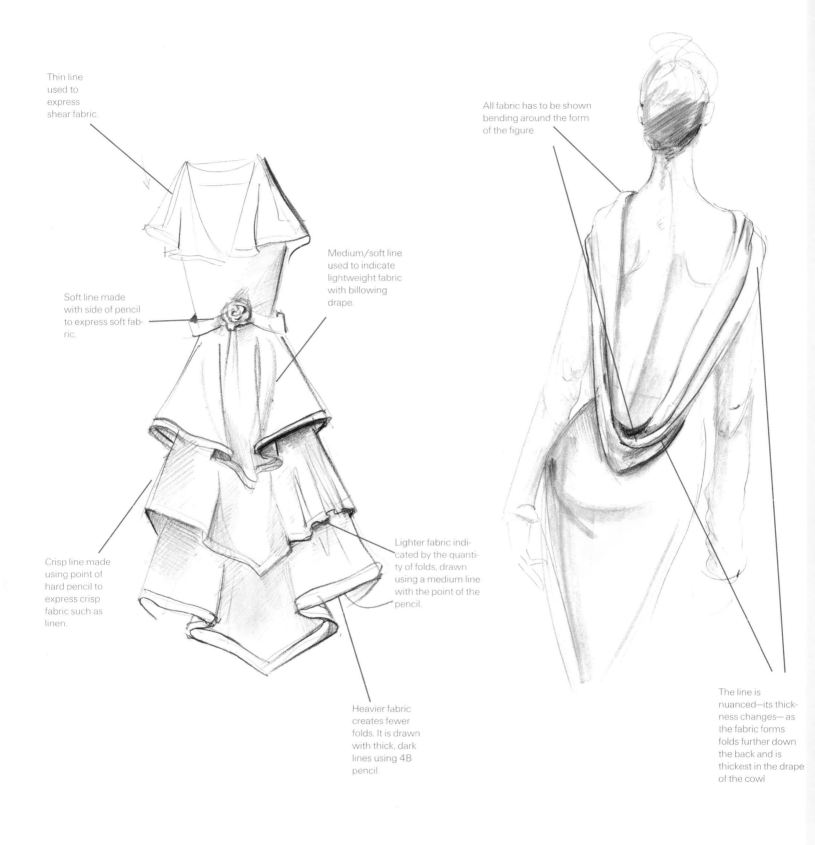

Thin line used to express shear fabric.

Soft line made with side of pencil to express soft fabric.

Crisp line made using point of hard pencil to express crisp fabric such as linen.

Medium/soft line used to indicate lightweight fabric with billowing drape.

Lighter fabric indicated by the quantity of folds, drawn using a medium line with the point of the pencil.

Heavier fabric creates fewer folds. It is drawn with thick, dark lines using 4B pencil.

All fabric has to be shown bending around the form of the figure

The line is nuanced—its thickness changes— as the fabric forms folds further down the back and is thickest in the drape of the cowl

construction/drape/shading/
single point drape

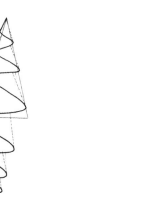

Cascade drape, vertically suspended
1. Draw an inverted cone shape.

2. Draw the outline of the drape as a line snaking down between the sides of the triangle and extending beneath.

3. Draw in the shapes of each section of the drape with sides sloping towards the center-top. Shade in the interior of each fold.

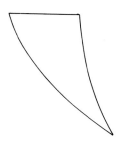

Cascade drape, diagonally suspended. 1. Draw a dagger shape

2. Draw in the shapes of the drape, bending diagonally towards the suspension point.

3. Shade in the interiors of the folds.

DO. Correctly drawn cascade drape.

DO NOT DO. Incorrectly drawn cascade drape. The folds are drawn at different angles. The sections of drape must all be aligned in the same dirrection.

Cowls are examples of two-point drape. The fabric is suspended from two points and drapes fluidly with wider folds at the bottom. Here the drape of the cowl is correctly drawn.

DO NOT DO. Incorrectly drawn cowl—there are too many lines. Lines relate to individual folds and cannot intersect other lines.

Side cowl, correctly drawn..

DO NOT DO. Incorrectly drawn side cowl. The cowl is not drawn to bend around the figure and appears stiff. Both the silhouette and the interiors of the folds should curve round the figure.

Gathered fabric. When fabric is gathered into a seam it flares out from the seam into a series of cone-shaped folds, radiating from the center of the seam. At the edge of the fabric these cones curve out and then back in on themselves. The cones left of the center radiate out to the left and those right of center radiate right. When drawing, first draw a second line parallel to the hemline to mark the height of the folds, and draw the folds between that line and the hem.

The gathers are drawn as loops, also radiating to left and right.

DO NOT DO. Here all the folds face to the right and the gathers are not drawn radiating from the seam; gathers must be drawn emerging from the seam.

drape and shading/
ruching/do not do's

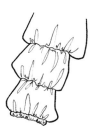

Ruching (also spelt rouching) is where areas of bunching and rippling in the fabric are caused by gathers on both sides of a seam.

DO NOT DO. Here the silhouette does not accurately reflect the gathering. With this amount of gathering there would be more fabric in the sleeve and it would puffout more.

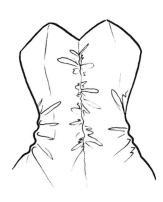

Ruching .

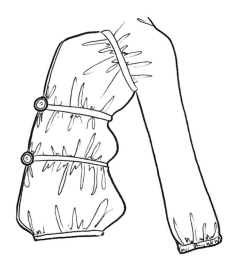

Ruching .

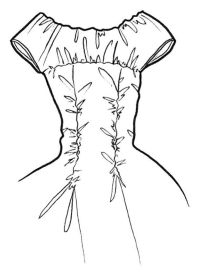

Ruching .

DO NOT DO. Here also, as above, the silhouette does not accurately reflect the construction of the garment. Fashion drawings are technical drawings and all parts must be consistent with each other.

DO NOT Do. No seam is drawn for the sleeve to connect to the main body of the garment. The position of the seam connecting the sleeve to the body of the garment contains essential information on the drape–and how it is shading– of the garment.

DO. Note in the skirt, which is correctly drawn, that a large amount of fabric in the body of the garment means the hem will be wide.

DO. Note the correctly placed shadow along the overlap of the opening of the jacket, indicating depth and that the shading on the right side of the jacket and the left side of the skirt indicates that the garments are larger than the body underneath , i.e. they are loose-fitting in these areas.

crisp fabrics/cotton voile/
silk organza/linen

CRISP FABRICS

A thin line is used when drawing the silhouettes of garments made of crisp fabrics. The slight stiffness of crisp fabric causes it to drape in folds that are more angular than softer fabrics: soft flowing curves are not present.

Dress made of cotton voile, a light open-weave fabric that is crisp and has a wiry feel. Note the angular appearance of the points of the handkerchief hem indicate the crispness of the fabric. The lightness of the fabric causes numerous folds to form; these are drawn in with a light touch. :
Value range; 8–6

Tiered skirt with unpressed pleats made of silk organza with paillettes. Fabric is lightweight so can be gathered into numerous narrow pleats that form numerous folds. Draw with sharp lines using the point of the pencil.
Value range: 8–6

Handkerchief linen scarf with rayon velvet ties. The gathers are drawn with thin crisp lines.
Value range; 7–6, Velvet, 8–7

crisp fabrics/
cambric/sateen

The top is cambric, a closely woven ,smooth cotton fabric; the skirt is made of canvas linen, a heavier weight linen with a soft finish, with stitched-down pleats The skirt is drawn with heavier straight lines to indicate the flatness of the stitched- down pleats and the weight of the fabric. Note the beads are drawn with a crisp edge to indicate the hardness of the material they are made of.

Value range : skirt , 6–4; top and beads, 7, 3,2,

Sateen dress. Sateen is a smooth, tightly woven fabric with a sheen that drapes with numerous crisp folds that are rendered using a light line.
Value range: 7–3

prints, plaids and stripes

PRINTS, PLAIDS AND STRIPES

Prints are designs that are printed onto a range of fabrics, including cotton, silk, wool but also many others. Prints can be applied in numerous ways, as repeating patterns or randomly, in the body of the garment or along a border.

There are no fixed rules, but generally if a print is larger, with a limited number of repeats on the garment, it can be fully rendered. If the design is small and with large numbers of repeats then, both from the point of view of the ease of rendering and also ease of viewing, it is usually best to render only a portion of the overall printed surface. To gauge the size of the repeats for repeating patterns it is easiest to hold the fabric to the body and count the number of repeats. This is the number that will appear in the drawing.

When drawing garments made of printed fabrics, it is best first to draw the outline of the garment and then to shade it so it will be clear where the folds will appear. The garment is shaded in the same way as a plain unprinted garment in the same fabric would appear, for example, wool/mohair is shaded with soft, broad shadows, silk taffeta with sharp, angular, highly contrasted shadows. Once the shaded garment has been drawn the print design is plotted onto it. A simple shape is chosen to represent the design of the repeat—for example, flowers might be represented by circles. It is easiest to plot the position of the pattern repeats using a grid system, making sure that it is adjusted to follow the curves of the body. The hem provides the horizontal axis for the grid and lines should follow its curves.

Remember that patterns on printed fabric break up and fall out of register in the folds of the drape. Surprisingly, it is actually easier to draw prints on fabrics with abundant drape as it is not as necessary to be as precise as when rendering a print on a flat surface, where every tiny error of measurement can be noticed.

Both coats are wool cashmere, and the top and skirt are cotton shirting.
The print on the coat is only partially rendered: it is usually too time-consuming to render the whole garment, and often makes the drawing look too busy. The coat on the left is a paisley print that *has* been fully rendered: sometimes the final result is worth the effort! Print designs must always be positioned parallel to the curve of the hem of the garment, as seen in both garments here.
Value range: Coats, 7–6; skirt/top, 8–5

The skirt and the body of the top are printed with vertical stripes that change width below the yoke; the sleeves have horizontal stripes. Note that the stripes follow the drape of the fabric as it curves over the bustline and into the seam of the yoke. The stripes form a v-shape where the fabric is gathered into the seam at the princess line and bend around the pockets and into the folds of the skirt.

prints, plaids and stripes/
silk crepe/cotton/jersey

This dress is made of floral-printed silk crepe. The design on the print is randomly placed; the repeats are irregular. The skirt of the dress is full, with numerous folds; the top is more fitted with fewer folds. It is important that the print repeats correspond with the drape of the fabric: they break up in the folds of the skirt and are seen bending around the bust in the bodice.
Value range: 6,5,1

The plaid design of this cotton top is made up of a mesh of vertical and horizontal lines of different widths. The easiest way to draw plaids is first to sketch in the position of the widest vertical and horizontal lines and then to place in the secondary lines.
Value range: 9–1

The collar of this sleeveless jacquard jersey dress has diagonal stripes that bend in towards the knot; on the tie the stripes change angle and on the belt are again parallel to those of the collar. The stripes on the body of the dress are vertical and wider-spaced. With stripes of varying widths and directions it is important to make sure they appear even. This is done by first drawing in the center stripes and then drawing in the number of stripe repeats making sure they are evenly spaced.
Value range: 7–5

shiny fabrics/
silk velvet

SHINY FABRICS

Shiny fabrics, as part of their own definition, show values at the high end of the
scale—the highlights are bright white,
shown in a drawing by leaving the white
of the paper unmarked (and occasionally
enhanced with the use of white-out or
similar). For dramatic effect, the bright
highlights are often juxtaposed with the
darkest shadows, so the contrast of values is most extreme.

A number of different types of fabrics
are shiny, for example: velvet, taffeta,
leather, fabric with metalic thread, satin
and others. Although they are all shiny
they do not all reflect light in the same
way: as they drape differently, with folds
of different widths, angularity and softness, so they reflect light in different patterns. *Shine* should also be differentiated from *sheen*. Shine is a sharper reflection of light, often in highlights, whereas
sheen is a broader diffusion of light
across a larger surface. Examples of fabric with sheen are: silk charmeuse,
velour, cotton velvet, jersey, cashmere.

When drawing garments made of shiny
fabrics it is best to plan out where the
areas of light and dark will fall before
beginning the drawing. Remember that
light is reflected at its brightest on the
top of the folds and shadows are darkest
in the interiors of folds. As mentioned, to
highlight the contrast of dark and light,
the darkest shadows of folds are often
place next to the lightest highlights on
the tops of the folds.

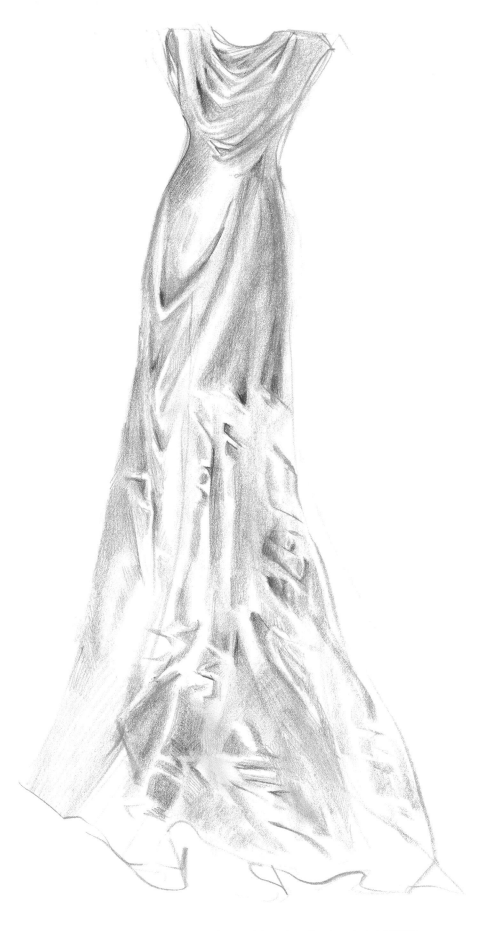

This long evening dress shows a variety of types of drape, from the elegant cowl neckline
to the complex folds in the train. It is made of silk-velvet and is lit from left of center so a
wide range of values appear on both sides of the garment and in the folds of the drape.
The fabric itself is of a medium value; the reflected shine is of high value and the shadows
in the drape are of the lowest value.
The fabric is soft and forms soft, rounded folds, the shadows in which are drawn using the
side of a very soft (6B) pencil.
Value range: 9–6, 3–1

Long-sleeved, off-the-shoulder, long evening gown made of four-ply satin crepe. The garment is lit from the right and is drawn using the same technique as the garment on the preceding page except that the folds are gathered from the side seam, creating horizontal drape so that the planes of light and dark also form horizontally. Satin crepe also has slightly more texture than velvet, with crisper drape drawn with more angularity of line.
Value range: 9–6, 3–1

This sleeveless, knee length dress is made of crushed velvet, a fabric with a slightly textured surface that reflects light unevenly across its surface. Light is reflected more as *sheen* than shine, with a broader area of light forming on the tops of the folds. The uneven quality of the surface texture is drawn by making short strokes with the side of a soft pencil slightly raised to the tip, creating a smaller mark, and using a tapping motion. This technique is used in all the areas of the garment. A 4B pencil is used in the darker areas and a 2B in the lighter, and the white of the paper shows through in the lightest areas.
Value range: 7, 6, 2

shiny fabrics/taffeta/ patent leather

In this ensemble the skirt is jacquard taffeta, the jacket is felt, trimmed with hand-crocheted balls; the hat is also felt and the muff is faux fur. To draw the jacket and hat use the side of a 4B pencil; the folds are soft and rounded and the highlights on the tops of the folds are narrow. The skirt, by comparison, has crisper, more angular folds.
Value range: 9,3–1

Patent leather is one of the highest gloss shine fabrics, meaning it has a very high degree of value contrast. Light reflects from its surface as thin, sharp highlights on the tops of the folds, and shadows form directly adjacent to the highlights. The highlights are shown by leaving the white of the paper unmarked. The shadows have to be a dense black to show the correct level of value contrast; there is minimal gradation of tone, and the areas of shadow are completely filled in with a heavy application of the softest available pencil—a 6B. The flatter areas of this jacket reflect its intrinsic color, and are represented using an even application of a medium value that is not gradated where it meets the darker and lighter areas.
Value range: 9,6,1

shiny fabrics/cottons/
sequins

Different decorative elements. The sleeve is tied with rat tail cording; it is very black, drawn with a 6B pencil leaving a little light on the surface of the bows. The belt is studded with sequins and seed pearls. These are both drawn as half-circles, with the sequin as a flat circular shape and the pearls as spheres. Both have round highlights. The flowers on the sleeveless shirt have interlocking petals that cast soft shadows creating a spiral effect.
Value ranges: 9, 2, 1

The garments in this gypsy outfit are made of a variety of fabrics: the blouse is cotton gauze, the vest is cotton felt, the skirt is cotton. Sequins are sewn onto the border of the vest, belt and skirt. The fabrics themselves are *not* shiny, but the numerous sequins are, and each has its own bright point of light. The sequins are drawn as a half circle with the point of the pencil (the other half is left undrawn to represent the reflection of light). Place a dot in the middle of each sequin to show the thread securing them to the garment. Each sequin has its own small cast shadow also in the shape of a half-circle.
Value range: 9, 6, 5

shiny fabrics/satin

These dresses are made of satin, a shiny smooth fabric. Satin is not as shiny as the shiniest fabrics, and light is reflected more as a sheen over a broader surface of the folds rather than thin, crisp lines.

The overall value range is less than for shinier fabrics. The softer appearance of the fabric is achieved by using the side of the pencil to create the shadows of the folds and leaving larger areas of the paper unmarked to show the tops of the folds. No heavy lines should be used in drawing these garments.

Value range: 7,6,1

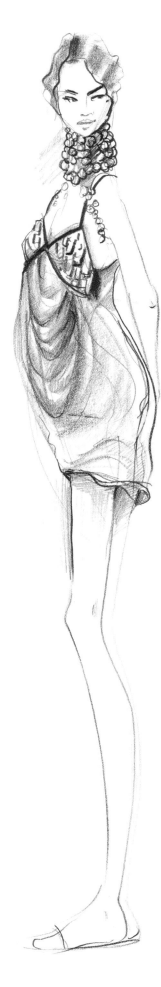

The skirt part of this minidress is silk-knit, the bodice is metallic brocade. Silk yarn is shiny and when knitted into fabric displays a sheen across the surface. It is lightweight, forming soft folds, and is shaded using the side of the pencil to avoid hard lines; shadows should be rounded. The metallic brocade bodice is shinier and has a wider range of values; shadows in this part of the garment appear more angular and geometric. The surface texture of the metallic brocade is not smooth and this creates numerous uneven areas of shadow and light. Here it is lit from the left side which has the effect of creating deeper, more dramatic shadows. Shading is drawn in with the point of the pencil to pinpoint precisely the small areas of shadow.
Value range: skirt, 6, 5, 3; bodice, 9, 2

This ball gown is made of silk taffeta, a fabric that forms folds with more angular shapes than other fabrics: it has almost the feel of paper. Note that in this garment there are three types of folds: horizontal, diagonal and vertical. Keep the line crisp.
Value range: 7,6, 1

transparent fabrics/
chantilly lace/exercises

"Transparent fabric" is oxymoronic, a self-contradiction: if a fabric is really transparent it cannot be seen, so cannot be drawn. So-called transparent fabrics (also called "sheer" fabrics) are in fact rarely fully transparent; they range from partly or semi-transparent to almost fully transparent. Generally speaking transparent fabrics are more opaque in the parts where they fold over themselves—in the drape, hems and seams—and more transparent on the flatter areas. The more transparent parts of garments made of these fabrics are shown by indicating the presence of the shaded body underneath; the less transparent parts are shaded with subtle value ranges depending on the fabric.

Note that a common mistake when drawing transparent fabrics is to omit the constructional detailing: these features are in fact made even more pronounced by the transparency, so all seams, hems and tucks should be clearly shown.

EXERCISES
1. Draw on the croquis a leather jacket with fur trim over a lace blouse, matched with cotton pants. Draw twice over varying the fabrics of each of the garments.
2. Draw a tiered skirt with the top tier made of a shiny fabric, the middle of a matt fabric and the bottom of a transparent fabric.
3. Draw a tailored suit using plaid fabric for the jacket and a textured fabric for the skirt or pants.

This sleeveless party dress is made of a fine Chantilly lace. Chantilly lace is the finest of laces, often appearing in the shapes of leaves or floral motifs. It is drawn with the finest point of a hard pencil and a very light touch. Refer to the description of the Alençon lace dress in this section.
Value range: 9,4,3,

transparent fabrics/alençon lace/silk chiffon

This evening dress is made of Alençon lace—a handmade French lace that has solid patterns where the lace is more tightly woven and bordered with cording (*cordonnet*). The garment is drawn by first outlining the repeat of the lace pattern on a grid, in a similar way to drawing a print. The design of the pattern is then drawn using a hard pencil to give clear, precise lines. Most patterns in lace are so complex that they can be drawn abstracting much of the actual detail, while preserving the overall scale and shape, and indicating the thickness of the lace by the thickness of the line used to draw it. The net ground beneath the lace is indicated with very fine cross-hatching. This does not have to be rendered across the whole surface; it can be effectively shownby drawing in those parts where the garment touches the body and the shadow of the body underneath shows through.
Value range: 9,4,3,

This high-waisted, sleeveless evening gown is made of silk chiffon, an extremely light and soft, transparent fabric. The lightness of the fabric makes it billow and flow across the body. All the curves of the drape are rounded, and shadows are thin and soft. The whole garment is drawn using a very light touch. The silk has a slight iridescent quality that can be accentuated by using the sharp edge of an eraser to bring out the thin lines of light on the tops of the folds.
Value range: 9,7,6

transparent fabrics/
vinyl

Transparent vinyl raincoat. The fabric has angular, rigid folds that must be clearly seen in the silhouette. Shadows are drawn to express the body under the garment with a light touch and even value. Do not outline the body under the garment. The reflective areas of the vinyl at the tops of the folds are drawn in by erasing the pencil to leave the white of the paper to show through. Darker shadows are applied in the deepest parts of the folds.
Value range: 8, 5, 4

textured fabrics/
faux crocodile/faux fur

TEXTURED FABRICS

Textured fabrics range from all kinds of knits, to furs and other animal skins, to fringe, beading, quilting, cording and numerous other natural and man-made fabrics.

Of all fabrics, textured fabrics are those with the most direct impact on a garment's silhouette. The surface quality of the fabric is uneven, in varying degrees, and this can be clearly seen in the fabric, so has to be clearly reflected in the silhouette.

When drawing textured fabrics more line and shading is used than other fabrics as the surfaces are often broken up and more edges are seen. These outlines generally require the use of harder, HB or 2H pencils.

This faux crocodile/alligator jacket with faux fur collar is drawn with two contrasting techniques: Once the silhouette of the garment is drawn the fur is rendered using the side of a soft pencil with long strokes. The pressure of the strokes lightens towards the end of each stroke (here from left to right) to show the lighter area of the fur on the right side where it is closest to the light source. The silhouette and interior texture of the fur is brought out using the point of the pencil to show the individual fur fibers (different animal or faux animal skins have different lengths of individual hairs). The body of the jacket is drawn using the side of the pencil to create the squares that represent the individual crocodile scales. Only one pencil is used—a soft, 4B, for example—but the squares cover a wide range of light to dark values that represent the shiny parts and darker areas, so the pencil must be used with a correspondingly wide range of pressures to capture this variety.
Value range; 9,3–1

textured fabrics/
shearling/feathers

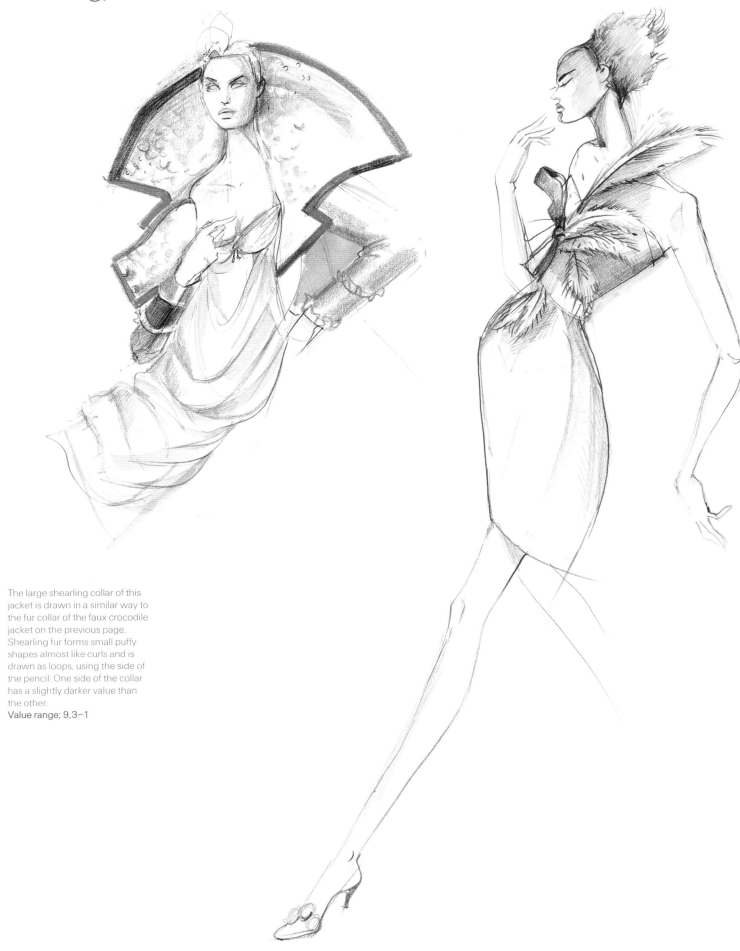

The large shearling collar of this jacket is drawn in a similar way to the fur collar of the faux crocodile jacket on the previous page. Shearling fur forms small puffy shapes almost like curls and is drawn as loops, using the side of the pencil. One side of the collar has a slightly darker value than the other.
Value range; 9,3–1

Feathers are drawn by first lightly tracing the silhouette of each feather, remembering that some feathers overlap, then defining the outside strands of each feather using a hard pencil with an extremely light touch. Where feathers overlap the topmost feather casts its shadow onto the feather below.
Value range 9, 6,5,4

textured fabrics/mohair/
fagoting/denim

This short dress has a fitted bodice with fagoting—an open, decorative stitch used here along the side seam—and a fringed skirt. Fringe and fagoting are textures made up of linear elements. Fringe can be drawn with a more fluid, diagonal stroke, indicating that it can move freely. The fagoting is drawn with more control to indicate its precise structure that is an integral part of the garment. Value scale 9, 5, 4.

This top is made of crocheted mohair "granny" squares with rosette appliqués of the same fabric attached to the center of each square. The crochet pattern is drawn with the point of the pencil using a circular motion; denser applications are made where the crochet is thickest and appears darkest.
Value range 9, 7,6,2,1

The texture of denim is due to its twill weave—a weave with diagonal ridges—that gives the fabric a slightly rough surface. Denim is a medium-weight fabric that drapes in wide folds. It is drawn by first filling in the silhouette of the garment with an even application of shading of a medium value using the side of a soft pencil and then indicating the darker values of the folds using smaller, circular strokes. Indicate the twill—the white cross yarn—by removing thin lines from the rendering using the fine point of an eraser.
Value range: 6,5,4,3

soft fabrics/suede

SOFT FABRICS

Soft fabrics include wool, angora, cashmere, suede and felt, and other fabrics that are soft but without the distinctive texture of furs or some bulky knits. As their name suggests, everything about soft fabrics is soft. Soft fabrics generally do not have shine, but can have a subtle sheen, so their value range are closer together than those of shiny fabrics. They are usually drawn using the side of a soft pencil.

Suede is a very soft fabric that forms wide shadows. In the finished garment no lines are visible except those of constructional details; the silhouette is defined by the edge of the shadows. Suede is drawn by applying successive layers of pencil to express first the value of the intrinsic color of the garment and the shadows and subtle sheen on the surface of the folds. Using a blending (smudging) technique with a stump or cotton swab, layers of tone are then added inside the folds to create the shadows. The sheen on the top of the folds is created by lightly removing some of the pencil with the sharp point of an eraser.
Value range: 6, 4, 2

soft fabrics/gabardine/ suede

Gabardine has a tight weave with a flat surface so drapes in shallow folds that form wide shadows with relatively little contrast with the color of the body of the garment. The silhouette is drawn with clear edges but avoiding sharp lines. Fill in with an allover even value and apply shadows into the interiors of the folds with wide pencil strokes.

Suede has a similar surface quality to gabardine but is drawn with wider shadows and has a slightly softer edge than gabardine.

Value range: gabardine, 8-5; suede, 6–3

chapter seven: men
and men's clothing

drawing men/men and women/men's poses

DRAWING MEN

It is important not to confuse men with women, and vice-versa. Women often draw men that look like women and men often draw women that look like men. Like fashion itself, looks come in and go out of style, and one season men's looks can be masculine and muscular and the next thin, sensitive and more feminine. Despite these seasonal variations, though, there are clear physical differences between the sexes that are independent of fashion, and these must be clearly shown in drawings. As a rule, the male of the species is built more for "fight and flight" than the female, and is larger, harder and more angular. Although the figure is still a nine-heads one, a few of the proportions are slightly different. Here are the main differences:

1. The male head is slightly larger than the female head. It is squarer, with flat planes and more prominent features. The jaw is wider, the nose stronger, the forehead more prominent, cheekbones higher. The mouth is wider and the lips, particularly the upper lip, are not as full as in the female face; the eyes are less rounded. The neck is thicker than the female's.
2. Men's shoulders are wider and straighter than women's, closer to two heads wide as opposed to a woman's one and a half heads. In contrast to women the shoulders are also wider than the hips. The arms are thicker and more muscled and the hands are larger.
3. The chest is wider than a woman's, as is the back.
4. The torso is slightly longer than a woman's. The waist is lower and not as tapered; the hips are not prominent and the pelvis area is smaller.
5. Male legs are slightly shorter than women's, with much larger muscles, knees and feet. Hands are wider and fingers thicker than women's.

MEN'S POSES

With the exception of active sportswear poses, where it is effective to use poses from a "frozen moment" when legs and

Men should be drawn to look like men.

men and women/
men's clothing/exercise

arms can be extended in a number of planes typical of the sport, filling a large portion of the page, men's poses tend to be straighter and more conservative than women's, with arms and hands closer to the sides of the body: Men are angular and poses do not have the same sensuous curves of women's bodies. This is not to say that men's poses are not graceful and sophisticated, however: men should not be drawn stiffly; rather, their poses are more "ready for action", often with legs slightly apart to balance the body weight (rarely seen in female poses except for younger women)

MEN'S CLOTHING

Although the variety of men's clothing continues to grow rapidly, there is still not the same range of garments as is available for women. Tailored suits and other garments continue as important staples of men's wardrobes—basic uniforms with a long lineage dating back to heraldic times when they were a form of body armor. Increasingly, though, tailored garments have come to be adopted for less formal occasions or to be worn in combination with more casual clothes; for example, a tailored jacket might be paired with a t-shirt.

When drawing men's tailored garments, other than the differences in silhouette corresponding to the different body poportions, there are remarkably few differences from women's tailored garments, the main one being that closings on men's clothes are from right to left on the drawing (left to right on the body). Suits are often drawn worn with formal shirts and ties. When drawing the shirts, make sure that the shirt collar covers most of the neck and is placed above the jacket collar. In front view, little, if any at all, of the neck is visible between the jaw and the top of the collar: long, elegant necks do not feature in fashion poses for men. The same attention to detail, precision of line and symmetry are present in men's tailored garments as in women's.

EXERCISE

Study the croquis over the next few pages and then copy three front, three side and three three-quarter views.

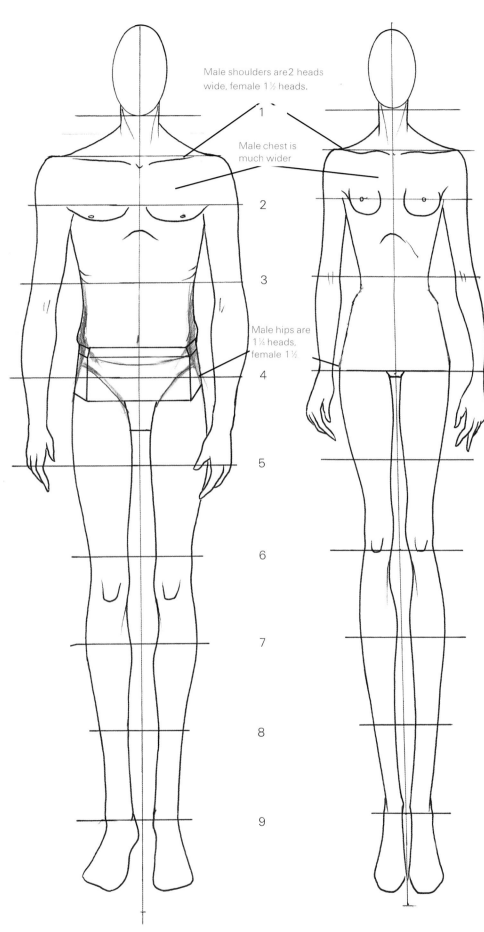

Male shoulders are 2 heads wide, female 1½ heads.

Male chest is much wider

Male hips are 1¼ heads, female 1½

The male fashion croquis is about the same height as the female but most of the features are bigger and broader. The torso is longer but the legs shorter than a woman's. Men should be drawn to look like men, and it is worthwhile to study the main physical differences between the sexes in order to draw them accurately.

malecroquis/front/side view/ three-quarter S curve

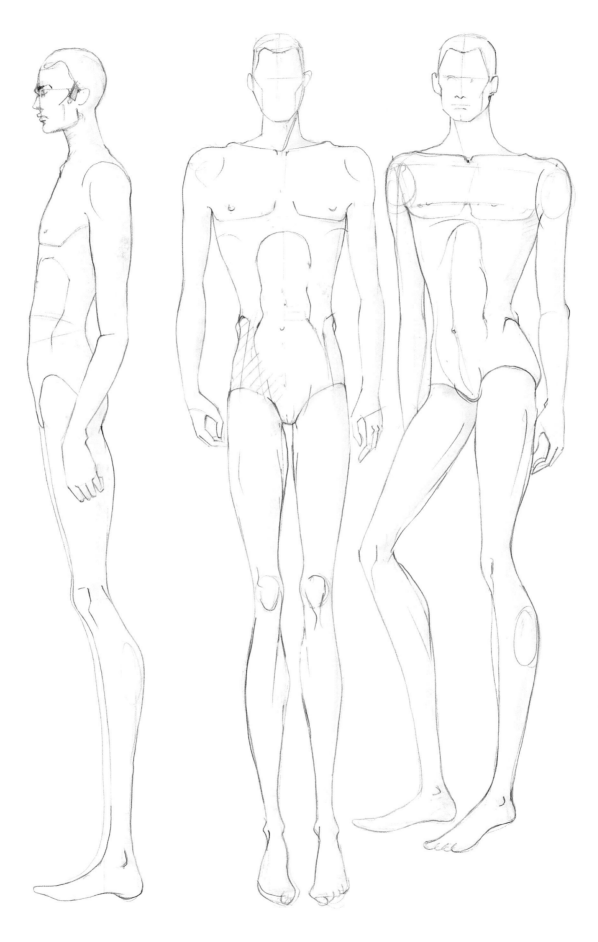

Male croquis—side, front and three-quarter view.

male croquis/front/back view/three-quarter S curve

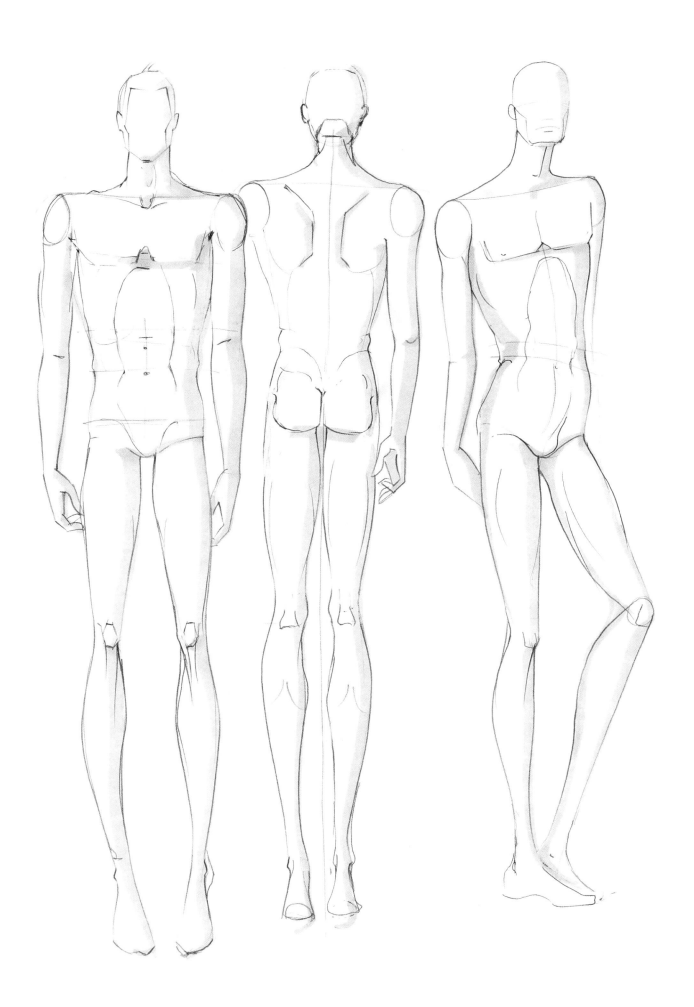

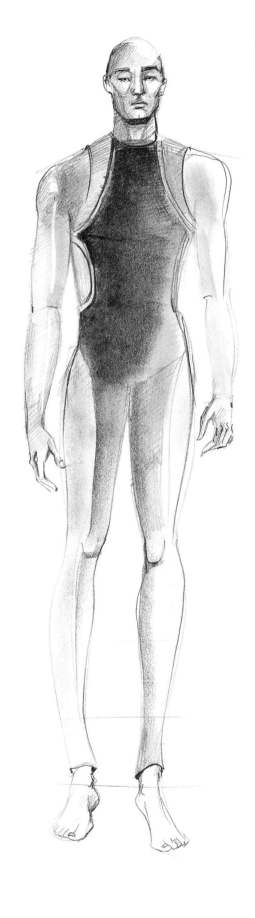

male croquis/ front view—
fleshed-out

male face v. female face

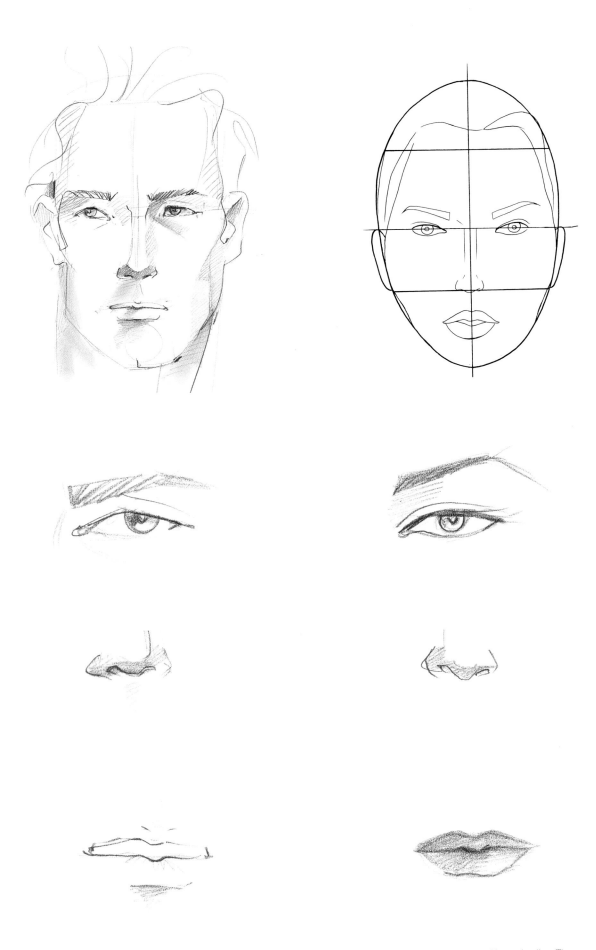

Male face v. female face. The male face is more rectangular, with a wider brow, larger chin and squarer and lower jawline. The features are in the same locations but are more horizontal. To give a particularly masculine look the planes of the face can be drawn in, from the sides of the eyes to the nose, and then straight down to highlight the cheekbones. **Eyes/eye-area**. The male eyebrow and eyelid are more horizontal than the female and the eye is more recessed—there is more shadow under the eyebrow. **Nose**. The male nose is more horizontal at the bottom—it does not turn up. **Mouth**. The male mouth is more horizontal. If the upper lip is drawn then it is more squared off at the edges.

male face/three-quarter view/exercises

EXERCISES

1. Copy three front, three side and three three-quarter view faces from this section.
2. Choose pictures of different types of men from a magazine or newspaper (e.g. college student, businessman, soldier) and draw their faces.
3. Fill a page with men's eyes, noses and mouths.
4. Draw a three-quarter croquis wearing an outfit (i) for the weekend, (ii) for a business meeting (iii) for travel and (iv) to play a sport.
5. Draw a young man dressed to go out to a club in leather and denim.

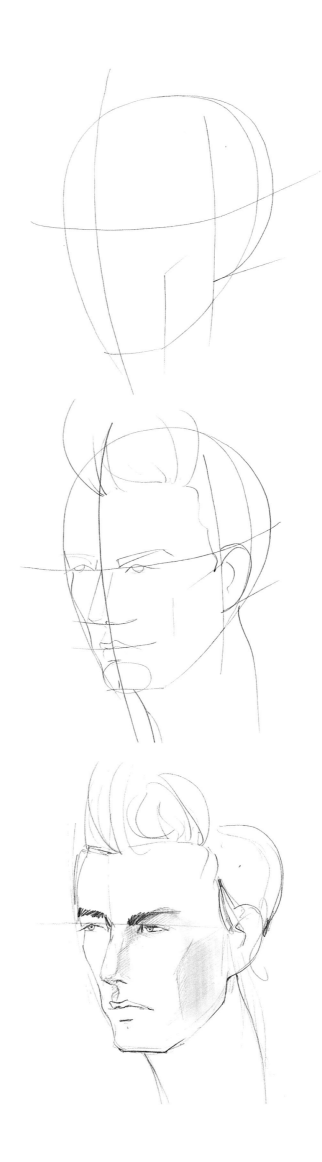

male face/
various views

male face/
front view

337

male face/
various views

Position of lapels in front and three-quarter /three-quarter-side figures. Make sure the lapels are correctly placed in relation to the center-front line in all angles of poses.

Men's suits do not always have to be drawn with stiff, formal poses.
Relaxed poses are often effective for showing off more formal garments.

men in suit/jacket
contemporary poses

Note the position of the belt and pant cuffs—lower than for women: the cuffs break over the top of the shoes.

young man in jacket/pants
contemporary pose

This figure is seen from a slightly lower eye level, making the line of the jacket bend upwards and giving the drawing a more dynamic feel, almost as though captured in a walking pose by a camera.

young men/
contemporary poses

Using poses with more diagonals—outstretched arms, bent knees, bodies leaning away from the vertical—suggests motion, creating a more dynamic and youthful look to the garments.

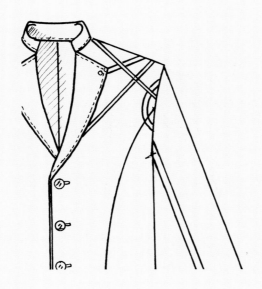

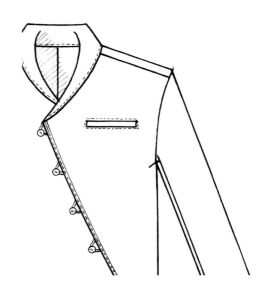

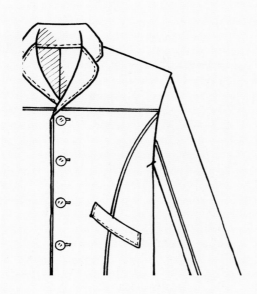

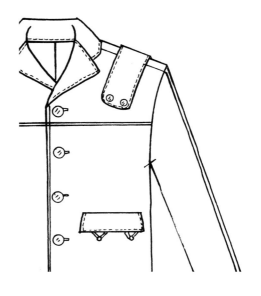

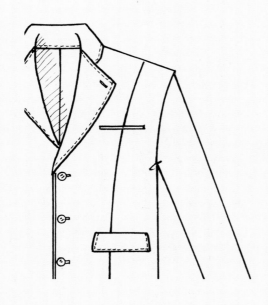

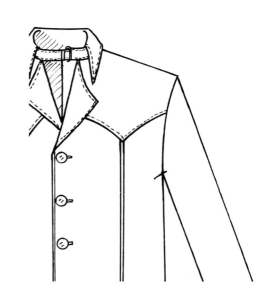

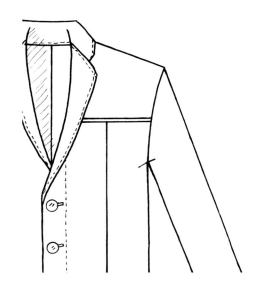

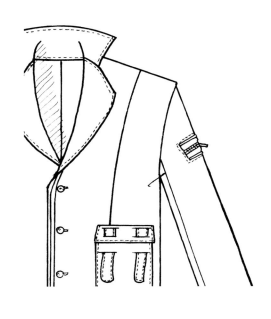

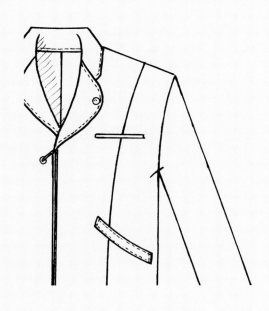

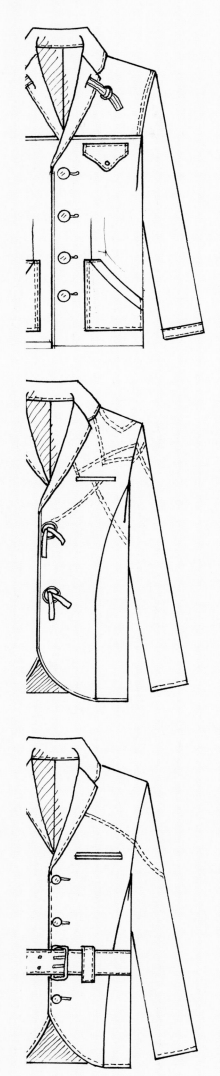

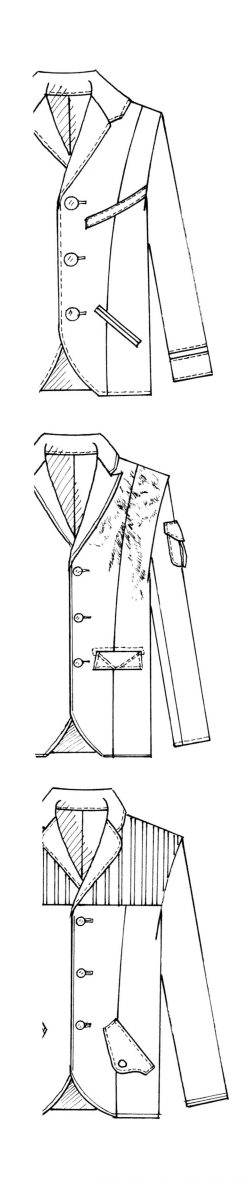

mens' jacket styles— designer and retro

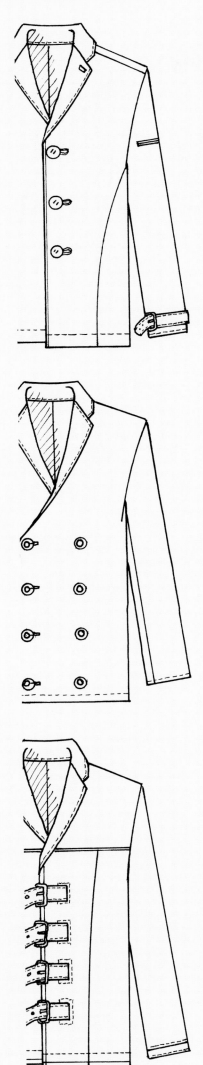

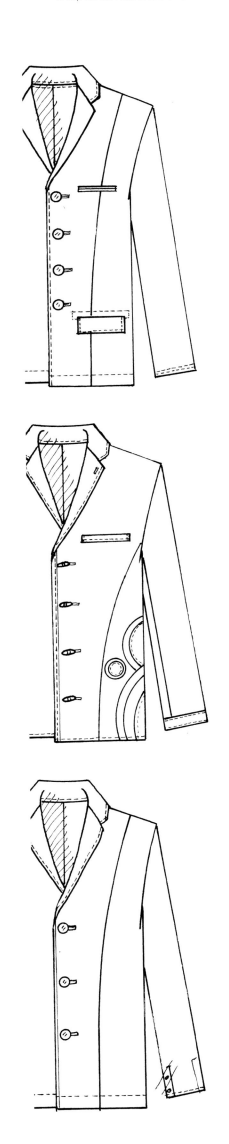

shirts

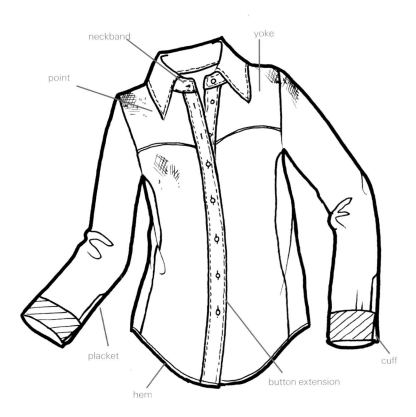

Parts of shirt with tailored, rolled collar.

SHIRTS

Shirts, though now often worn by women, are traditionally one of men's staple garments and are worn in a wide variety of formal, informal, casual and active sporting occasions. Traditional shirts close in front, others close behind or pull on over the head; some shirts have long hems that tuck inside the pants and others have hems of varying lengths worn either in or out of the pants. In men's shirts long hems are common, in women's less so (though they sometimes imitate men's). Remember that men's shirts button left over right, women's right over left.

Most shirts contain some degree of tailoring: dress and formal shirts are fully tailored, and other less formal shirts have less. The con-structional details common to most shirts are the following:

YOKES.

The yoke is the part of the shirt that fits across the shoulders. Yokes extend in varying lengths down the front or back of the garment, or both, and the back and front parts of the shirt are attached to them.

COLLARS

Shirts are made with a wide variety of collar types—they continually change shape and size with fashion trends. Some shirts are made with detachable collars and others without collars. Collars are usually attached to the yoke with a neckband that allows the collar to stand up over the body of the garment. The collar neckband is closed either with a button or stud aligned with the buttons on the band that runs along the placket—the opening—at the front of the shirt. (A placket is the name for any of the slits inserted into shirts or blouses to make them easier to put on and take off; they can be located at the sides, front, neck, back or wrists.)

BANDS/BUTTONS/BUTTONHOLES

As a rule the buttons are sewn onto the exten-sion, or band, that extends down the front of the shirt from the neckband to the hem. Buttons should be placed at equal distances down the band; the size of the buttonholes varies with the size of the buttons. Men's dress shirts usually have small buttons and button-holes.

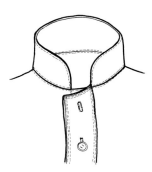

Band collar

Rolled collar

Rolled collar

wing collar

Spread collar

CUFFS

Sleeves end in cuffs, either made of a separate piece of fabric sewn onto the sleeve or formed by folding over the end of the sleeve. Cuffs are a prominent fashion feature of shirts and there is a large variety of types. Make sure that cuffs are curved—drawn as ellipses around the arm—and are seen peeking out of the bottoms of jacket sleeves, sometimes adorned with cufflinks.

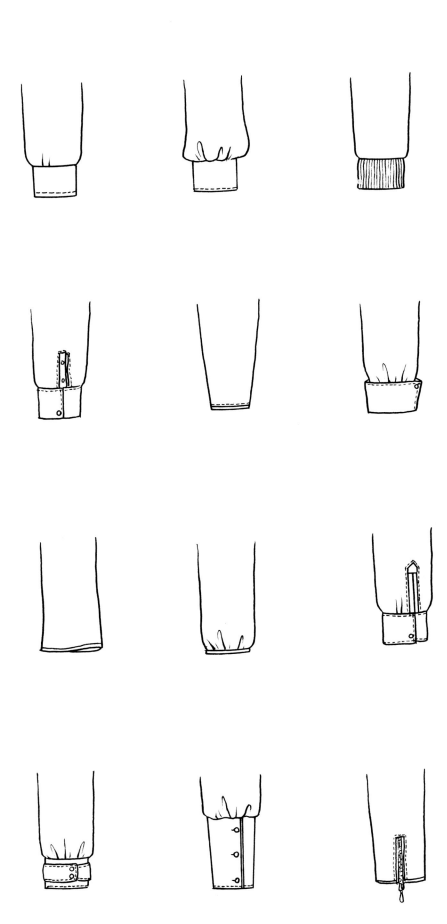

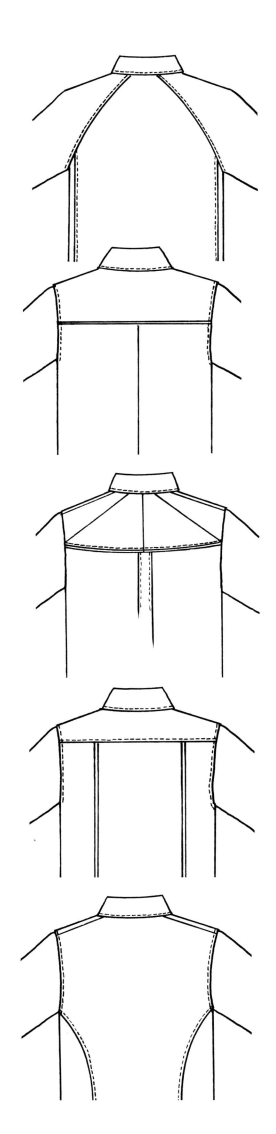
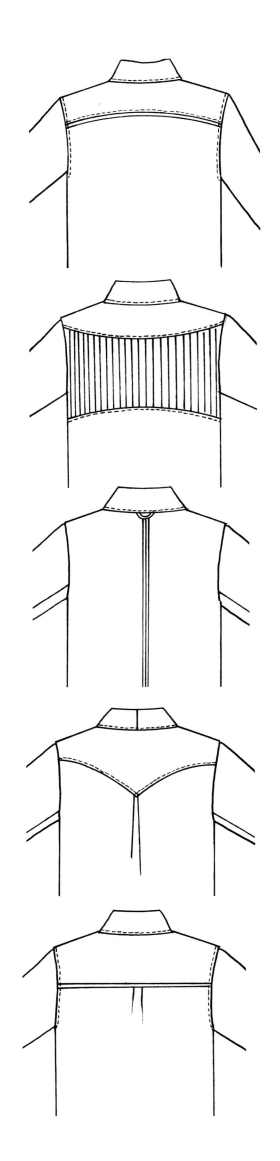

young man/
contemporary pose

A typical male pose—hand-in-pocket. Note how this pose affects the shape of the jacket: it opens up the front of the jacket, revealing the silhouette of the pants and their fit at the waist and the details of the shirt.

The variety of poses for young men's fashion reflect the variety of young men's attitudes: youthful, energetic, athletic, happy, tough, nonchalant, street-wise, thoughtful and more.

young men/
contemporary poses

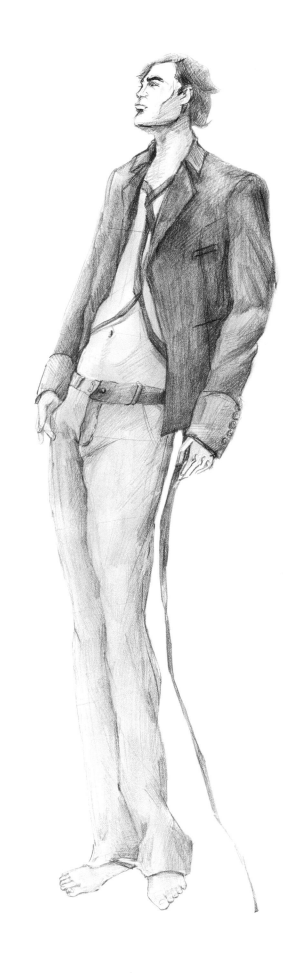

young men/ contemporary poses

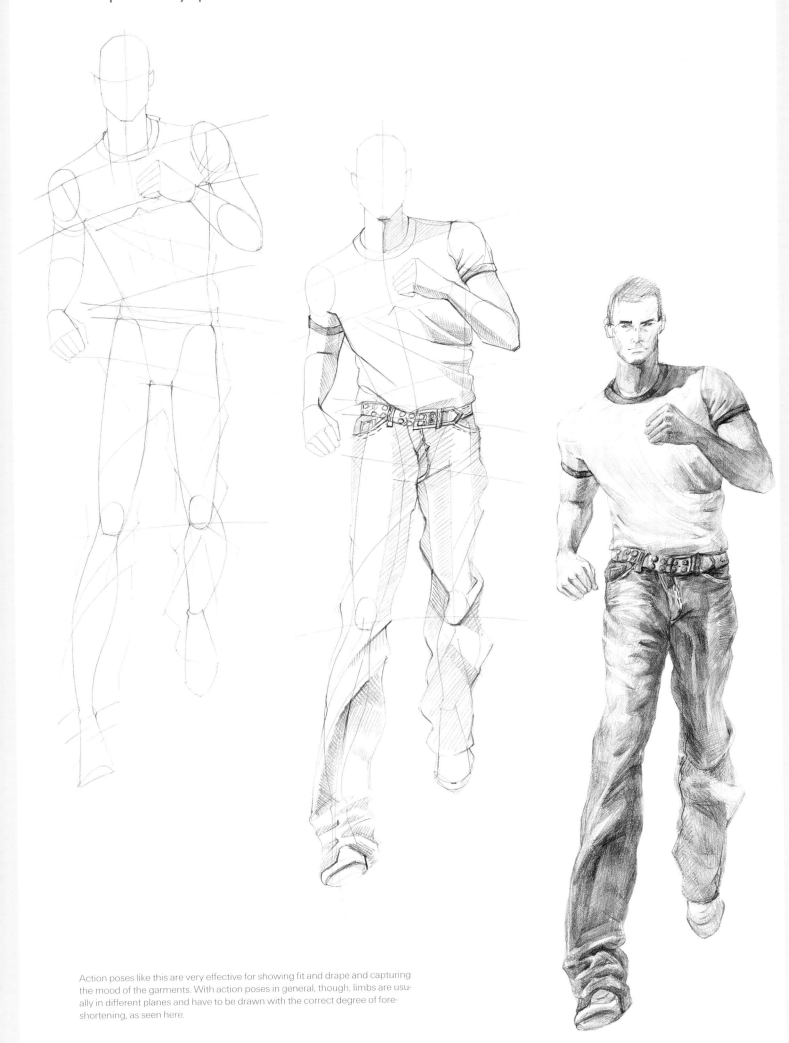

Action poses like this are very effective for showing fit and drape and capturing the mood of the garments. With action poses in general, though, limbs are usually in different planes and have to be drawn with the correct degree of foreshortening, as seen here.

men´s accessories

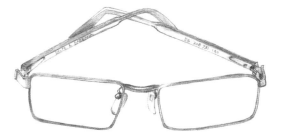

men's flats/ templates

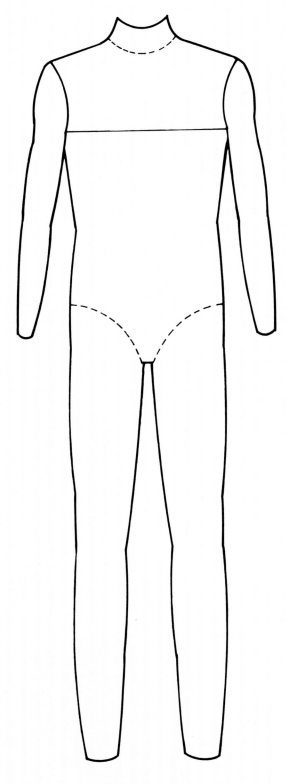

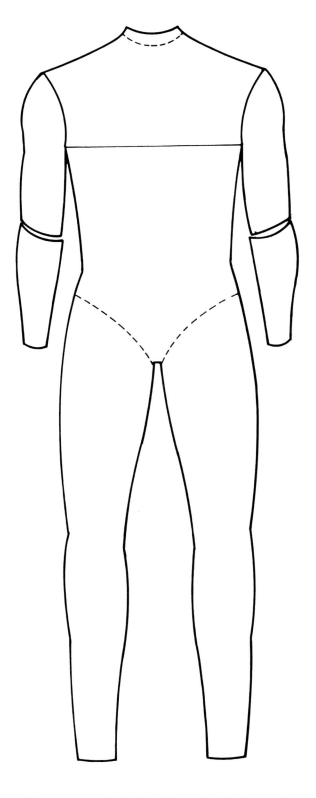

Traditional men's eight-head flat template. Most of the examples of flats included in this section are developed on croquis of this size or a slightly slimmer young man's template..

Contemporary men's eight-head flat template. The chest and shoulders are broader and waist relatively slimmer than the traditional template. Used frequently when drawing active sportswear.

men's flats/
jackets

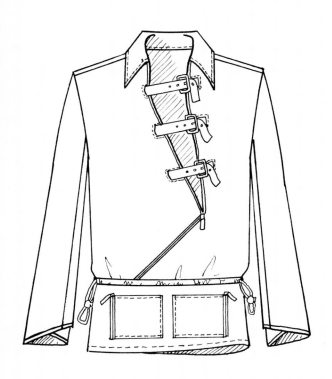

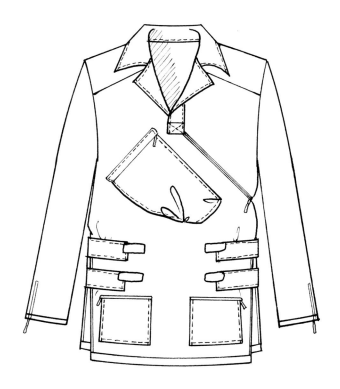

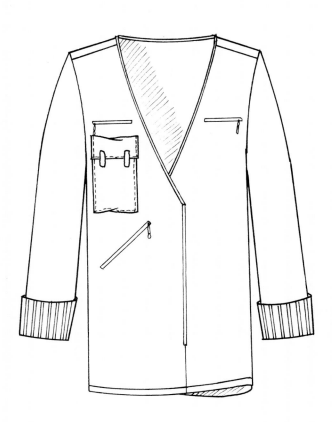

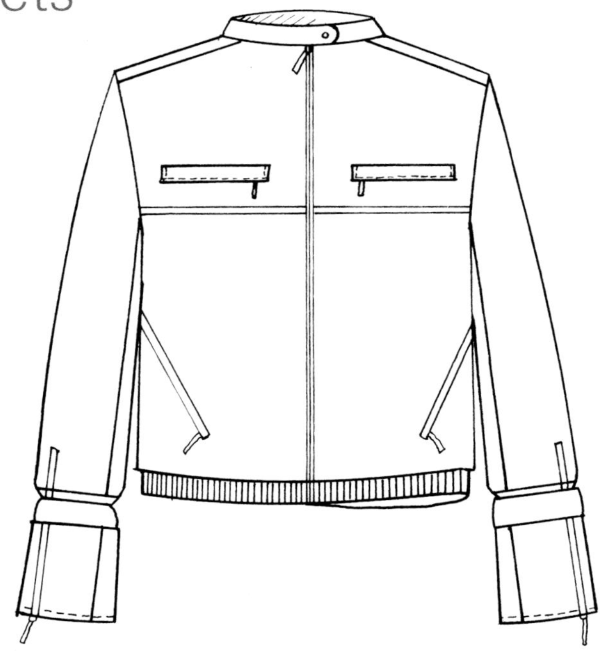

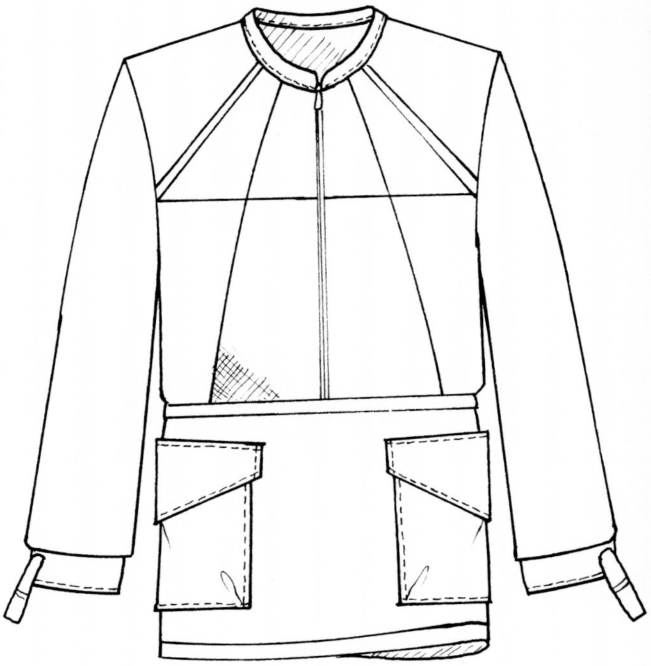

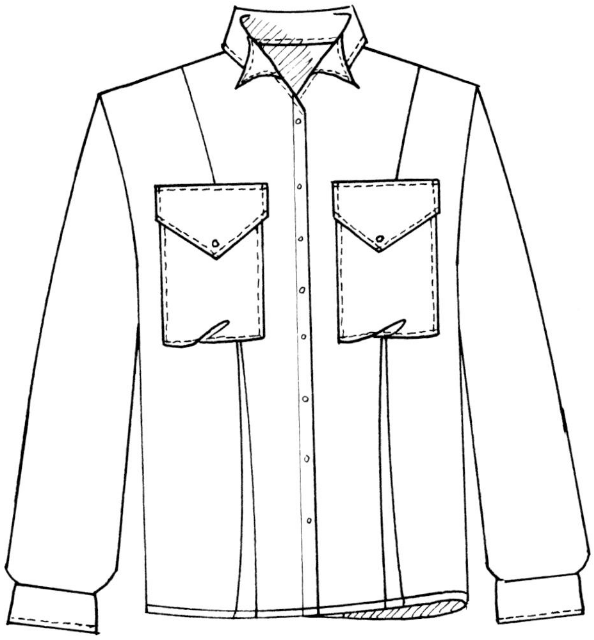

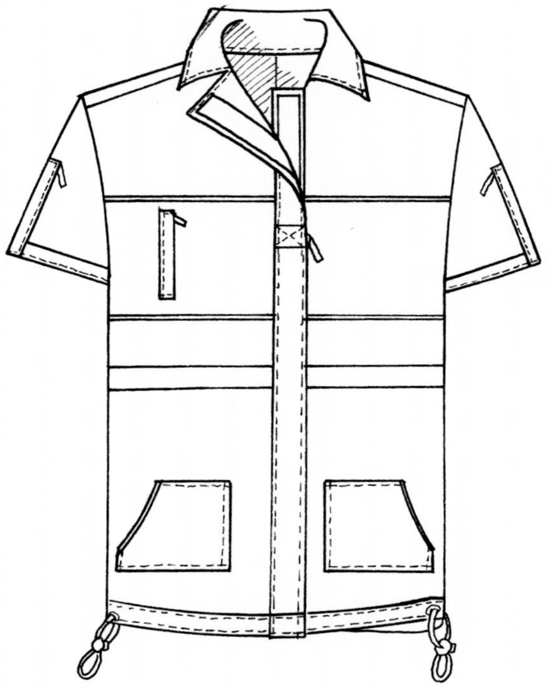

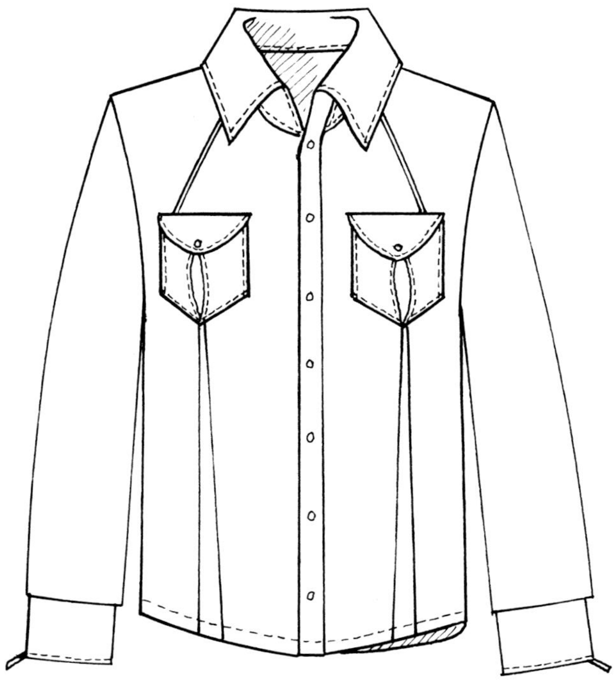

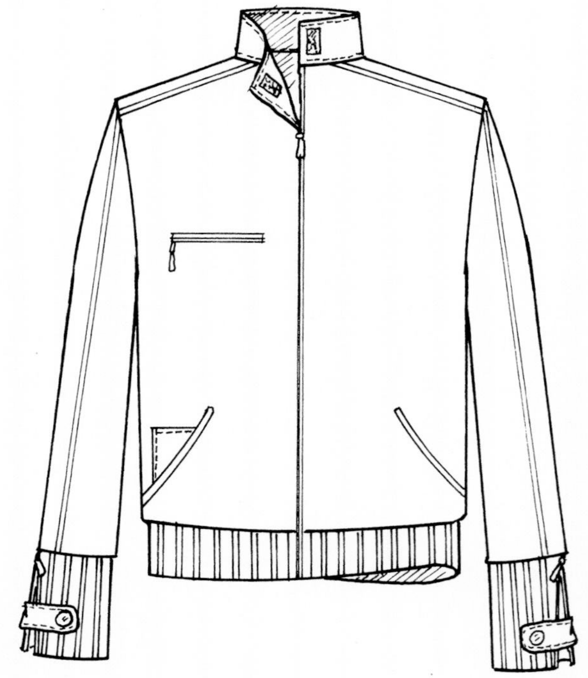

men's flats/ jackets

men's flats/
shirts

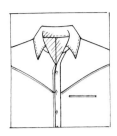
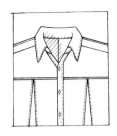
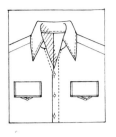

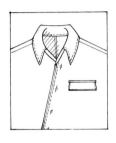

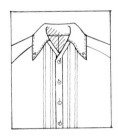
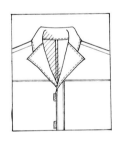

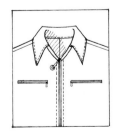

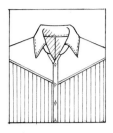

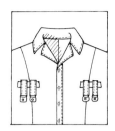

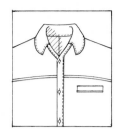

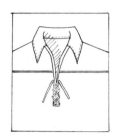

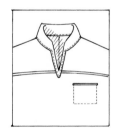

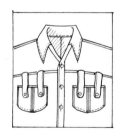

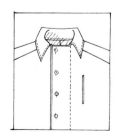

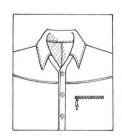

men's flats/
underwear/swimwear

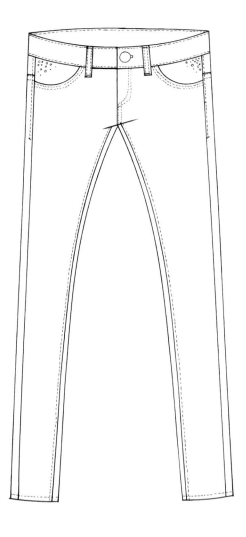

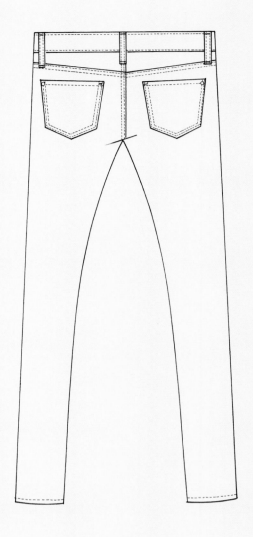

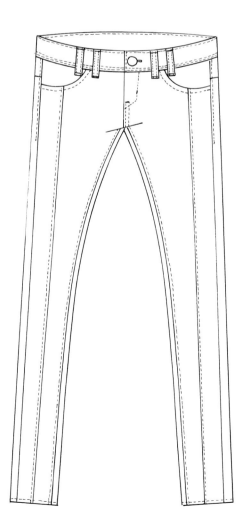

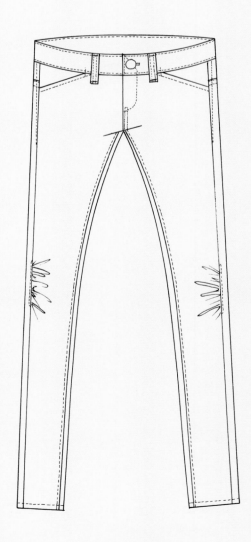

men's flats/
pants

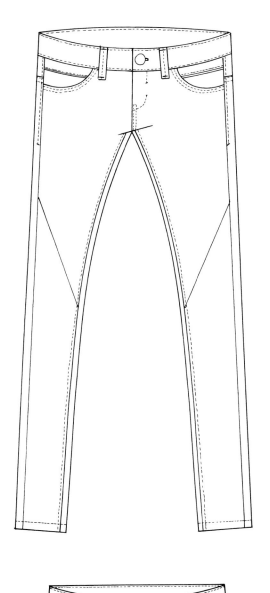

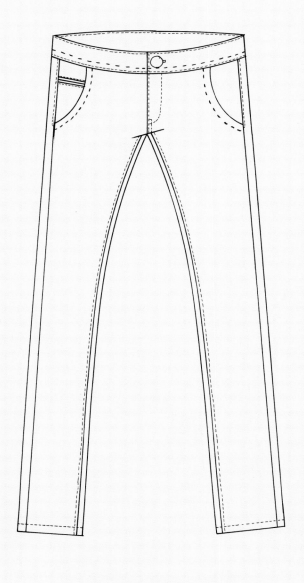

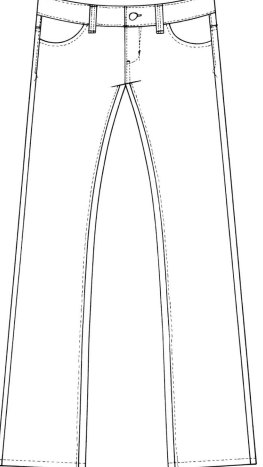

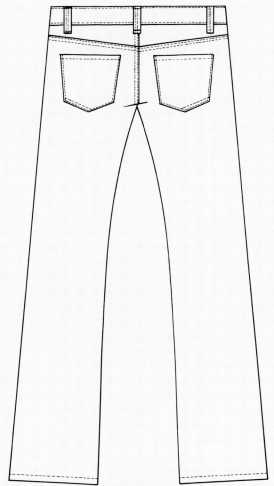

chapter eight: children and children's clothing

drawing children/
young children's croquis

DRAWING CHILDREN

Renaissance artists—the great Leonardo da Vinci just as much as lesser artists—were able to master the complexities of perspective drawing and drawing the adult figure and face, but for the most part, for some unexplained reason, never mastered the art of drawing children: most of the children in Renaissance paintings look like little old men and women. Children do not really look like old men and women, of course, and artists in following centuries were able to capture their likenesses admirably, but we must avoid the Renaissance (or any other approach) that distorts how children actually are; children are different from adults in many ways, and must be drawn with care if they are to look natural and convincing.

Children's bodies and faces have different proportions, shapes and textures to adult bodies and faces. Children's faces and facial features are soft and round with few planes. Until they are almost into their teens, little bone structure can be discerned in their faces, or muscles on their bodies (That was the main mistake the Renaissance artists made—they drew scaled-down, developed "adult" facial and body features rather than real children's features.) Because of this, children should be drawn with a light touch to convey the softness of their features. The shapes of the accessories—toys, bags and so on—that children favor at different ages can often be used effectively in a drawing to echo the rounded shapes of their faces and bodies. Children's bodies change quickly from year to year and so care has to be taken to draw the croquis that corresponds to their age. The different croquis are shown here and the differences between them should be studied.

The ways children differ from adults other than the purely physical are also significant when portraying them in fashion drawings: Children are not sophisticated in their facial expressions and bodily poses; they are loose-limbed and playful and often pose in ways that

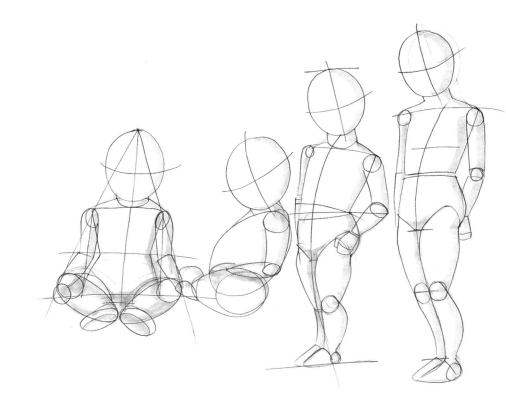

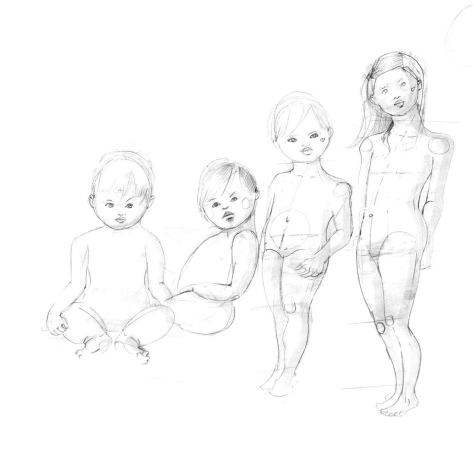

Young children's croquis: infants; toddler, small child.

older children's croquis/exercises

would look silly or awkward in an adult. This is not to say, though that they do not have personalities: children are (usually, but not always!) sweet and innocent, but also complex and multi-dimensional: modern designers create beautiful garments for children that recognize and respond to this. To do justice to them, then, children's croquis should be drawn with typical natural poses and attention to detail.

EXERCISES

1. Copy photos of babies, toddlers, small children, older children and teenagers from magazines and copy.
2. Draw a page of babies and children of different ages and sexes.
3. Select five garments from the flats at the end of this chapter and draw on children of three different ages.
4. Draw a group of children in pants and sweaters and the same group in party dresses.
5. Show a little girl and a little boy of different ages going to (i) school, (ii) a party, (iii) the beach and (iv) to church or a wedding.

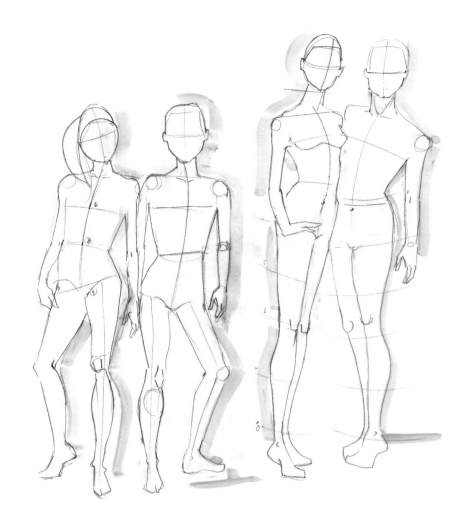

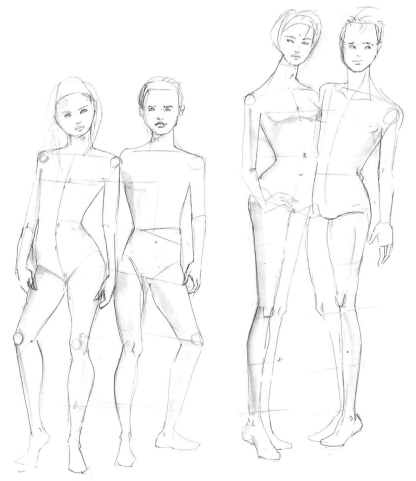

Older children's croquis: 7–9; 11–12.

children/characteristics
of different ages

PHYSICAL CHARACTERISTICS OF
CHILDREN OF DIFFERENT AGES
The usual age group categories for chil-
dren are INFANTS/LAYETTES,
TODDLERS, YOUNG GIRLS AND BOYS
(3–6), OLDER GIRLS AND BOYS (6–12),
JUNIORS/TEENAGERS (12–18).
The croquis and main physical features
corresponding to the different categories
of children are as follows:

INFANTS/LAYETTES.
Generally drawn with 3 – 3½ head croquis. Small children have low eye levels—
about two-thirds way down from the top
of the head (adult eyes are half way down
the head). Heads and limbs are rounded
so they will bounce off hard objects. No
necks are visible. As they do not yet walk,
crawl or stand infants are usually shown
sitting or laid down with feet pointing
inwards. Infants have little hair, and the little hair they *do* have is fine and close to
the head.

TODDLERS.
The croquis is about 4½ heads. Growth
from infant has occurred mainly in the
legs. The face is round and there is very little definition in the features. The eyes
appear disproportionately large as they
are the same absolute size as adult eyes.
The limbs are rounded and well padded;
still no necks are visible. Hair is thicker and
more evenly spread over the head.
Toddlers can be shown sitting or in rather
awkward standing or "toddling" poses.

Top—infant/layette. Small babies cannot sit or hold up their heads and have to
be supported in any position. Note that there are no hard edges to any of the
features. Bottom—infant, 3–6 months. By this age infants can support their
own heads and sit comfortably. Note the position of the legs—they splay out
from the body and then bend back in from the knees so the feet are together.

children
children's clothes

YOUNG GIRLS AND BOYS: The croquis is about 5 ½ heads. This age group has become longer in the torso than toddlers and necks are defined. Children start to participate in decisions about their clothes around this age. Accessories start to become important-bows, hair pieces, backpacks, belts, shoes and so on. Small boys start to have angles and planes in their faces (up until this age there is very little difference in the physical appearance of the sexes). Although still awkward in many poses, children of this age are now fully mobile and can be shown in a range of standing, walking and running poses.

OLDER GIRLS AND BOYS: The croquis is 6½–7 heads. Girls especially start to grow in their legs around 8 or 9 years old. Bone structures become more defined, poses are more graceful. Eye levels have moved up to about the same level as adults—half-way down the head. Vanity reigns: clothes become extremely important and a wide and increasing range caters to the children's and parents' whims.

JUNIORS/TEENAGERS: The croquis is 8 heads. The appearance is almost exactly like an adult except the facial features are slightly more rounded. Poses are generally more exuberant than adults, with arms and hips akimbo and considerable attitude displayed. Colors in general are saturated and vibrant; skin tone is healthy and rosy.

CHILDREN'S CLOTHES
The variety of children's clothes has grown enormously. Children wear a full range of clothes designed exclusively for them as well as miniaturized versions of adults' clothes. The market for children's clothes continues to grow rapidly with parents' increasing affluence and generally lower cost of clothing.

Children's clothes are usually made from soft and simple fabrics. Head openings are usually proportionately larger than in adult clothes, otherwise there is little difference between children's and adult's clothes.

Top—positions of babies' legs; bottom-study of (high fashion) toddler's face.

Toddlers have little sense of balance. They are very naughty and make cute, awkward poses. Feet turn in and limbs are akimbo. All limbs and features are rounded.

children/
toddlers' poses

More toddlers. Note that at this age children are still wearing diapers; clothes
have to be roomy enough to accomodate them, and they should be indicated
by fullness around the bottom.

children/
little children's poses

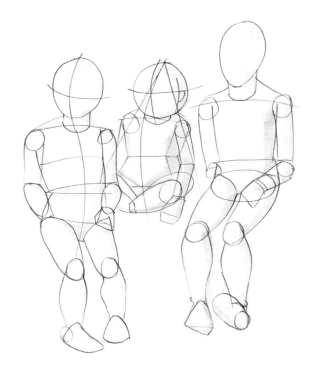

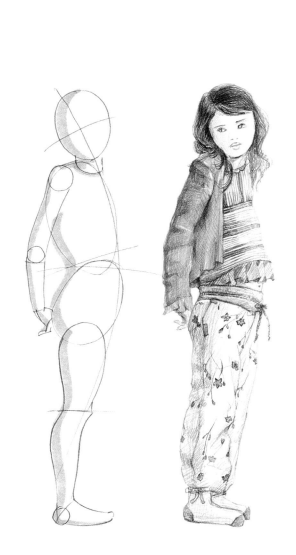

Top, little children—2, 3 and 4. Attitudes are playful with mouths turned up in smiles. Bottom, left and right, slightly older children—4 and 6. Limbs and features are still rounded at these ages.

children/
little children's poses

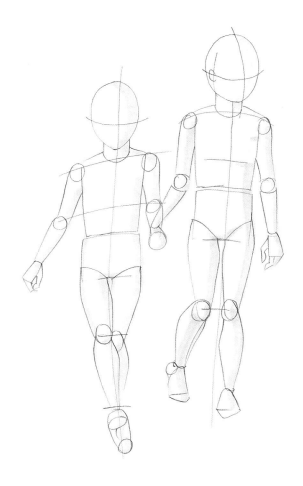

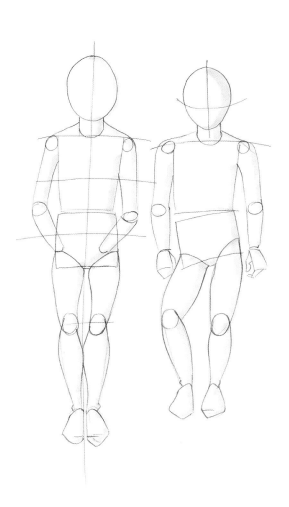

Clothes for different seasons. Top, summer clothes; bottom, autumn clothes. Children about 6.

11–12 year olds

Party clothes, 11–12 year olds.

Fashionable outfit, 12 year old.

Teenagers. Note that men's faces start to
square up in mid to late teens.

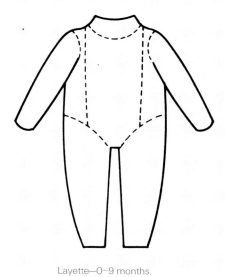

Layette—0–9 months.

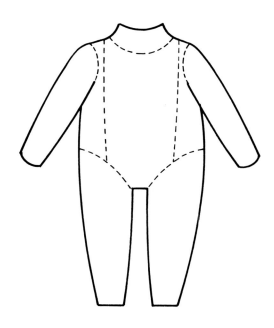

Infant—9–24 months.

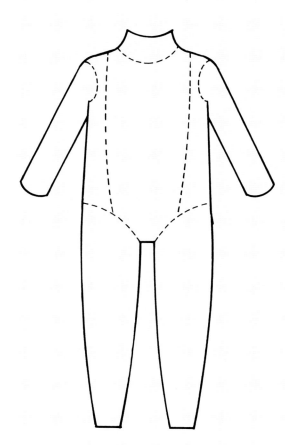

Toddler—2–4 years.

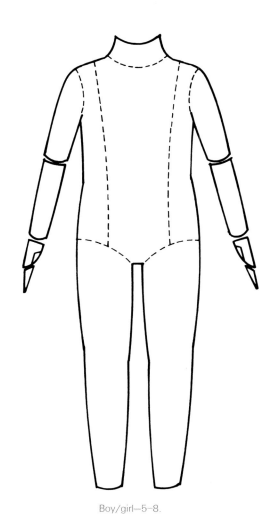

Boy/girl—5–8.

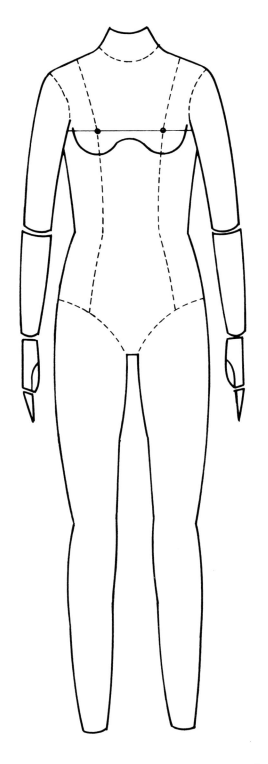
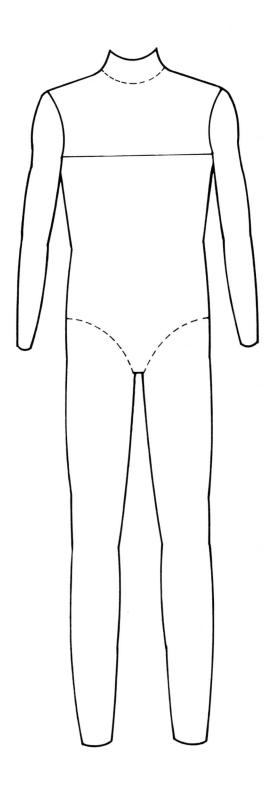

Junior girl and boy flat templates.

children's flats/
pants/dungarees

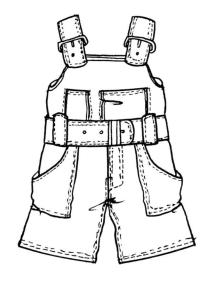

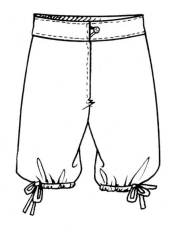

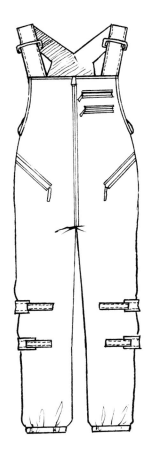

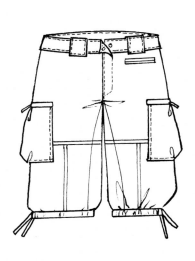

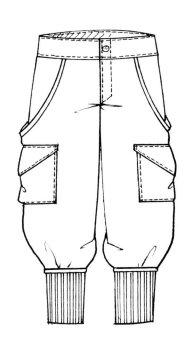

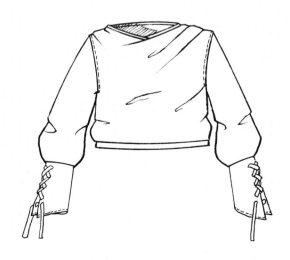

children's flats/tops/
jackets/skirts

chapter nine:
fashion drawing
in the real world

interviews with

ruben alterio
artist, fashion illustrator, designer

mona may
film and theater costume designer

bernhard willhelm
fashion designer

jean-charles de castelbajac
fashion designer

fashion drawing in the real world

Fashion drawing is seen extensively the world over. It is a universal language used in many industries. As well as in the fashion, apparel and textile industries: we find it in the fashion press, TV, the film industry, theater, opera, multimedia, toys, advertising, publishing and many other areas of business. This chapter gives a glimpse into the lives of some people who use fashion drawing in their daily work.

The people interviewed here are from different backgrounds but are all well established in their professional careers. What they have to say will interest, and is relevant for, anyone who plans a career in fashion or who is already using fashion drawing in their daily work. Although each of those interviewed here has a strongly individualistic approach to his or her profession, shining very clearly through all the interviews is the love of fashion, the passion to express ideas about fashion and art, and the understanding of the importance of drawing as a tool of communication and self-expression in their work.

Gucci

Badgley Mischka

Guy Laroche

ruben alterio

NR: Ruben, please tell us about yourself: How did you come to be a fashion illustrator?

RA: I was born in Buenos Aires. When I was 13 years old my father, a painter, registered me in the National School of Fine Arts (Escuela Nacional de Bellas Artes) where I spent 6 happy years. In 1969, after an exhibition in Buenos Aires, I travelled to Brazil, where I learnt to live by drawing decorative objects and also from my painting. Some years later, in Paris, where I now live, I was introduced to the theater, music, poetry and other 'happenings' without leaving aside my pencils and brushes. One day, already installed in my "atelier" (studio), the editor at the time of a magazine called "Fashion in Painting" (" La mode en peinture") suggested I work there. I was surprised because my painting really did not try to be illustrative. I was doubtful, but I accepted, thinking that if I did it I should approach illustration in the same way as painting, in a minimalist manner, with few references.

NR: Were your major influences fashion designers, artists or illustrators, or maybe all three? Could you tell us some of the greatest influences on your work.

RA: My influences come from the history of art, my father and, above all else, observation.

NR: For me your work is extraordinary. It has so many abstract elements, and reminds me often of beautiful abstract expressionist paintings. Yet it conveys a wealth of information on line and silhouette, color and texture and invariably captures that intangible mood and essence of a garment. Despite the abstract elements, how important to you in your work are the basic rules of the croquis and drawing technique?

RA: They are important because they allow you to return to the essence of things in order to arrive at a freer state.

ruben alterio

Alberta ferretti

Couture Givenchy

NR: When you make a painting of a garment do you first draw it?

RA: It depends on the subject and the occasion.

NR: What is the difference in approach to drawing or painting a garment which already exists and drawing to express ideas in one's imagination?

RA: Creation or execution ? I believe there is creativitiy in the execution, but all this would take a long time to fully discuss.....

NR: Do you work directly with designers in the creation of garments, helping them to express ideas which they cannot express themselves because they lack the necessary drawing skills?

RA: No, that has never happened to me in fashion as such, but it has happened in other areas like decorative book design.

NR: How do you view the increased use of computers in fashion design? What do you think is the future of fashion illustration—does it have one?

RA: Why not let the different ways of working co-exist? Why photography yes, painting no.... cinema yes, photography no....cinema no, video yes.... and finally, eveything no and the computer yes? Enough of totalitarianisms—let the future unfold! (Voila l'avenir!)

NR: Maestro Alterio, what for you are the elements which most contribute to a fashion illustration being truly excellent? What advice would you give to someone who wishes to make good fashion drawings from their creative ideas?

RA: To show from within his or her nature as an artist the nature of the "other" as in a portrait, a landscape or other subject which we have to draw. Fashion illustration is not my principal means of creative expression— I dedicate most of my time to painting. But as in all the other "plastic" arts and expressions in which I am happily asked to collaborate with other artists, they are closely connected, like the branches of a tree, and complement each other.

NR: Thank you Ruben.

Issey Miyake

mona may

Mona May in her closet.

CAREER BACKGROUND:

Mona May graduated from the Fashion Institute of Design and Merchandising (FIDM) in Los Angeles in 1985 with a degree in fashion design. She grew up in Germany, her mother is Polish, her father German. After graduating from FIDM, she went to Berlin and worked as an apprentice fashion designer for two seasons. She returned to the LA in 1987 and started working on commercials, videos and low-budget films.

Mona returned to LA because she was in love, not because of the lure of Hollywood. At the time of her return, she had had no involvement in costume design: her return to LA set her in a new direction.

Costume designers, like many of the professions working in Hollywood, are independent freelancers. Mona's big career break came when she designed the costumes for the film *Clueless* directed by Amy Heckerling. *Clueless* was a hit and put Mona, as well as many of the actors and crew, on the Hollywood map. Mona is now much in demand by Hollywood film studios.

NR: Mona, what exactly *is* costume design for a movie?

MM: Costume design is the whole process of creating the look of the clothes used throughout a movie, TV or commercial, even if it's a contemporary and not a period movie. The clothes create the characters. They tell us what sort of people they are, where they live, where they shop, whether they buy their clothes at K Mart or buy designer clothes. It really is a matter of getting into the psychology of the characters and helping the director and actors to get across the idea, very clearly and quickly, of who a person is. The costume designer also has to show the change characters go through during the movie in the way they dress. In *Never Been Kissed*, a movie I worked on with Drew Barrymore, there were forty six costume changes. It's a great example. It's a contemporary movie and you begin seeing her as a mouse, a bookworm, then through the film you see her transformation into a beautiful, mature young woman.

NR: Mona, walk us through the process of designing costumes for a big movie.

MM: Well, first I get a request from the producer or director of a film to meet up and discuss ideas for a movie. I always read the script before I attend the meeting, and at the meeting we discuss what the costumes should look like.

NR: And when do you put pencil to paper?

MM: Right away. Sometimes in the meeting. Sometimes I even bring my sketch artist to the meeting, if time is pressing and I have to get my ideas across. Also it depends with whom you're working. Sometimes you're working with very creative people who understand your ideas. A lot of times you can be working with men who have no idea about fashion. You have to present directors with ideas which you think are fashionable but also agree with their sensibility and vision of what the leads should look like. So straightaway I start doing very simple sketches myself or hire someone to do them for me if I don't have time. I usually have between six and eight weeks of preparation time from being hired to starting to shoot, and there is an enormous amount to do. As well as design, I am involved with budget and accounting and also supervise the making of the clothes. Besides this I have to involve the actors, shop, get swatches. I usually take 35mm photos of all the fittings and then present them to the director and the actor. It's one big elimination process until we get what we want. I also present boards with the pictures showing the scene numbers and all the possibilities we should look at.

I do a lot to prepare for a movie—more than most other designers I'm sure. That's the best part for me, doing the sketches, getting the swatches, reading *Collezioni*, finding out what's happening in Europe. The movie *Loser* was shot in New York City and I met with underground designers, people whose clothes might be seen in Barneys in a year's time. It's about taking the extra step. A lot of costume designers don't go as far as I do. Often there's no need. A small town movie, a military movie, even a James Bond movie—he wears the same beautiful Brioni suits the whole time. You just call when you need a new one. The babe has a couple of gorgeous dresses and the designers send them to you and you get a couple for the doubles because they're always getting wet.

NR: What about working with the actors?

MM: Actors can be very insecure. They see themselves on a huge screen where every imperfection is magnified a thousand times. You have to work with them so they feel comfortable in their clothes, so when they walk on the set they feel like the character and they can really do the best job possible for the director. So that's my job. If wool makes them feel itchy we can't use wool. I'm as much a psycologist as a designer. I often have to give them pep talks to make them feel good before going on set.

NR: Tell us about the clothes you design.

MM: What I do is quite wild. I often set the tone of the movie and a lot of my movies are known for the wardrobe. A movie is made a year ahead of release so I have to predict, almost as fashion designers predict, what's going to happen a year from now and what kids are going to like. I have to really be on top of things and do my research well—focus on the street life. As I go to clubs in London, Berlin or LA, I am constantly absorbing new fashion trends and ideas.

NR: And what about actually making the clothes?

MM: A film is shot over a three-month period, so you have to make sure that the clothes fit well, that they are made well, that they can be dry-cleaned several times over a period of three months. It's all about construction—it's not about creating something which looks good for five minutes and then is thrown away, as might be the case for a garment you're showing on a catwalk. You're really into detail because on the movie screen everything is big. Unless you want your stitching to look messed up for a purpose it has to be done professionally. I have to use certain people I trust for alterations. There are people I've worked with over the years who can take my sketch and make something that looks just like it. I think that's how you move ahead in this business—by providing this attention to detail.

NR: Most of your clothes are made to couture standard, then?

MM: Yes, I think so. Look at the clothes in *Clueless* for example. They all fit beautifully. Also, what I didn't mention is creating the *illusion* of beauty. You get actresses with all kinds of bodies—bigger boobs, smaller boobs, big butts, small butts. It's up to me to create the best proportion, the best fit and the best illusion of their amazing beauty (as well as

Concept drawing

Mia Sorvino and Lisa Kudrow in *Romy and Michele's Highschool Reunion*

Concept drawing for *Clueless*

Stacey Dash and Alicia Silverstone in *Clueless*

make-up and hair). A lot of these actresses do not have a perfect body, but after going to fashion school I know what to do to make the most of their looks. Where the skirt should end, where to push the bra, where to pad.

NR: What influences you in your designs?

MM: Everything can inspire me. I travel a lot between films. I go to Asia, to India. Berlin, my home town, is one of the pulsating places in Europe. There's the most amazing underground culture going·on there with the East meeting the West. It's what London once was.

NR: Do you usually come in on budget in your films?

MM: I have to take care. I will go to any lengths to get exactly what I need—it could the latest thing from Japan and I have to pay $500 for it. People know that I'm like that, but I usually come in on budget. But it's difficult to come in under budget because making clothes is expensive. Fabrics are very expensive—they can cost $150 a yard. And budgets are getting smaller—the economics of the film business is changing.

NR: I saw the movie *Romy and Michele (Romy and Micheles's High School Reunion)* and noticed the shoes. Do you have someone who builds things like that from scratch?

MM: Sometimes. Sometimes we just get the glitter and the spray paint if we don't have the actual shoes. That's movie-making: you have to be spontaneous and ready for anything. Maybe the actress is bloated and decides that the dress she loved yesterday now makes her look fat and she's not going to wear it. So you have to have the skills of craft and painting and making anything out of anything. A bad hair day— what can you do?—maybe divert attention with earrings or a headband. The process is also very interesting because it's group-oriented. A fashion designer can force ideas. Here, you have to work with maybe a hundred people and interact with each one of them so it comes together. Most of the films cost twenty-five million dollars. *8MM* cost sixty million. My budgets range from two hundred thousand to five hundred thousand and I am completely responsible for the full amount. Things have to be delivered on time. If something does not

arrive I cannot say Kasha or Irena didn't do it. It's my .... on the line—they'll fire *me*.

NR: How much sketching do you have to do?

MM: It depends on the film. I can make between forty and one hundred sketches per movie. It depends how much time I have, how much money I have to hire a sketch artist, how involved the design process is. For example, in the movie *The Loser* I only had two characters who had really important transformations, so I really didn't do a lot with the other characters—or example the roommates. I really concentrated on the Loser and the love interest. Her clothes were very specific. She was a young girl who was influenced by the 80s, but in a new millenium way. She never went home, she always had a rucksack with clothes in it. She worked as a waitress in a strip bar and by day went to college. You had to believe that all her clothes were in the rucksack. Very interesting. I also do 'mini-sketches'—what happens each day with a person. Say one day she is wearing a skirt and pants, but she never went home and the next day she is wearing the skirt with tights, and it is just another outfit.

NR: Whom do you work with most on the movie?

MM: The most important person I work with is the Production Designer, and also the decorator. They set the look of the place-the exterior and interior of the house, whether the bedding is Calvin Klein or Laura Ashley. How does that go with the clothes? A character can't have dime-store clothes and Calvin Klein sheets. Everything has to work colorwise, too. We can't have someone sitting on a couch wearing green if the walls are green. We go into the details of each scene and setting.

NR: Do you use a computer in the design process?

MM: I have little personal time to sit at a computer. If I were very advanced, maybe the computer could make the design process quicker. But everything is still in early stages. What would be good is if I used a digital camera and then print the pictures from the computer and maybe have a flip book instead of my boards.

NR: There must be a lot of sensitivity to color.

Loser concept drawing with pantones

Jason Biggs in costume on the set of *Loser*

mona may

MM: Yes. I work with pantones and present those in a fan or book. The final process can be very different. I have to be fluid. The final product might be dyed and then look horrible on the actor. Or the director of photography might say, "No, with the lighting we're using you have to punch up the color". Also there is often a palette. In *Clueless* we did not use any browns or grays. As a result the film looked beautiful, just very vibrant colors. In *Loser* we did not use any blue, so we created a very warm "Fall-in-New York" type palette. The kids couldn't even wear blue jeans. The director of photography used a lot of yellow light and I used greens and burgundies. Creating a palette and texture is very important. I worked with Joel Shumacher on *8MM* and everthing in the film has been over-dyed and dirty. Everything is gray, mousy and dark, giving the film the kind of "ickyness" he wanted it to have.

NR: What skills should someone have to do what you do?

MM: Well, they have to know how to draw. At first I could not afford to hire Felipe (Felipe Sanchez, Mona's sketch artist) so I had to do everything myself. Even if they're very simple drawings or collages, sketches help you to sell an idea for a costume. A lot of times by saying
"I want to use an A-line skirt", people don't understand what you're talking about. The way you show how to draw textures is really important. Are the clothes flowing and light or are they heavy? Even if you're not a great drawer it's important to be able to get your idea over in some form. I also think you have to have the sensibility of proportion: who people are, race, culture, where they come from. Body type is important.

NR: It's important for you, then, to have drawing skills as a fashion designer?

MM: Yes. A lot of costume designers don't have those skills because a lot of times there is not a lot of preparation time, but for me drawing is important.

NR: Mona, how did you get your foot on the first rung of the ladder in Hollywood?

MM: It was just through hard work. I didn't really have a portfolio to start with. Getting started involves hustling, going to interviews, schmoozing, constantly go through the battle being creative, assisting on films a lot. I didn't get an agent until I did *Clueless*, after people could see that I could make money for them. That's what the film business is about. You have to have a sense of humor, not to take what you're doing too seriously. If Drew Barrymore comes onto the set one day and hates your costume, you can't let it get to you. If all those things got to you you would go to pieces.

NR: Which costume designers do you most admire?

MM: Edith Head is the most famous one. I'm the young Edith Head (laughs). I like Colleen Atwood. She does a lot of interesting projects: *Edward Scissorhands, Mars Attack, Sleepy Hollow*. Interesting fantasy worlds. I love the *Star Wars* costumes. Trisha Biggar should win an award for them. Sandy Powell, the designer who did the costumes for *Elizabeth, Orlando* and *Velvet Underground* is amazing.

NR: Thank you Mona.

bernhard willhelm

NR: Bernhard, please tell me about your background and how you came to be a fashion designer.

BW: I am from a small city in Bavaria, Germany, called Uim—right out in the countryside. I really came to fashion by accident. I actually wanted to study biology but 2 of my friends went to fashion college in Germany, and I followed them.

NR: What are the major creative influences on your work? Is art a big influence?

BW: Right now I'm most influenced by print, fabric and graphic ideas. I think patternwork, graphics and fabrics should have the same value. I'm really into craft, childrens' and embroidery books at the moment. I also like traditional German costume , which is actually still worn in the area I come from. My favorite artist right now is Attila Richard Lukacs, an artist from Canada.

NR: How does drawing feature in the creative process?

BW: An idea just can be written in a sentence.

Drawing is more for the pattern process. Normally the first sketch is the best.

NR: How important is it for a fashion designer to acquire drawing skills and be able to express his or her ideas in this medium?

BW: For me creativity works best in a team. Drawing helps you to communicate easier. I realized at school that I have a quite good geometric memory. For me drawing and space go well together. Even when my drawings are always looking very flat there's a three-dimensional idea behind them.

NR: Do you use computers at any point in the design process? Is there a role for computers in the design of haute couture?

BW: We don't do haute couture . We don't use computers . They are only used in making an industrial pattern from a hand drawn one to cut the garments.

Thank you Bernard.

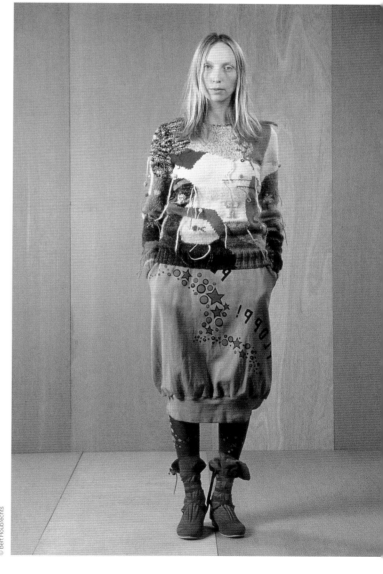

jean-charles de castelbajac

NR: Jean-Charles, please tell me about your background and how you came to be a fashion designer.

JCC: I come from a military background— my family have worn helmets for over one thousand years. Partly in reaction to that, and a wish to enter a more artistic field, I entered fashion. Also, I had a beautiful Swedish girlfriend who left me and I saw fashion as a convenient way to meet other beautiful girls.

When I was seventeen I went to Paris. It was May 1968—the time of the "evénèments", the student troubles, like you had at Berkeley. It was a shock for me. I found everyone wearing workclothes and military fatigues. I had not even finished my high-school diploma, but I knocked on the door of Raymond Lewy and became a cutter for four days.

I created my first collection for my mother—who had a fashion house, Ko and Co, in Limoges. My inspirations were my memories from boarding school, where I had spent twelve years from the age of five. I made a raincoat from a shower curtain and a coat from a blanket. These were my roots and the beginning of a tradition. Traditions and origins are very important for me today.

NR: What are the major creative influences on your work? Is art a big influence?

JCC: Art is a great influence. When I began working in fashion I became friendly with Robert Malaval and Alain Jacquet—French "Pop" artists. Later I became friends and worked with Andy Warhol and Robert Mapplethorpe. I always asked artists to do the invitations to my shows. I have also worked with artists who drew on muslin as part of a pret-a-porter collection. I have always been influenced by the functionality of clothing. My work was popular in the 1970s in America because clothing there is so influenced by function and my work was intuitively grasped by the American public. Madame Chanel was also inspired by functional working clothes.

An example of function spilling into design was the clothing I designed for *Charlie's Angels* and Farrah Fawcett-Majors. That clothing is functional but sexy. Function is not a prison —the function of a garment can be to seduce rather than protect. I like to bring humanity to functional clothes by adding luxury—to bring back the touch of the hand which gives clothes their human quality.

NR: How does drawing feature in the creative process?

JCC: For me drawing is the magic connection between inspiration and expression. Now I draw more freely, my designs are also more free and expressive. I am now moving into couture and am less generous in my drawing—expression comes from the "moulage"—the cutting process itself. Much of my work is almost sculptural—at the moment I am working with the architecture of the square.

NR: Do you use computers at any point in the design process? Is there a role for computers in the design of haute couture.

JCC: I delegate all the computer work. For me the magic is between pen and paper. I flirt with the computer but do not make love to it. My work tends to be iconoclastic. I do not like perfection, nothing too new, nothing definite. I like to explore contradictions and harmonies. If I were to work with a computer it would be as a way of making a print, but then to hand embroider it or have it beaded by Lesage.

NR: How do you see the future of fashion drawing and illustration?

JCC: I love fashion illustration. I am greatly inspired by Milton Glaser and Paul Davis (two well-known illustrators). I think there is a big revival of fashion illustration going on in Europe—we are bored with what is produced by computer. You are beginning to see advertisements and even magazine covers

drawn by hand. There is a much greater need for individuality and experimentation. When I taught recently at St. Martin's in London I saw much more enthusiam for new graphic techniques.

I think the revival of interest in fashion drawing is the expression of a new humanity, a sensuality and revival in genuineness, individuality, in sharp contrast to what was happening in the fascist 90s with minimalism. My new collection of pret-a-porter is based on fashion illustration—there is no photography.

NR: Who and what have been your American influences?.

JCVC: I admire Charles James, Geoffrey Beene and Stephen Sprouse. They stayed true to their own inspirations and did not bend to market forces. I have a great sympathy with US designers because of their love of function. America has a tradition of

thinking how clothes must perform in the work-place. In France clothing is about fashion: Napoleon, the Musketeers, the design of their uniforms had more to do with the art of love than the art of war. They were more concerned with seducing women than being dressed for battle.

My first blanket came from Pendleton. My work can be seen as layering American functionality with French ideas of fashion.

NR. Thank you Jean-Charles.

appendix:
face/body templates
specs/women's flats

body templates/large size/
pregnant front & three-quarter views

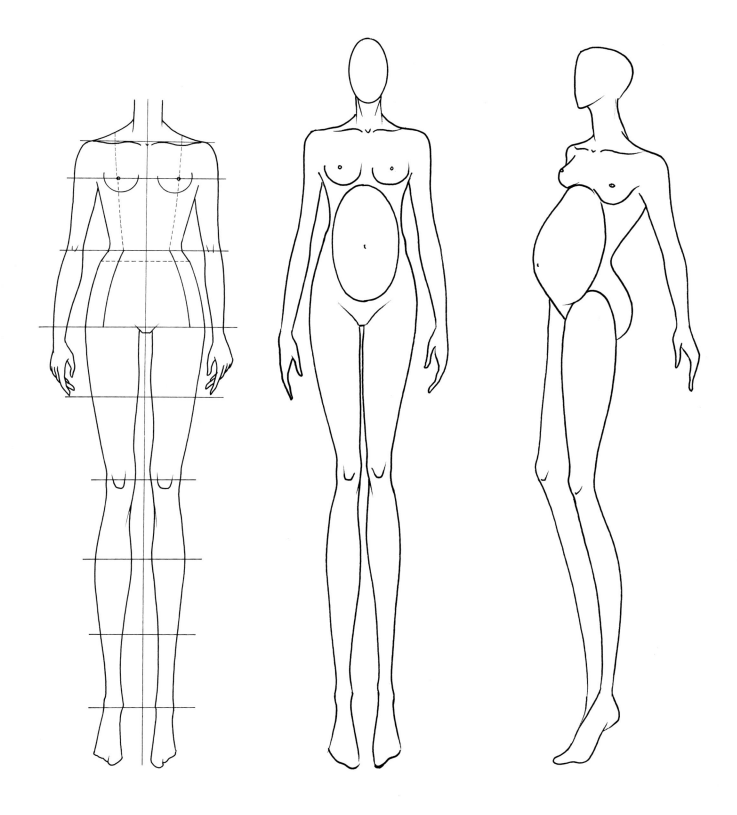

SPECS

Included in this section are flat drawings of the main women's and men's garments, with indications of where measurements are usually taken to provide specifications— specs— to manufacturers. These diagrams have been adapted from systems presently in use by major garment manufacturers. It should be noted however that the location of measuring points varies between companies. If specs are accompanied by flats showing the exact location of measuring points, as here, the risk of confusion is minimized.

The letters on the drawings show the places where garments are measured. The tables below give the description of the measurement and if it is a front or back measurement or both. Garment measurements are made with the garment spread out flat on a flat surface.

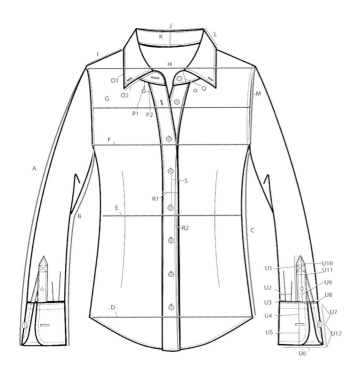

	Front	Back
A Outside sleeve	x	x
B Inside sleeve	x	x
C Side seam	x	x
D Waist	x	x
E Rib cage	x	x
F Lower torso	x	x
G Mid chest	x	x
H Across shoulder	x	x
I Shoulder length	x	x
J Back collar length	x	x
K Collar width	0	x
L Side collar width	x	x
M Armhold length	x	x
N Yoke length	0	x
O1 Front collar length	x	
O2 Front collar width	x	
P1 Button placement vertical	x	
P2 Button placement horizontal	x	
Q Stand up collar width	x	
R1 Placket width	x	
R2 Placket spacing	x	
S Placket length	x	
T Back collar bottom length	x	

CUFF	Front
U1 Placket length	x
U2 First tuck location	x
U3 Second tuck location	x
U4 Cuff length to button hole	x
U5 Cuff length from bottom to button hole	x
U6 Cuff width	x
U7 Button location from top of cuff	x
U8 Top cuff width	x
U9 Button location from top	x
U11 Placket width	x
U12 Button placement from bottom of cuff	x
V Cuff length	x

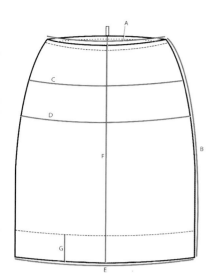
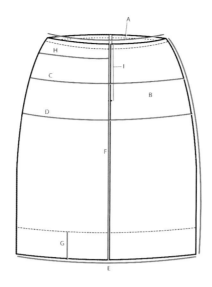

	FRONT	BACK
A Waist width	x	x
B Side-seam	x	x
C High hip	x	x
D Lower hip	x	x
E Hem width	x	x
F Skirt length	x	x
G Hem length	x	x
H Zipper location from side- seam	O	x
I Zipper length	O	x

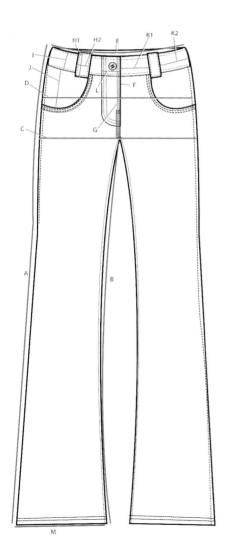
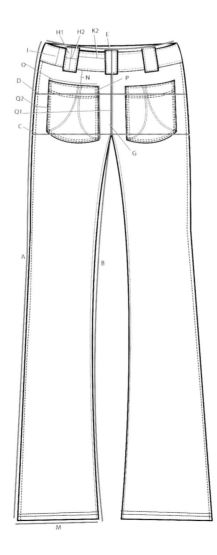

	FRONT	BACK
A Outside side-seam	x	O
B Inside side- seam	x	O
C Lower HIp	x	x
D Pocket opening	x	O
E Waistband	x	x
F Crotch length	x	x
G Zipper placket length	x	O
H1 Belt loop height	x	x
H2 Belt loop width	x	x
I Waistband width	x	O
J Length to pocket placement	x	O
K1 Center front to belt loop	x	O
K2 Spacing between belt loops	x	x
L CF zipper width	x	O
M Bottom width	x	x
N Waist band to top back pocket	O	x
O Pocket width	O	x
P Pocket length	O	x
Q1 Pocket to center back	O	x
Q2 Pocket to side-seam	O	x

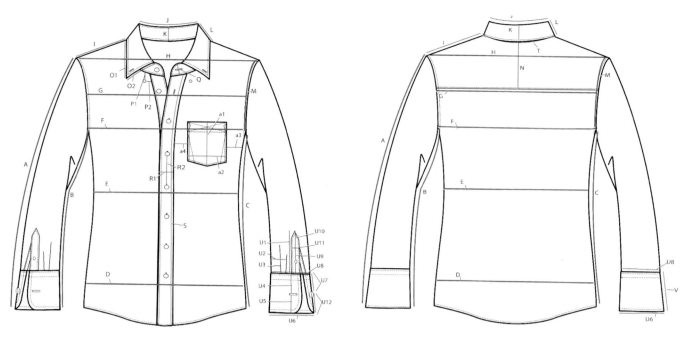

	FRONT	BACK
A Outside sleeve	x	x
B Inside sleeve	x	x
C Side-seam	x	x
D Waist	x	x
E Rib cage	x	x
F Lower torso	x	x
G Mid chest	x	x
H Across shoulder	x	x
I Shoulder length	x	x
J Back collar length	x	x
K Collar width	x	x
L Side collar width	x	x
M Armhold length	x	x
N Yoke length	O	x
O1 Front collar length	x	O
O2 Front collar width	x	O

	FRONT
P1 Button placement vertical	x
P2 Button placement horizontal	x
Q Stand up collar width	x
R1 Placket width	x
R2 Button spacing	x
S Placket length	x
T Back collar bottom length	x
CUFF	
U1 Placket length	x
U2 First Tuck location	x
U3 Second Tuck location	x
U4 Cuff length to button hole	x
U5 Cuff length from bottom to button hole	O x
U6 Cuff width	x
U7 Button location from top of	x

	FRONT
U8 Top cuff width	x
U9 Button location from bottom	x
U10 Button location from top	x
U11 Placket width	x
U12 Button placement from bottom of cuff	x
V Cuff length	x
POCKET	
a1 Pocket length	x
a2 Pocket width	x
a3 Placement from side-seam	x
a4 Placement from center placket	x

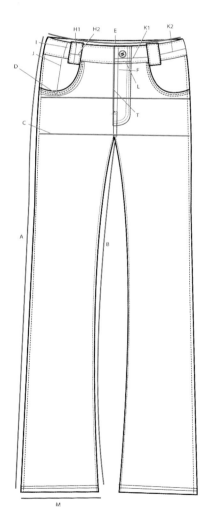

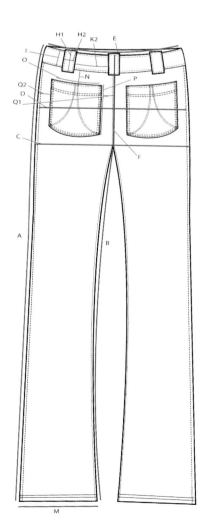

	FRONT	BACK
A Outside side-seam	x	O
B Inside side-seam	x	O
C Lower Hlp	x	x
D Pocket opening	x	O
E Waistband	x	x
F Crotch length	x	x
G Zipper placket length	x	O
H1 Belt loop height	x	x
H2 Belt loop width	x	x
I Waistband width	x	x
J Length to pocket placement	x	O
K1 Center front to belt loop	x	O
K2 Spacing between belt loops	x	x
L CF zipper width	x	O
M Bottom width	x	x
N Waist band to top back pocket	O	x
O Pocket width	O	x
P Pocket length	O	x
Q1 Pocket to center back	O	x
Q2 Pocket to side-seam	O	x

Ruffled jean skirt

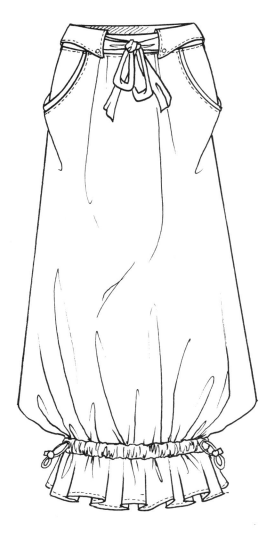

Sash tie bubble skirt

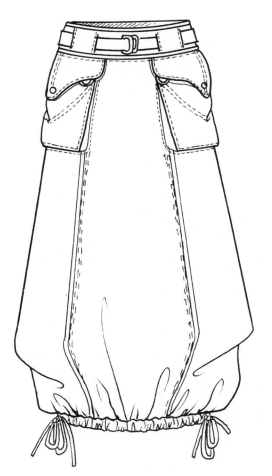

Toggle lock bubble skirt

Tiered ruched skirt with
string ties and cargo pockets

Whip stitch pockets

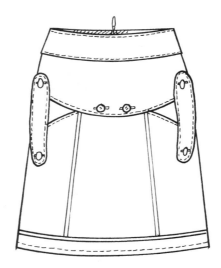

Yoke with button tab detailing

Saddle pocket mini with fringe

String tie novelty pocket

Tab pocket mini

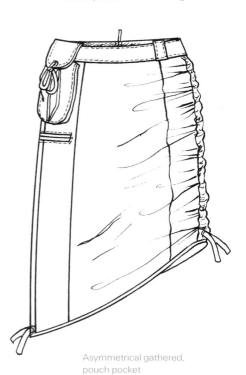

Asymmetrical gathered, pouch pocket

Spaghetti wrap broomstick

Ruched dropped yoke

Mini with fringe

Tabbed yoke

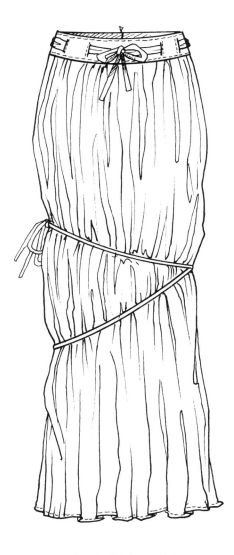

Spaghetti tie broomstick

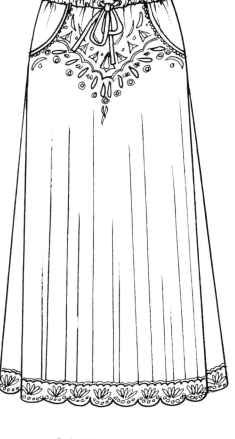

Embroidered yoke, drawstring

Short, side tie detail

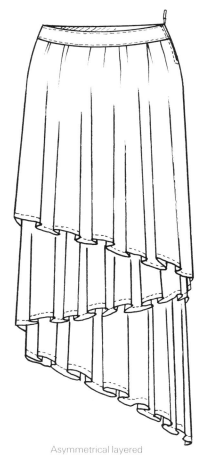

Asymmetrical layered

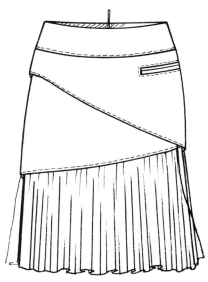

Asymmetrical

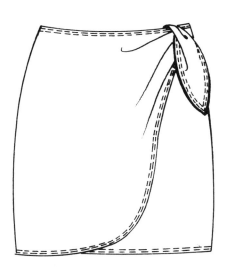

Sarong

Self tie belt side slit

Fringe

Short flounce

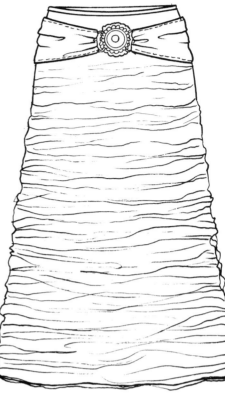

Crystal-pleated

Asymmetrical layered

Yoke floral print

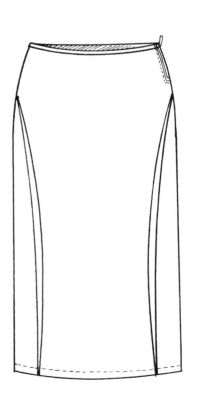

Paneled, slim

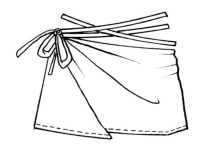

String tie wrap mini

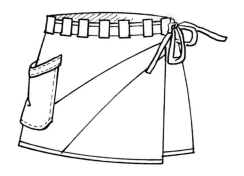

Ribbon tied mini
sarong, patch pocket

Mini with flounce

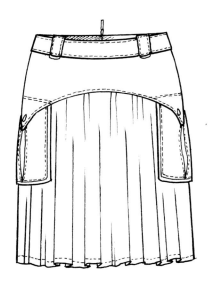

Yoke with bellows pockets

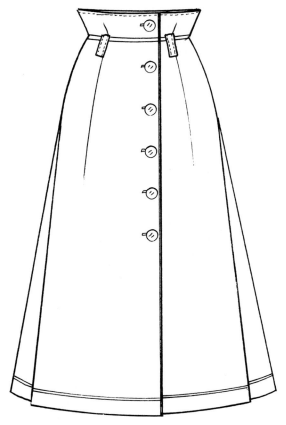

Buttoned wrap

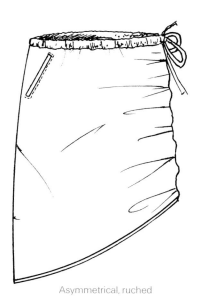

Asymmetrical, ruched

Tiered yoke

Loop detail dropped yoke

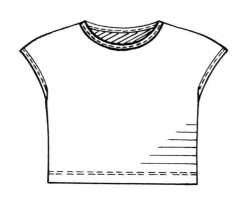

Cropped sleeveless T

Sleeveless pullover

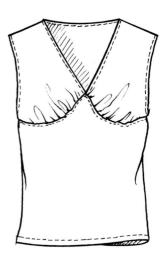

V-neck pullover, slip-
inspired shell

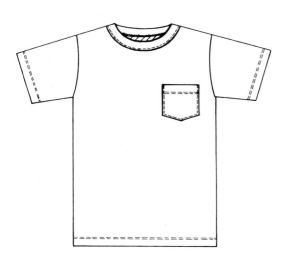

Patch pocket sleevless T

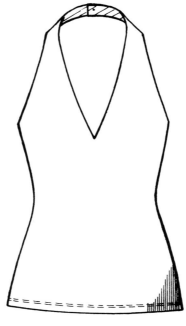

Halter

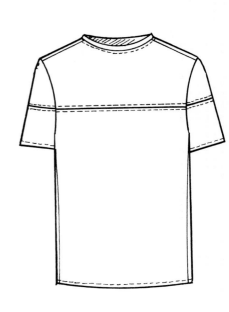

Short sleeveyoke T

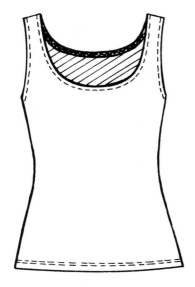

Tank

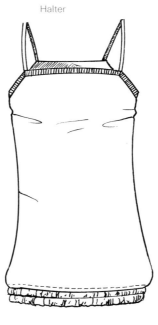

Blouson cami

Halter

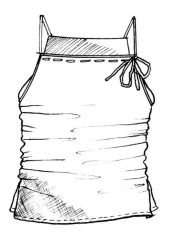

Lace-up cami

Tie detail pullover

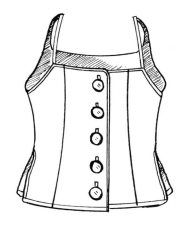

Button front spaghetti strap

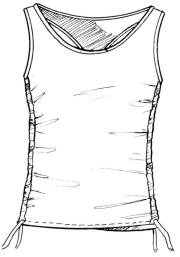

Ruched swimmer-back tank

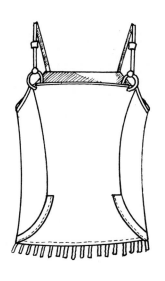

Beaded and fringed cami

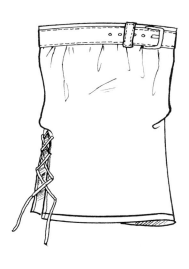

Belted, side-laced, off-the-shoulder

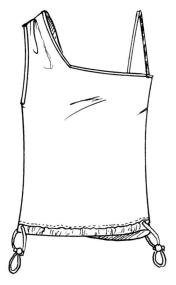

Asymmetrical cami/tank with
drawstring waist

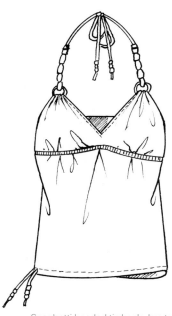

Spaghetti-beaded tie back , bra-top
halter

Ruffle scoop neck

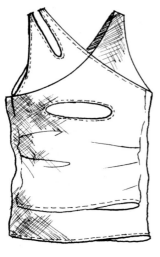

Layered cut-out crossover tank

Spaghetti-laced short cami with
ruched brassiere

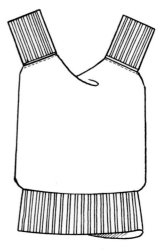

Rib-strapped and waisted tank

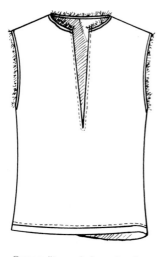

Deep split mandarin neck pullover

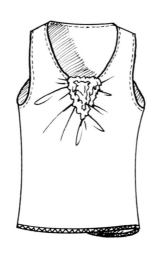

Medallion front tank

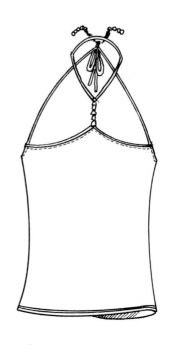

Beaded spaghetti-laced cami

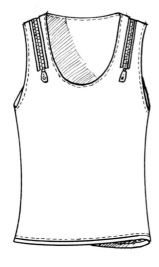

Zipper tank

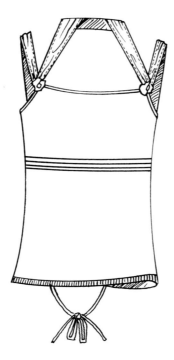

Halter neck tank

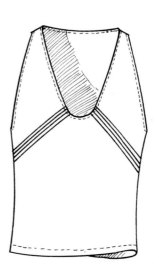

Deep v-neck tank

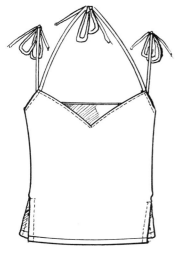

Spaghetti tie cami/halter

Bustier with spaghetti tie at waist

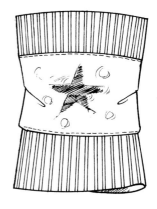

Tube with ribbing panels

Asymmetrical cami/halter

Asymmetrical with appliqué

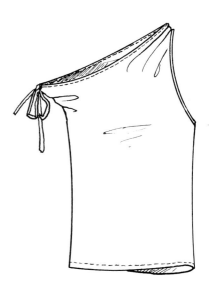

Asymmetrical off-one-shoulder

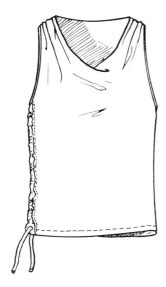

Tank with beaded side detail

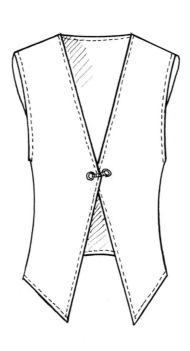

V-neck vest

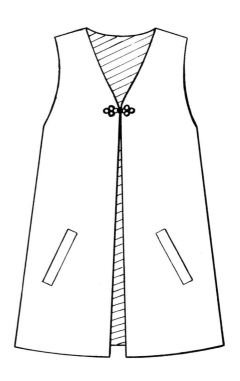

Vest with frog closing

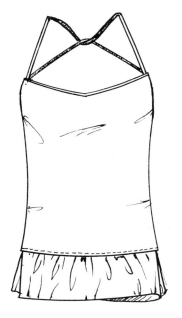

Spaghetti strap gathered
hem cami

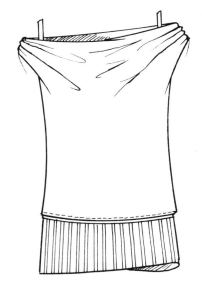

Off-the-shoulder cowl neck

Slip style cami

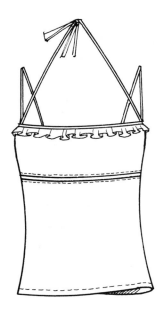

Ruffle-trim spaghetti-tie cami

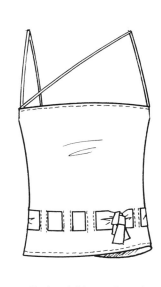

Enclosed ribbon sash cami

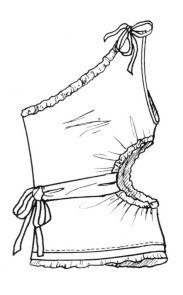

Single shoulder cut-out tank

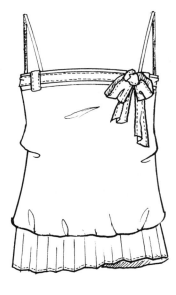

Cami with flounce

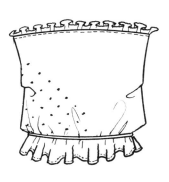

Ruffled tube top

Cap sleeved, tie detail pullover

Chinese lounging jacket

Rib trim short sleeve
pouch pocket pullover

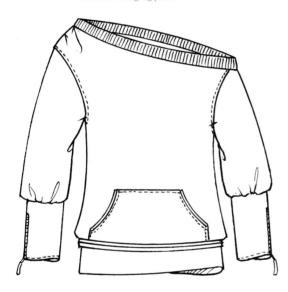

Asymmetrical neckline with
bound kangaroo patch pocket

Off-the-shoulder blouson with
sash belt and matching cuffs

Split neck long raglan sleeve

Cropped long sleeve
with rib trim and waist

Ruffle neckline/cuff

Cowl neckline

Retro housecoat with
patch pocket detail

Cut-out puff sleeve blouse

Tie-front shirt

Off-shoulder raglan sleeve top

String tie flutter sleeve top

Cropped blouson

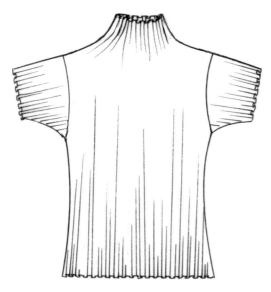

Rib knit

Cropped puff sleeve

Baby doll v-neck pullover blouse

Puff sleeve wrap blouse

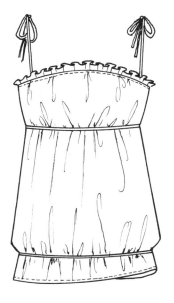

Tie string ruffle trim empire

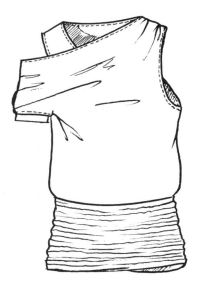

Asymmetrical wrap pullover

Wrap neck pullover

Off-the -shoulder yoke asymmetrical sleeved string tie top

Short sleeve lace trim

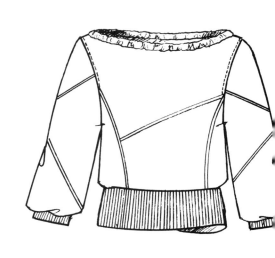

Asymmetrical paneled

Empire-waisted wrapped
spaghetti detail

Grecian one shoulder
flutter sleeve

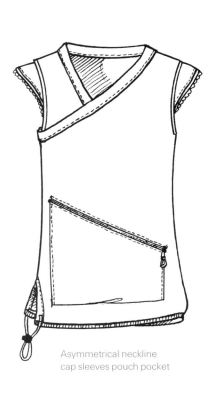

Asymmetrical neckline
cap sleeves pouch pocket

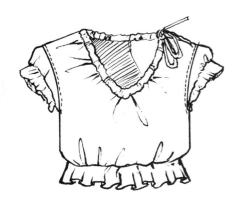

V-neck short puff top

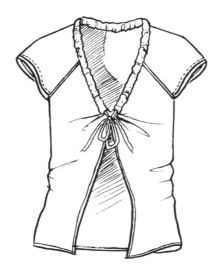

Ruched tie-front v-neck top

Shaped tube top

Double slash neckline puff sleeve

V-neck puff sleeve shirred empire

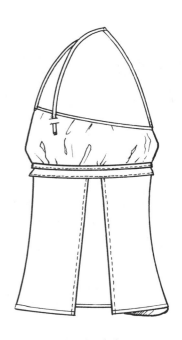

Bandeau halter

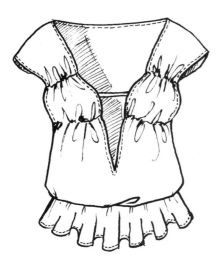

Grecian style plunging neckline pullover

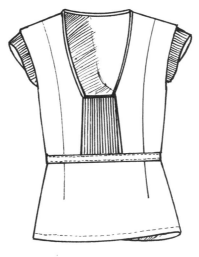

Drop sleeve square neck

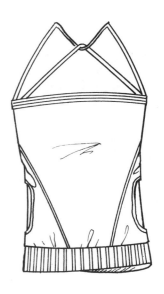

Spaghetti tie halter

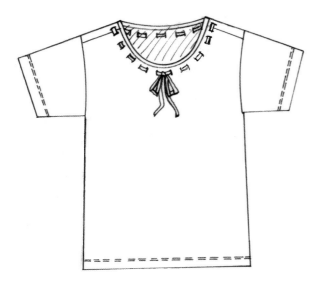

Jewel neck short sleeve T

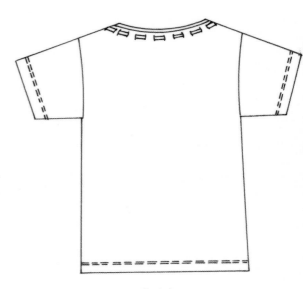

Back view

Ruffle trim Paris graphic

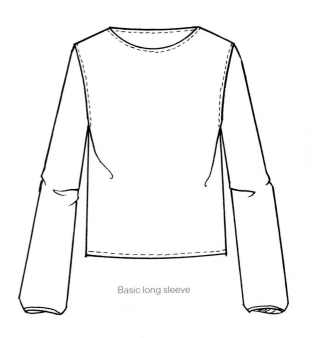

Basic long sleeve

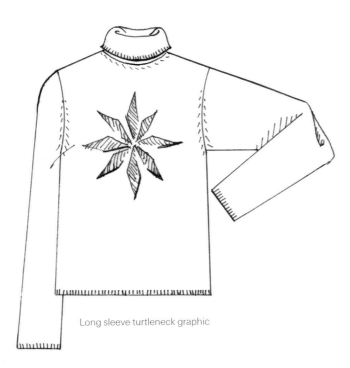

Long sleeve turtleneck graphic

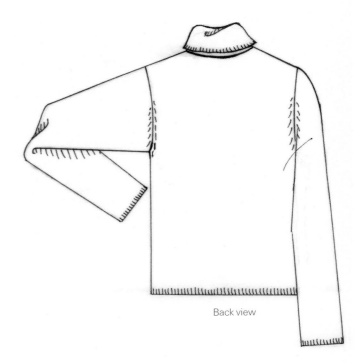

Back view

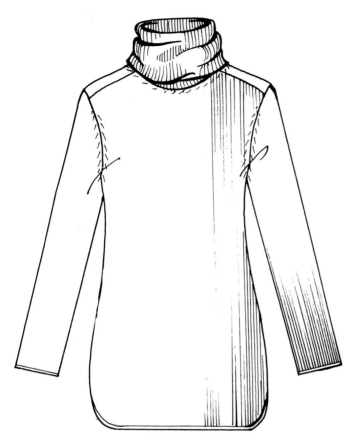

Ribbed turtleneck tunic pullover

Pirate shirt

Bandeau

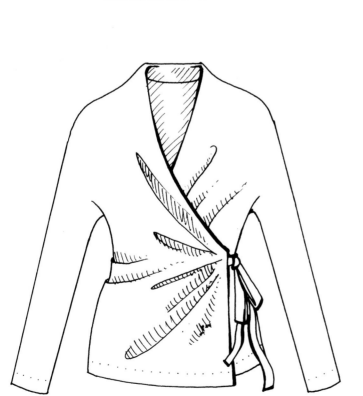

Dolman sleeve wrap

Ruffle front vest yoke shirt

Cropped sleeveless T

Sleeveless pullover

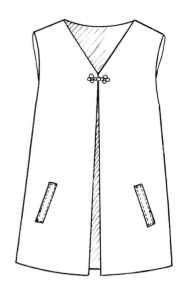

Frog closure vest

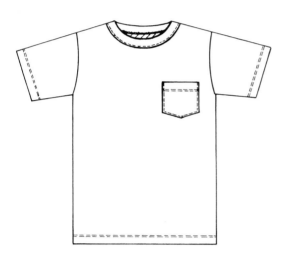

Classic pocket T

Sleeveless halter

Bolero sweater

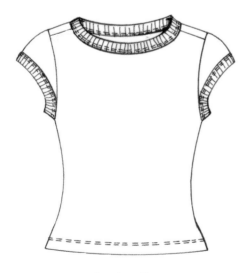

Cap sleeve T

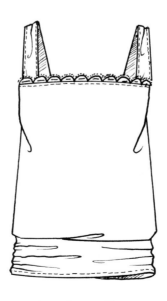

Lace trim sun with
gathered waistband

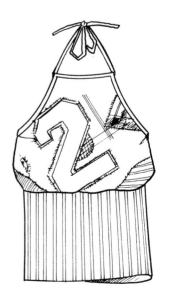

Graphic print halter
deep rib waistband

Beaded string halter

Button front sun

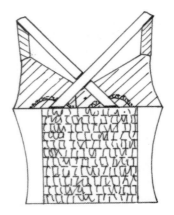

Back view showing
gathered back

String-laced cami

Tie detail pullover

Rib trimmed short
sleeve pouch pocket

Ruched swim-
mer back tank

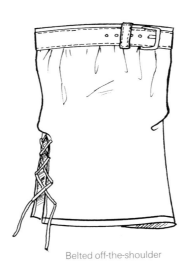

Belted off-the-shoulder

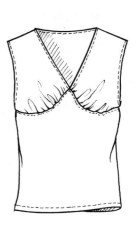

Lingerie-inspired shell

Mock wrap graphic pullover

Ruffled short
sleeved blouson

V-neck short sleeve pullover

Tie closure long-sleeved

Cropped blouson

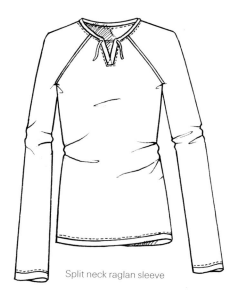

Split neck raglan sleeve

Puff sleeve empire

Floral print tie-belt blouse

Cut-out layered

Spaghetti-laced
short sleeve

Rib-banded tank

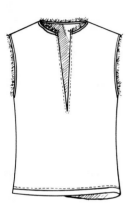

Split neck sleeveless
pullover

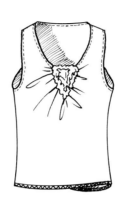

Medallion front tank

Spaghetti tie beaded cami

Zipper tank

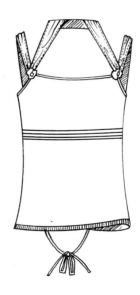

Halter neck tank

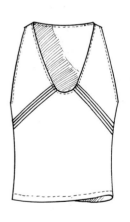

Deep U-neck tank

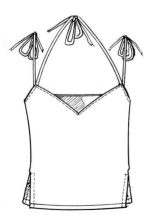

Spaghetti strap cami

Stapless self tie

Graphic tube top

Spaghetti strap ties side darts

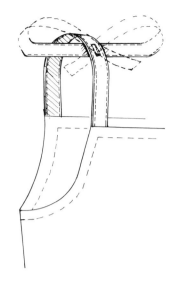

Detail

Smock blouse gathered empire waist

Off-the-shoulder raglan sleeve

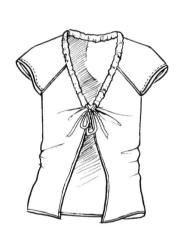

Gathered v-neck raglan short sleeve

Puff sleeve blouson ruffled hem

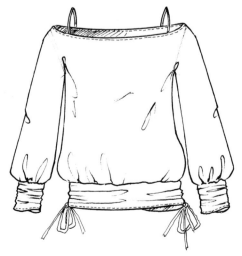

Off-the shoulder long sleeve gathered cuffs waistband

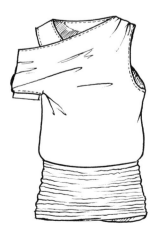

Asymmetrical opening crystal pleated waistband

Short sleeve asymmetrical tie wrap

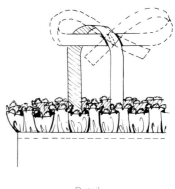

Detail

Fitted sun ruffled lace trim

Back view

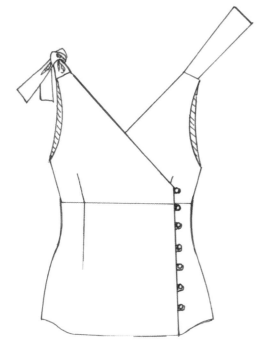

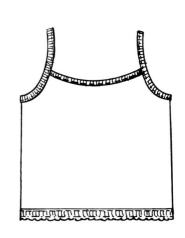

Banded rib tank

Asymmetrical button closure sun

Back view

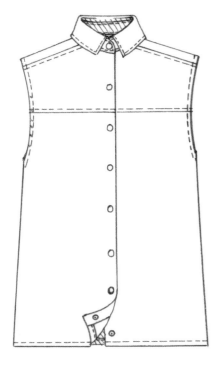

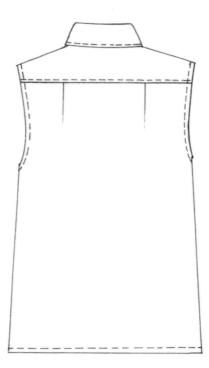

Ribbed pullover

Sleeveless shirt snap closures

Back view

Peasant blouse

Back view

Set-in sleeve top-stitching

Dolman sleeve top-stitching

Knit turtleneck

Short sleeved top-stitching

Pintuck detail tuxedo

Ruffle placket blouse

Hidden placket pocket shirt

Banded collar shaped shirt

Pintuck yoke

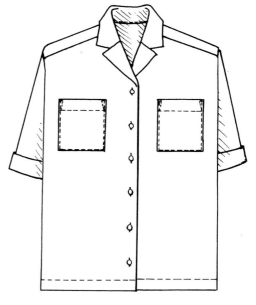

Camp shirt

Sleeveless ribbed trim

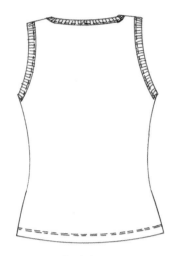

Back view

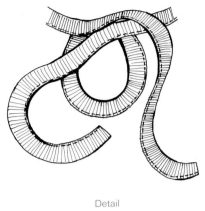

Detail

Button front printed cropped

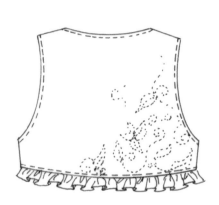

Back view

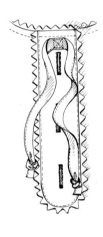

Detail

Puff sleeved yoke

Back view

Sleeveless smock

Knit turtleneck raglan sleeve

Rolled cuff cardigan sweater

Cable-knit cardigan

Bow tie blouson pullover

Knit vest with cable feature

Fringe poncho

Turtleneck turned up sleeve

Popcorn-stitch knit cardigan

Military

Western style

Bishop sleeve fold cuff

Peplum bell sleeve

Long sleeved polo

Pocket T

Long sleeve turtleneck

Two pocket placket

Fur-trimmed parka

Back view

Detail

Vest

Gathered yoke double
button cuff

French cuff multibuttoned

Tab roll-up sleeve

Fitted princess seams
welt and flap pockets

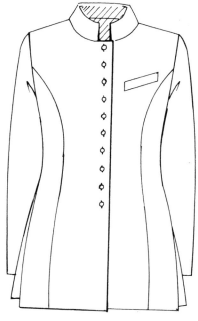

Nehru jacket

Double breasted
peak lapel fitted

Pea coat

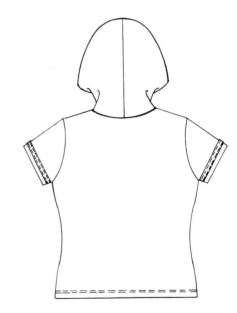

Back view

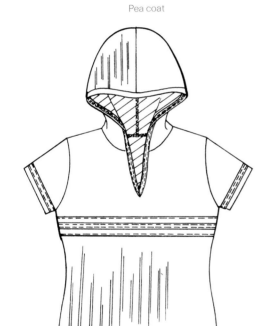

Ribbed hoodie

Back view

Fur-trimmed jean jacket

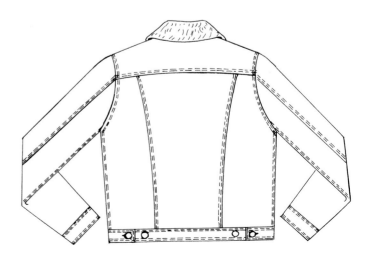

Back view

Tab detail safari

Back view

Motorcycle

Back view

Varsity jacket

Kangaroo pocket hoodie

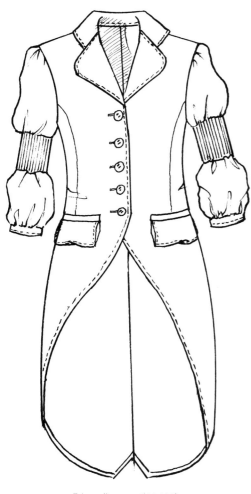

Edwardian morning coat

Piping-trimmed jacket

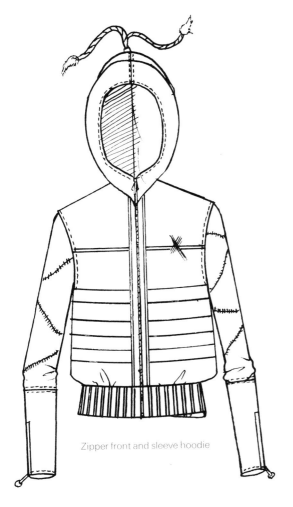

Zipper front and sleeve hoodie

Racer/members only jacket

Tailored tab pocket shawl collar

Princess seam short blazer

Asymmetrical button front

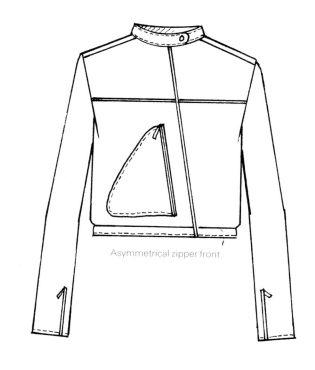

Asymmetrical zipper front

Scarf tie capelet

Double-breasted fitted top-stitch

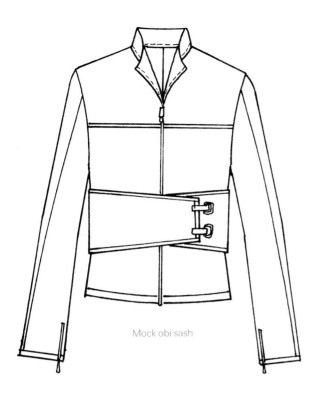

Mock obi sash

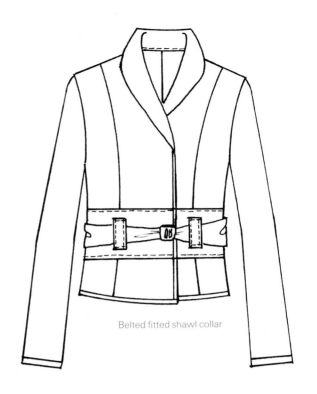

Belted fitted shawl collar

Stand collar with clips banded rib trim

Welt pocket cropped blazer

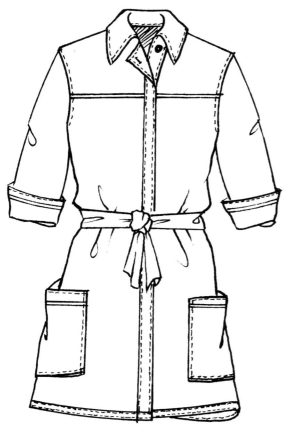

Dressmaker coat

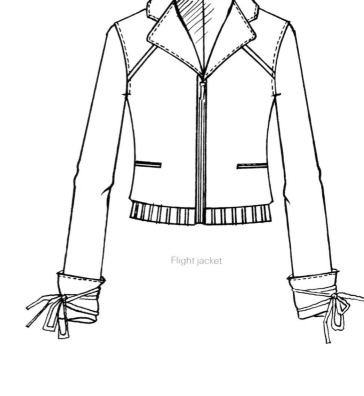

Flight jacket

Racing with juliet sleeves

Bomber jacket

Fur trimmed lapel
and hem tie closure

Double-breasted round collar

Sword peaked two-button

4-button D-ring belted pockets

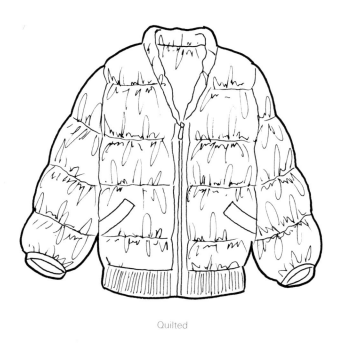

Quilted

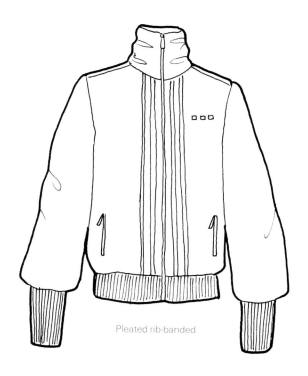

Pleated rib-banded

Fitted cloverleaf collar

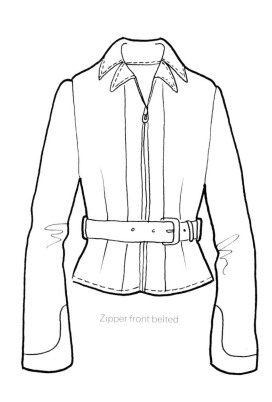

Zipper front belted

Racer jacket

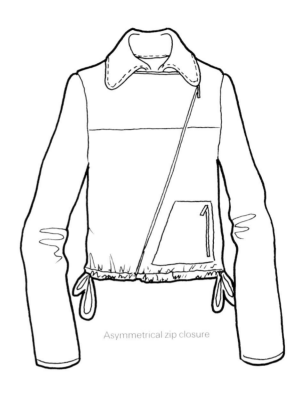

Asymmetrical zip closure

Zipper front

Double-breasted wide cuff

Daytona racing

Draped hooded belted

Fitted two button stand collar

Zipper front stand collar racer

Cropped shawl collar zipper

Zipper front rib-cuffed hooded

Coachman's pocket coat

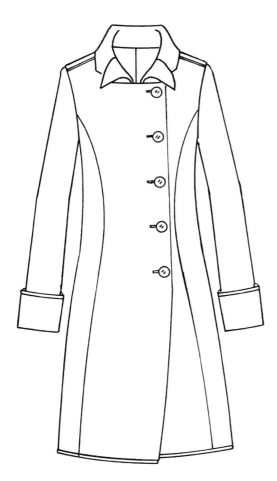

Asymmetrical button princess

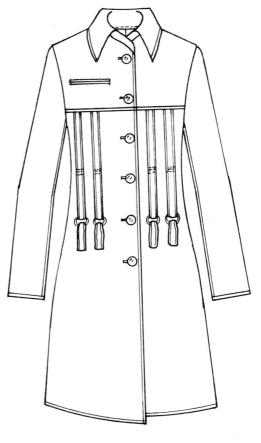

Banded tab retail coat

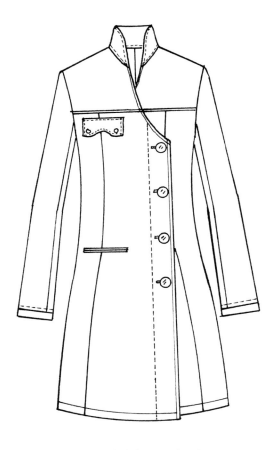

Asymmetrical closures yoke princess

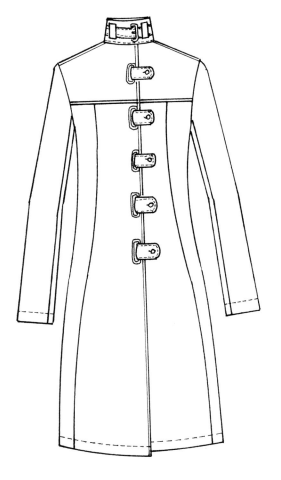

Band collar tab closure princess

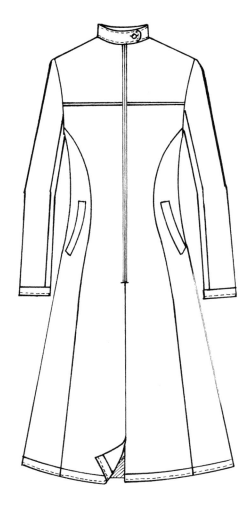

Zip front band collar princess

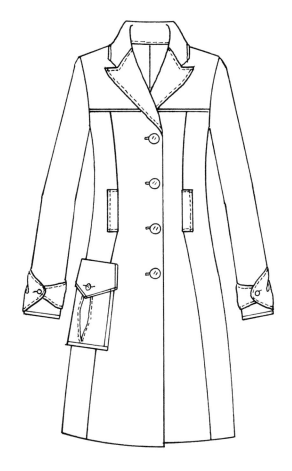

Peak lapel cargo pocket princess

Notch collar tie detail princess

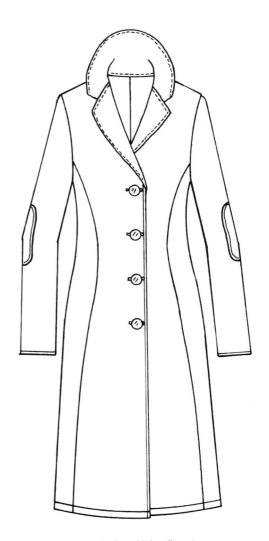

Patch elbow high collar princess

Zipper front obi-belted princess

Novelty equestrian

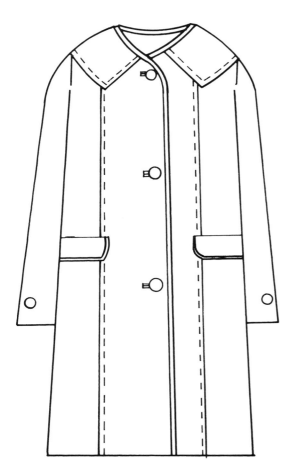

Three buton car coat

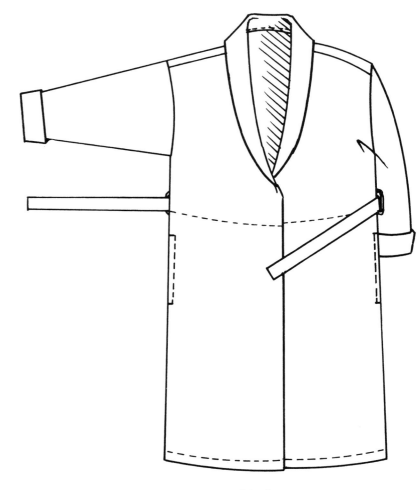

Belted lounge coat

Double-breasted notch collar car coat

Piped shoulder loop closure fitted topcoat

Yoke detail tie closure riding cape

Caped walking coat

Side button shawl collar jacket

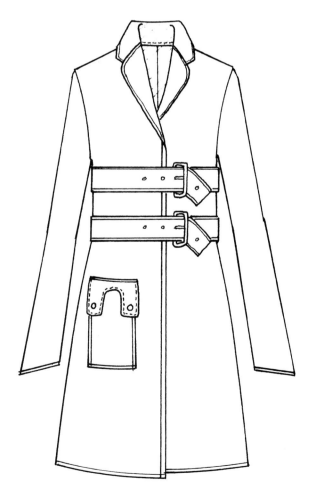

Double belted polo coat

Shawl collar capelet

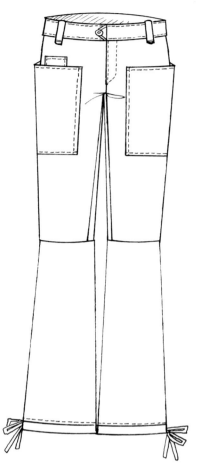

Patch pocket flared jeans

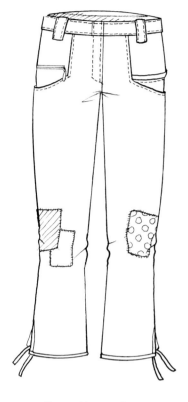

Cropped boot-cut jeans

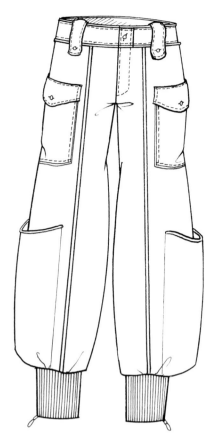

Urban cargo pants

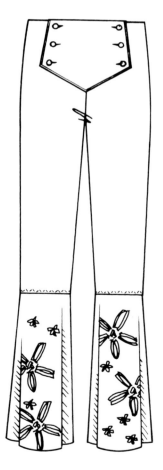

Sailor panel bell bottoms

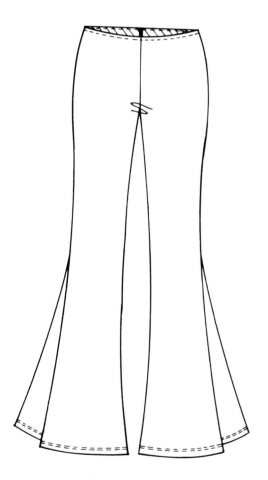

Low-rise bell bottoms

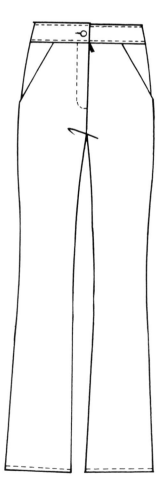

Boot-cut trousers

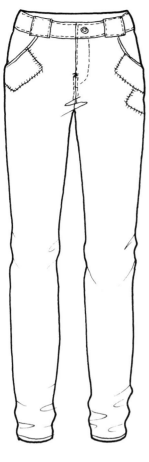

Slim leg jeans

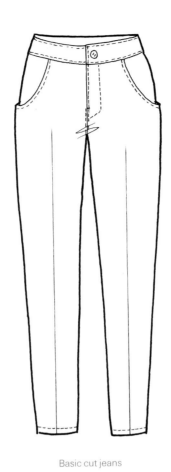

Basic cut jeans

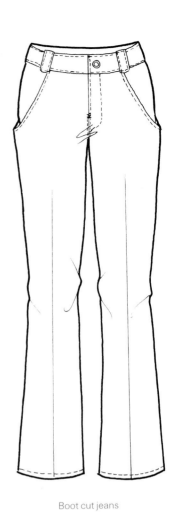

Boot cut jeans

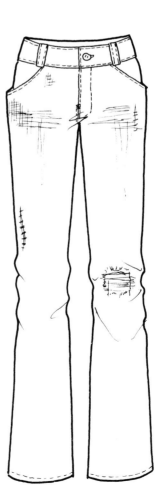

Logo detail sweatpants

Distressed boot cut jeans

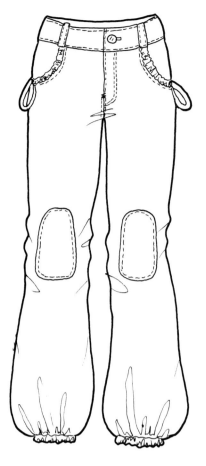

Jean style sweats

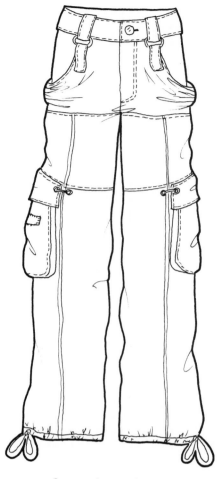

Cargo pocket parachute jeans

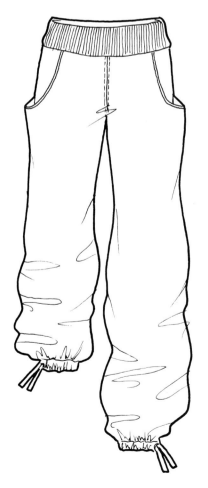

Rib banded yoga style sweatpants

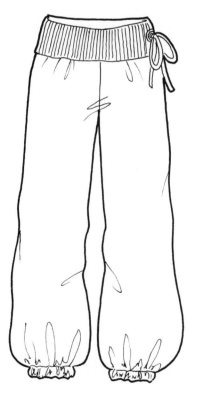

Drawstring cropped sweatpants

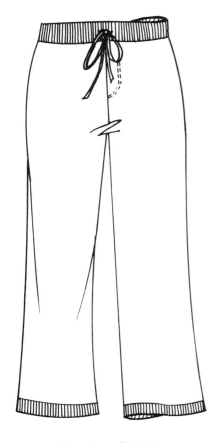

Drawstring pullon pants

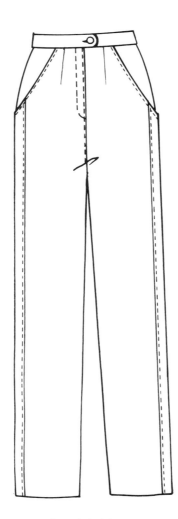

Extended tab trousers

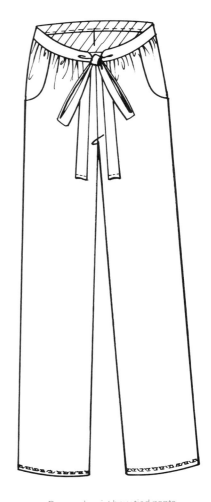

Dropped waist bow-tied pants

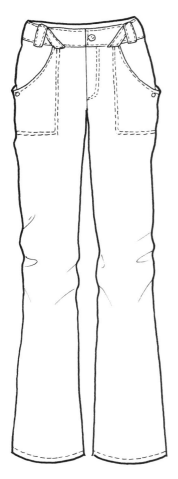

Boot cut jeans

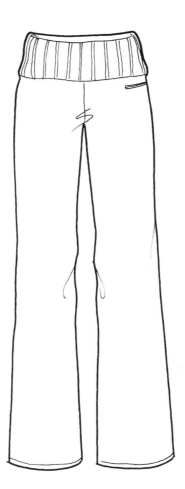

Yoga pants

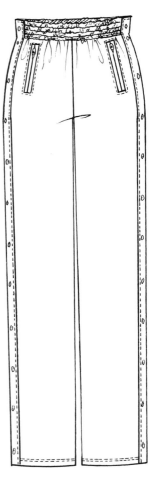

Side snap warm-up pants

Fringe cut-offs

Jogging shorts

Logo hotpants

Jean style shorts

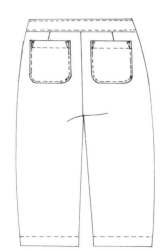

Patch pocket below-the-knee jeans

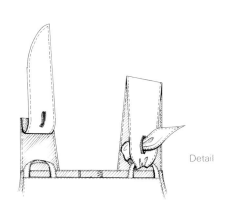

Detail

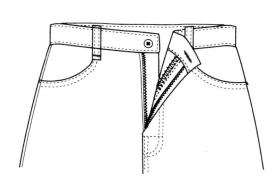

Zip detail

Four pocket baggie jeans back view

Dungarees/overalls

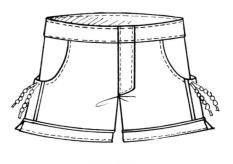

Daisy Dukes

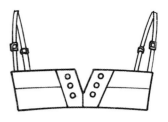

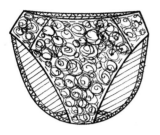

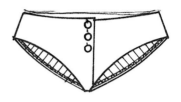

Retro two piece swimsuit/lingerie

Thong and underwire bra combo

Button detail two piece swimsuit

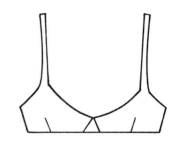

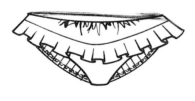

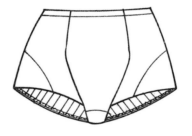

String tie detail bikini

Ruffle-trimmed two piece swimsuit

Girdle style retro swimsuit

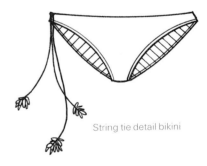

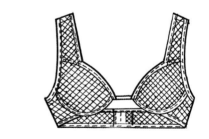

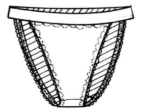

Strapless bra lace trimmed thong

Comfort mock wrap bra and thong

Tanner's two piece swimsuit

Satin edge retro bra front/back

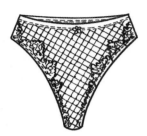

Lace panties front/back

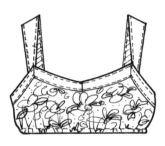

Retro bra swimsuit top front/back

Lace-up corset front/back

Racer back sports bra

Swimsuit bikini bottoms front/back

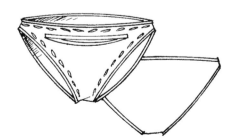

Strapless top boy-cut bottoms swimsuit

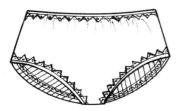
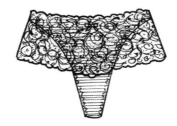

Lace trimmed underwire bra/panties

Lace strapless bra and thong

Ribbed bra and brief

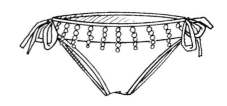

Full underwire bra/thong

Beaded fringe bikini

Sports bra/ trainer briefs

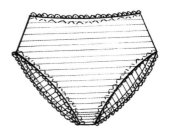

High-cut two piece swimsuit

Seamless bra/ribbed panties

Bra- cut swimsuit

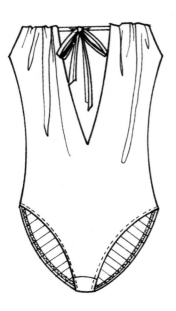

Pull-on strapless v-tie swimsuit

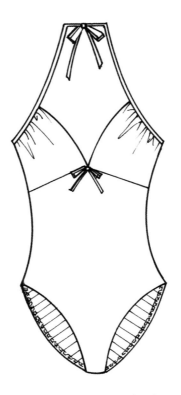

Spaghetti tie halter swimsuit

Underwire body suit

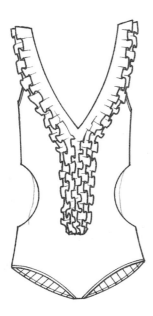

Ruffled deep-v boy leg swimsuit

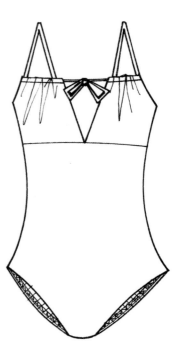

String tie swimsuit

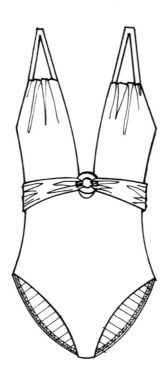

Deep v cinched waist swimsuit

Tie-back halter swimsuit

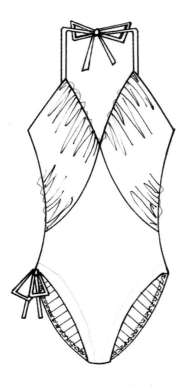

Spaghetti tie halter swimsuit

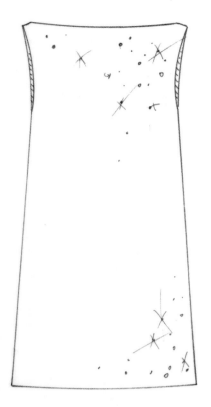

Beaded sheath

Cowl back (back view)

Empire with ruched trim

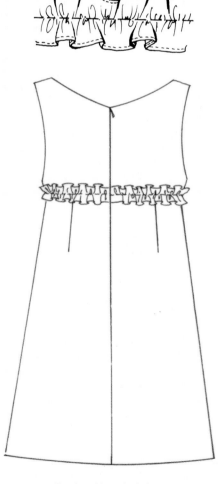

Empire with ruched trim.
Back view with detail.

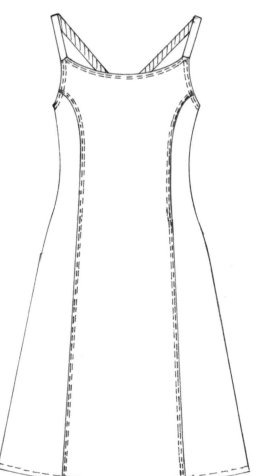

Princess seam sundress

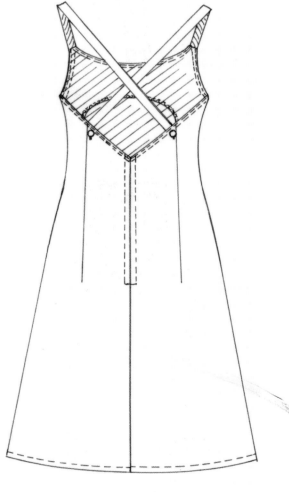

Back view

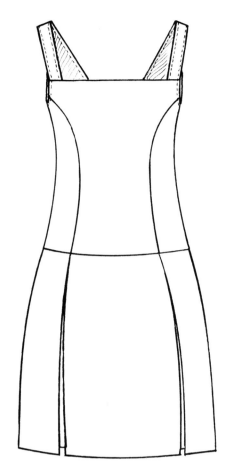

Sleeveless sundress inverted pleats

Back view

Empire flared skirt sundress

Empire flared skirt sundress. Back view.

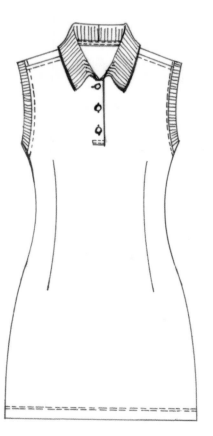

Ribbed collar placket fitted

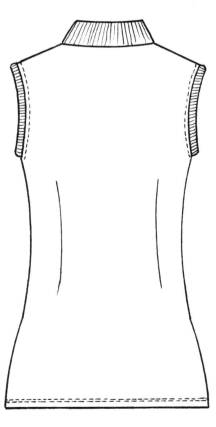

Back view

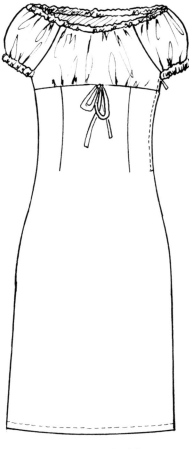

Empire baby doll

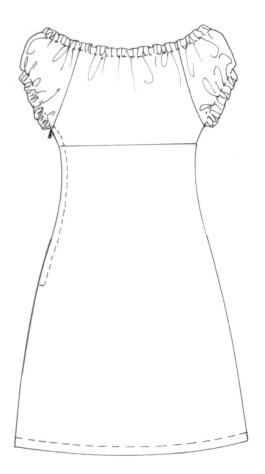

Back view

V-neck layered cocktail dress

Back view

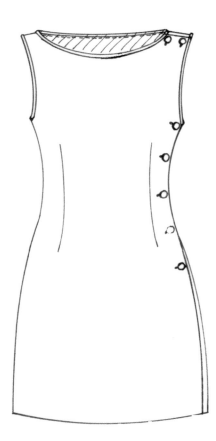

Side and shoulder button sheath

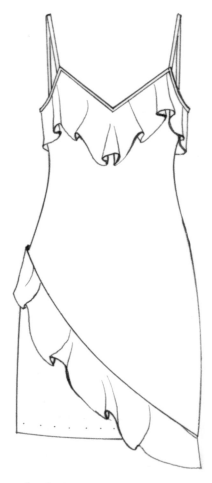

Spaghetti strap asymmetrical ruffle sun

Back view

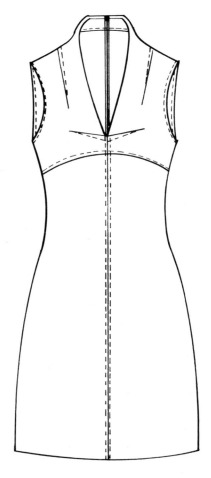

Deep v-neck dart construction Empire

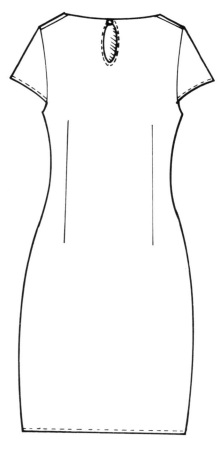

Keyhole neckline sheath

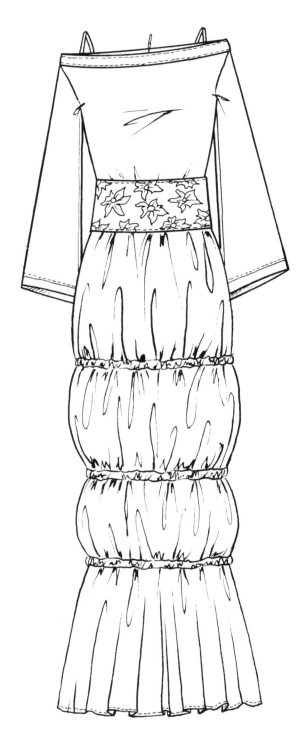

Modified obi ruched

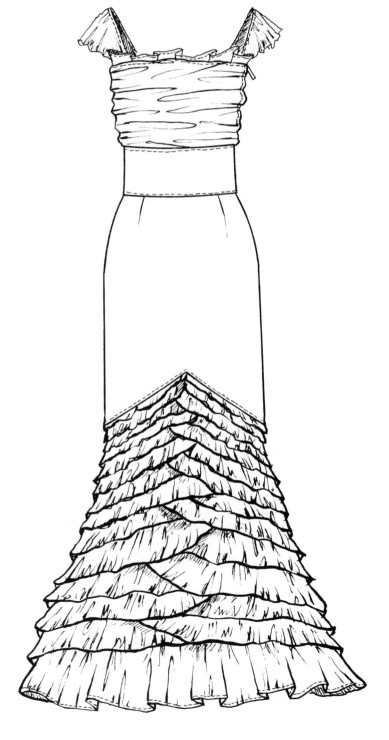

Retro layered flounce

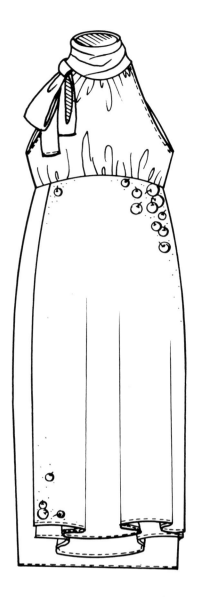

Bow detail mock apron cocktail dress

String tie halter neck wide waist

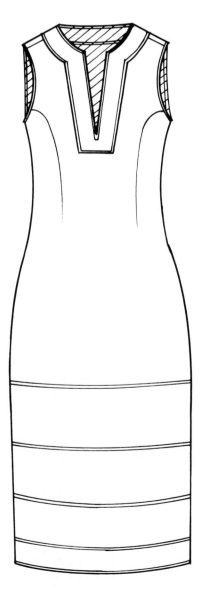

Slit neckline sleeveless princess seam

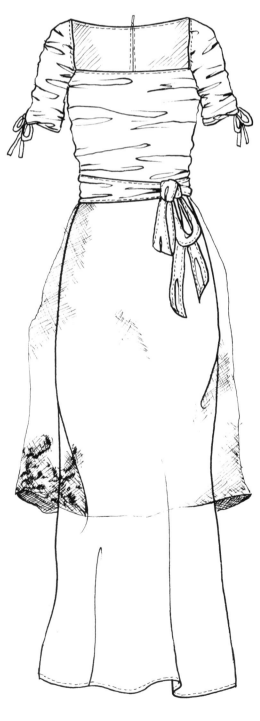

Square neck cinched waist apron dress

String tie halter, beaded waist full skirt

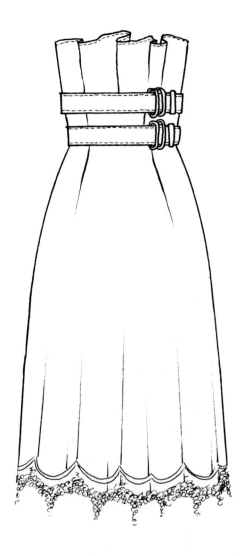

Strapless belted waist scallop hem

Mock wrap lace -trimmed

Ruched cinched waist beading and embroidery detail

Drop-v halter tiered skirt

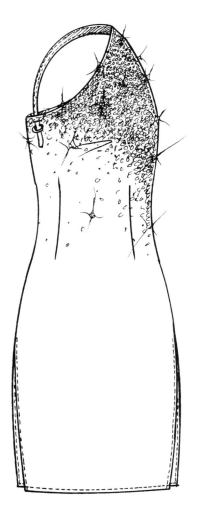

Beaded asymmetrical closure cocktail

Beaded waist strapless cocktail

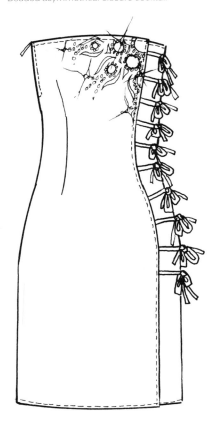

Strapless fitted beading side bows

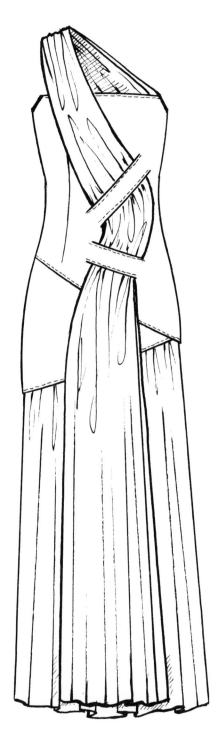

Grecian-inspired sash gown

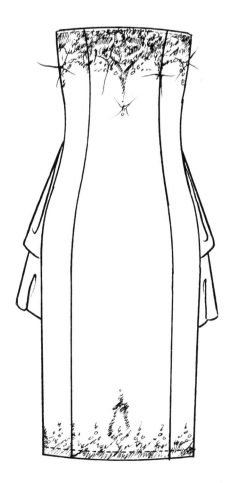

Strapless beaded cocktail

acknowledgments

The original project of *9 Heads* was an ambitious one, with a number of experimental parts, and in many ways a process of learning and discovery for me. Numerous question arose during both the planning and compilation stages of the book on what the best approaches might be: What were the best types of drawings to include as examples of how to draw the various elements of fashion-on-the-figure? What was the best overall format for the book? What was the best combination of text and images? How much technical information should be included? These, and many others, were questions for which, at the time, there was as yet no feedback, and which I had to answer—to the best of my ability—for myself, drawing on my experience and teaching instincts. Now six years have passed since the original publication, during which time I have used the book continuously in my fashion drawing classes in FIDM in Los Angeles, observing directly how students use it (and how I myself use it) and receiving extensive feedback from students, teachers, colleagues, designers and fashion professionals as to which parts work best, which could work better and what could be usefully added. All that feedback—both the critical as well as the complimentary—has been gratefully received and given careful consideration while designing and producing the content for this new edition, and I am most grateful to all those who supplied it.

I feel it is important to mention that the past few years have (so it seems to me) also seen a general improvement in the standard of fashion drawing, both in education and in the industry, a most gratifying trend that bodes well for fashion design in the years to come. This trend leads me to believe that two points of view on fashion drawing are receiving increasingly widespread recognition: a) fashion drawing is a powerful tool for fashion design, and that the better the tool the better are the end results, and b) considerable room for improvement in standards of drawing/design has existed and still exists. This improvement of itself (and it is heartening too that there also seems to be a widely held desire to continue this improvement) has also stimulated me to produce, with great pleasure and enthusiasm, new work for an increasingly critical audience.

This edition contains numerous changes from and additions to its predecessors and has proved to be another large and ambitious project in itself. It would not have been possible to complete in its present form without the close collaboration and contributions of three young designers with excellent design and drawing skills: Karolina Maszkiewicz, Jisook Paik and Johnny Singer. They are—each in their own special and unique way— highly talented and creative as designers and draftsmen. In meeting the exacting demands and deadlines for the work on this edition they all displayed a rare sensitivity to the style and content of the book and a committed professionalism. Together they have made a significant contribution to the book for which I am deeply grateful.

This new edition adds considerably to the body of technical information included in the previous editions, and I am particularly grateful for the help of James Clay, Patricia Good, Ofelia Montejano and Helene Reiner in classifying garments and garment details and answering technical questions on construction and design. My thanks also to Sebastian Flyte, Barbara Gutenberg and Jane Tsukamoto for their generous help and to Renée Weiss-Chase for her continuing kind support. Thank you also to Vern Anthony at Prentice Hall for his work in promoting the first editions of the book in fashion education in the USA and overseas and his helpful suggestions on new content for this edition.

Thank you again to Simon Johnston for his counsel and guidance on the design of this new edition. The original design for the book was most effective in bringing clarity and coherence to a large body of mainly freehand drawings in a clear, logical and attractive way, and it is a tribute to the strength of that original design that it has lent itself to extension and adaptation to the demands of a much-expanded volume.

Thank you to Stefani Greenwood, who made an invaluable contribution in the preparation, cataloguing and placement of the very large number of images, and to Serge Monkewitz for his kind help in cataloguing and preparation of the original artwork. Thank you also to Scott Council for the shots of drawing materials and to Willis Popenoe for his continuing help in refining the text.

Art Center College of Design in Pasadena continues, for me, to be an institution committed to the highest standards in contemporary design. Their expanded offerings to their graduate students of fashion-related topics over the last few years is both personally gratifying and, I am sure, as with the other types of contemporary design that are taught and developed there, will result in a meaningful contribution in this field. I would like again to thank Richard Hertz for his help and advice when he was chairman of the department of Liberal Arts and Sciences and Fine Arts Graduate Studies and to Richard Koshalek, President of the school, for his continuing kind support.

Although this edition contains many changes from the first two editions, not only, of course, would it not exist unless those editions had been made, but it is also grounded firmly on the foundation of that previous body of work. I continue therefore to be most grateful to all those who participated, in their many different ways, in the production of those editions. I would particularly like to mention again Mary Stephens and my colleagues at FIDM, as well as the FIDM library staff, whose help and support has never wavered over intense years of work on this and other projects. I would also like to remember Robin Pavlosky, who provided great help with technical matters for the first edition of the book but sadly passed away before its publication; she is sorely missed but not forgotten and her work is present in this new edition also.

I am also grateful to Ruben Alterio, Jean-Charles de Castelbajac, Mona May, Raymond Pettibon (whose work appears courtesy of Regen Projects in Los Angeles) and Bernhard Wilhelm, the interviews with whom and/or examples of whose work remain in this edition. I am also delighted that Demetrios Psillos allowed me to include one of his wonderful works in the introductory part of the book: his skill and keen wit are a great inspiration to all of us who draw fashion.

Finally I would like to thank my partner David Eno for his help in all stages of the preparation and publication of this edition of the book (except the drawing, for which he insists he is the single exception to my claim that anyone can learn to draw). The expanded scope of the book, greater rigor of both the drawings themselves as well as their technical fashion content, and the new depth of the accompanying explanatory text result, in large measure, from his keen observations and clear vision and insights. As with the first editions, without his help this new edition would not exist. Thank you.

Nancy Riegelman, Los Angeles, 2006

index